C01 5 57 5519 37

ABOUT THE AUTHOR

Formerly senior lecturer at the University of South Australia, Susan Mitchell has taught creative writing and scriptwriting for television and radio and Literary Studies. She has presented her own morning program on ABC radio and her own interview program, 'Susan Mitchell: in Conversation', on ABC television.

Her best-selling books include *Tall Poppies*, *The Matriarchs*, *Tall Poppies Too*, *The Scent of Power* and her first novel, *Hot Shots*.

Her heroines are Simone de Beauvior and Mae West.

ICONS, SAINTS AND DIVAS

ICONS, SAINTS & DIVAS

SUSAN MITCHELL

INTIMATE CONVERSATIONS WITH WOMEN
WHO CHANGED THE WORLD

An Imprint of HarperCollins*Publishers*

FOR MARY,
ICON, DIVA BUT DEFINITELY NOT SAINT

Pandora
An Imprint of HarperCollins*Publishers*
77–85 Fulham Palace Road,
Hammersmith, London W6 8JB

First published by
HarperCollins*Publishers* Australia 1997
Published by Pandora 1997
1 3 5 7 9 10 8 6 4 2

A catalogue record for this book
is available from the British Library

ISBN 0 04 440971 0

Printed in Great Britain by
Caledonian International Book Manufacturing Ltd,
Glasgow

CONTENTS

PREFACE

Adelaide, South Australia

'Marilyn French?'

'Yes.'

'I just want to thank you. You made me leave my husband.'

'Well, I'm sure there was a bit more to it than that.'

'No. I read *The Women's Room* and I decided I just wasn't going to take it any more.'

This conversation, repeated many times in front of me by many different kinds of women, sowed the seeds for this book. As chair of Adelaide Writers Week, an international writers' festival, it was my role to host and entertain visiting international writers, and 1994 was a special year. My home town of Adelaide, the capital of the state of South Australia, was celebrating the centenary of a major event: the granting of women's right to vote. A century earlier, not only had this relatively isolated state of a remote island contintent been among the first states in the world to grant women the right to vote, it was also, incredibly, the first in the world to pass legislation that allowed women to stand for parliament.

The suffragists in South Australia who had fought so bravely and so fiercely for women to gain the right to vote had remained largely invisible in our state's history and our education. It had taken 100 years for us to acknowledge and celebrate their achievements and, because of this, it was difficult for us to feel that we knew anything of the people responsible for these changes. Mary Lee, for example, who was a prominent spokeswomen for the suffragist movement, emigrated to Adelaide from England when she was almost sixty years old to care for her son, who was ill, but we know so little about her. Unfortunately, however, there were few first-hand accounts.

The Women's Suffrage Centenary Steering Committee decided to sponsor two international writers to attend the festival and chose Marilyn French, author of the feminist classic *The Women's Room*, and Deirdre Bair, the award-winning biographer of Simone de Beauvoir (author of *The Second Sex*, which laid the foundations for all the books of second-wave feminism that swept the world in the 1970s).

During the writers' festival, wherever I went with Marilyn French, women wanted to tell her that *The Women's Room* had changed their lives. I asked her if this happened to her in other countries. She said it wasn't always phrased in exactly the same blunt terms, and that hostile men often blamed her for the breakdown of their marriages, but that the book did seem to have had a dramatic effect on people's lives. I discussed this with Deirdre Bair too, who said that de Beauvoir's *The Second Sex* had been blamed for destroying the stability of western civilisation. When it was first published in May 1949, de Beauvoir could not sit in Paris cafés without people pointing at her and unleashing their derision in public.

I began to think of the power of certain books – seminal books – which in tandem with the activism of the second wave of the women's movement had changed the way that millions of women viewed themselves and their choices. In that sense they had changed the world. Forever.

Months later I found myself asking other women which books had done this for them. I checked my bookcases and began to compile a list. It all began in 1963 when Betty Friedan's *The Feminine Mystique* was published. The 'problem that had no name', the feeling of emptiness, the feeling of 'is this all there is?', the boredom, the frustration, the anger, the guilt, were all named. And in that naming, the power of women to believe they had a choice in how they wanted to lead their lives was rekindled. 'Who knows what women can be when they are finally free to become themselves,' wrote Betty Friedan in the book's conclusion.

It was this throwing off of the shackles and running headlong into the arms of freedom and adventure that concerned Germaine Greer in *The Female Eunuch*, first published in 1970. Shifting gears from steady reform to dramatic revolution, Greer set out to subvert, and to draw ire from all sections of the community. And she succeeded. She challenged every principle that women had been taught about womanhood, sex, love and their place in society. The economic, psychological, historical and social planks on which women's roles were determined were analysed and dismantled, one by one. Nothing was sacred. This book stripped away the hypocrisy, the sentimentality and the falsehoods that had cushioned women's lives. It was funny and wicked and bawdy and shocking and, for those reasons alone, compulsive reading.

Greer concluded: 'Liberty is terrifying but it is also exhilarating.'

It was also in 1970 that Robin Morgan collected and edited an explosion of women's voices in *Sisterhood is Powerful*, which blew asunder any notion that there was only one feminism. This book presented a multiplicity of viewpoints and no individual woman presumed to speak for the whole. It was both a celebration of diversity and a coming together of women's voices. In it Robin Morgan coined the phrase 'the personal is political'.

A PhD thesis on sex, power and patriarchy called *Sexual Politics* was the third book to set women on fire in 1970. Kate Millett took great delight in exposing the sexism and misogyny in the works of the 'great' male writers of the time. Her book became another rallying call of the biggest social and sexual revolution this century. In it she concluded: 'It may be that a second wave of the sexual revolution might at last accomplish its aim of freeing half the race from its immemorial subordination – and in the process bring us all a great deal closer to humanity.'

In 1971 Erica Jong's first book, *Fear of Flying*, embraced this same theme by tackling the fear of freedom – of liberation through the expression of sexuality. The term 'zipless fuck' entered the language.

In 1972 Phyllis Chesler challenged the psychiatric profession to re-evaluate and redefine the so-called 'madness' of women as they attempted to free themselves from the prisons of conformity, tranquillisers and shock therapy.

'How can women banish self-sacrifice, guilt, naiveté, helplessness, madness and sorrow from the female condition? How can a woman survive – and learn to value survival?' she asked in *Women and Madness*.

In 1977 all of these issues and themes appeared in a work of fiction by Marilyn French. It was called *The Women's Room* and it unleashed a tide of anger and dramatic changes in women's lives. It was a novel in the form of a political document. Or vice versa.

The search for spiritual understanding by a woman of colour won the Pulitzer Prize in 1983. In her novel *The Color Purple*, Alice Walker touched the souls of women as well as their minds. Feminism became part of a spiritual quest.

The beginning of the '90s saw the publication of the first books by a younger generation of feminist writers. Naomi Wolf exposed the Beauty Myth which imprisoned women. Her book challenged women to decide for themselves what to see when they looked in the mirror.

In her conclusion to *The Beauty Myth*, Naomi Wolf wrote: 'How to begin. Let's be shameless. Be greedy. Pursue pleasure. Avoid pain. Wear and touch and eat and drink what we feel like. Tolerate other women's choices. Seek out the sex we want and fight fiercely against the sex we do not want.'

She was followed by Susan Faludi, like Alice Walker a Pulitzer Prize winner, who named the 'backlash' that had been occurring against all these advances towards women's liberty. She pointed out that it was men, not women, who understood the profound force that a women's movement could exert and that's why they were doing their best to bury it.

In *Backlash: The Undeclared War Against Women*, Susan Faludi concluded: 'Whatever new obstacles are mounted against the future march toward equality, whatever new myths invented, penalties levied, opportunities rescinded or degradations imposed, no-one can ever take from women the justness of their cause.'

And finally in 1992, Gloria Steinem – who had been involved with Ms magazine from the beginning – published her first full-length polemic, *Revolution from Within*, where she reminded women of the necessity to maintain their self-esteem by looking within themselves and knowing that 'the political is personal'.

Rhodes scholars, Oxford firsts, Pulitzer Prize winners, graduates *summa cum laude* and Phi Beta Kappas; their work reflects their intellects. While they are all best known for one ground-breaking, best-selling blockbuster book, they have published many others and are all still writing new ones. Unlike those who seek to make their reputation by trashing these women and their books, they are not 'one-book wonders'. As extraordinary warrior queens they have been very vulnerable to attack, but they are also great survivors.

I rang Marilyn French, told her about my idea and asked if she would agree to be interviewed. She had been a guest on my ABC television programme 'Susan Mitchell: In Conversation' and she had read my first book, *Tall Poppies*, based on interviews with successful Australian women.

'Well,' she said after a long pause, 'I wouldn't normally agree, but because the interview I did with you was the best I have ever done, I will do it. For you.'

All I needed was this one act of kindness and generosity. Later that year, when I was in New York in October, I discussed my list with Deirdre Bair. Between her extensive network of contacts and friends, and those of my New York friends Nancy Grossman, the artist, and Arlene Raven, the art writer and critic, contacts and calls were made and I was vouched for. The world of international feminism and sisterhood, I found out, while vast and complex, is still accessible.

After the women's initial agreement, endless faxes and telephone calls to the writers' assistants or secretaries or agents followed to ascertain possible places or times for the interviews. Finally I had my list. Everyone I had asked had agreed except, I am sad to say, my countrywoman, Germaine Greer. She has stated publicly that biographers should at least have the decency to wait until she is dead before writing about her life. To my request to include her in this book, I received a negative response from her London agent.

By what seemed a small miracle, all of the writers who had agreed to be interviewed for the book were going to be in New York within the two weeks at the end of May and beginning of June in 1995, except Susan Faludi, who had an attachment to a newspaper in Stockholm; I could interview her on my way back to Australia. Arrangements and times were made. And confirmed. So too was my application for leave from full-time lecturing at the University of South Australia. I was not sure what lay ahead but I knew it would be different. Very different.

8 pm: Sydney Airport, New South Wales

Here I was, self-styled intrepid reporter, sitting in a Qantas plane on its way to Los Angeles and New York. Of course I was excited. And daunted. So I should have been. In the next two weeks I was to be a direct witness to ten political figures of contemporary social and literary history. Unlike the first wave of feminist writers and *agents provocateurs*, whose stories we never heard, the catalysts of the second wave would be together in one book, telling their own stories. And I would be the narrator of their lives and their work.

I knew that without their books I would not be who I am. Or where I am. All of these writers, in their various ways, had 'named' for me what I had known from the time I was four years old and made to lie down for a nap in the heat of the Australian afternoon next to my mother. I knew she was sick, but mostly she was sick of her life. I knew by the slant of the sun on the still, brown blind and the sluggish silence of the streets. I knew why my mother had ended up there in the sleeping suburbs. And I swore it would never happen to me.

But it wasn't until the women's movement swept the western world in the 1970s, surging with books that would validate my feelings and those of millions of other women, that suddenly we all knew we were not alone. And our lives were never the same again.

This was not to be just an interview book. Nor a book of profiles or literary analysis. If you want to know about these women's books, then read them. This book is different; in this book I want you, the reader, to come with me into the apartment or office or hotel suite and witness, first-hand, history as it is being told. Using the interviews as working documents, I will transform them into dramatic monologues so that each writer speaks directly to you in her most personal and intimate voice. It is the story of each woman's life as she told it to me. I will try to interrupt as little as possible. By getting behind the public masks of celebrity, it is possible to see the real women. I want them to leap off the pages as flesh and blood women, full of contradictions, fears, anger and hopes, but also full of joy, laughter, fun and sexuality.

I will not work from a list of set questions but I would like this book to explore the connection between their lives and their work. What did they think they were changing? What drove them? Have their ideas been translated into the kinds of changes they had hoped for? How have their own lives changed and evolved? What effects have fame, success and money had on them? What were the negotiations, the impasses between their work and their lives? As I sat there in my plane seat, a hundred other questions swirled around in my head.

This was a personal as well as a literary and political journey. I was in awe of these women and owed them a great debt for what they had contributed to my life. But I knew that my journey, although my own and eccentric, had pathways and choices that were more than familiar to millions of other women. The style and tone of this book should reflect this.

It was an enjoyable, orderly, uneventful flight. I ate, I drank, I slept, I watched a movie, I made notes. No Fear of Flying here. I was calm. Too calm, perhaps. In Australia when things go well, we wait for the axe to fall. Conspicuous success is a health hazard. I was, however, entering a totally different culture – where success was nurtured, where if you wrote one best-selling book you were encouraged to write another. And all of these women had done that. Neither Australia nor Britain trusted success, except in sport. Envy always seeks to destroy what secretly it most admires and we were countries eaten up with envy. Australia was a country in love with failure. All our heroes were failed men. But that is another book for another time.

8 pm: Los Angeles, California

On another continent, fourteen flying hours later, it was still 8 pm on the same day (something to do with the international date line). I loved Australia, but at times like these I wished someone would just hook it up and drag it a little closer to Europe and America.

Once ensconced in the global familiarity of the hotel-chain bedroom, I turned on the television. A reporter on CNN pronounced dramatically, 'There will be an empty chair on "CBS Evening News" tonight. Connie Chung has been removed from her co-chairing the "Evening News" with Dan Rather. CBS executives said that Dan Rather would return to his single anchoring of the news where the weeknight ratings had dropped from second to third position. Connie Chung said her removal was personally disappointing and unjustified and now she knew how Barbara Walters felt.'

Fresh from making notes on Susan Faludi's *Backlash* on the plane, I wondered about the timing of this event. Was this Faludi's worst-case scenario coming true? Why did they always blame the woman for the drop in ratings? In the entire history of American national television there had only been two women who had read the main evening news. And now they had both been dropped.

I rang Susan Faludi's Hollywood number. Her assistant was not sure whether Susan would have time to see me before her imminent departure for Stockholm but said it was worth trying to contact her. I left several messages on the answering machine and fell asleep. I dreamed I had replaced Connie Chung on the 'Evening News'. It was my first night, there was great excitement and expectation. And the Autocue broke down. I might have been in America, but it was definitely an Australian dream.

9 pm: New York City

Jane Galvin-Lewis was there to meet me at JFK Airport. Her smiling face, eclectic hats and bear-like hugs had come to signify New York for me. Ten years ago, she had stared at my friend and me from the other side of the room at a dinner party and, in spite of her politeness and cordiality, I knew we were being assessed. At the end of the evening she offered us a ride home. Sitting up there in her four-wheel drive Jeep, negotiating the New York traffic like a rodeo rider, she said, 'Normally I don't take to whiteys straight off. But I've decided I like you two Aussies. Would you like to have dinner and go to a show in Harlem some time?'

Would we?! We would kill for it! All our American friends had told us not to go into Harlem without a guide. And here she was. The next night, after dinner at Sylvia's, a Soul Food restaurant in Harlem, we went to a show at the Baby Grand where Lena Horne used to sing. When the lights came on we realised that we were the only white people in the room apart from another couple.

When they walked past our table we instinctively smiled and said, 'Good evening.'

They said, 'Bonjour,' and looked down their French noses at us.

Jane said, 'The one thing you can say about the French is they don't discriminate. They treat everyone like shit.'

When we left the nightclub, Jane drove us around the wide grand streets of Harlem, pointing out major landmarks from the civil rights movement. By day Jane worked in the department of housing and urban development, organising housing and shelter for the poor. At night she was an actor, and has now developed her own range of comic characters which she performs in small clubs in Manhattan. During the 1970s she was one of the black women with whom Gloria Steinem had teamed up to give talks and lectures all over America and Europe. There was a poster in her Brooklyn apartment with photos of Jane and Gloria under the heading 'Black and White Feminism'.

'Is that Liza Minnelli?' I asked Jane, ten years later, as we walked towards the luggage carousel.

'Yeah,' said Jane, with the nonchalance that comes from seeing stars of stage and screen, celebrities and international figures every day on the streets of New York.

Next to her again in the Jeep, gliding through the traffic with the occasional warning beep on the horn and the running commentary on the low IQs of other drivers who impeded her progress, I managed to talk to her about the book.

'I love it,' she said. 'It's a great idea. I can't wait to read it.'

There is a generosity of spirit in American feminists that is sadly lacking in Australia, where we have an obsessive tendency to cut down those who aspire to success. This 'tall poppy syndrome', now the subject of university research, seems to have arrived with the First Fleet. We, however, have turned it into a national sport.

I wondered if this was why all the women in my book were American, apart from Greer, who is expatriate Australian and still had not agreed to be part of it. Most of the British feminist writers had written one or two books and disappeared off the scene. Not only had all the women in this book written one ground-breaking best-selling blockbuster with which their names were synonymous, but they had gone on to write many other books and were all still doing more. Was it because once having made their name and been showered with fame and success their culture nurtured rather than destroyed them? Was it because New York was the epicentre of publishing and publicity and, in the words of Liza with a 'z', 'If you can make it there, you'll make it anywhere. New York. New York.'

And here I was, in the centre of what is indisputably the most exciting and vibrant city in the world, loading my luggage into the lift of the apartment building in West 69th Street, between Columbus Avenue and Central Park West, where my dear friend Bob Pugh had left his keys for me with a neighbour. He was in Glyndebourne at the Opera and had loaned me his apartment so that I would have a familiar sanctuary while I undertook the ten interviews in two weeks.

9 am: Upper West Side, New York City
I had one day before my first interview, with Erica Jong. A quick trip to Zabar's on Broadway ensured that the fridge and cupboards were stocked with delicious food. I even discovered some excellent South Australian wine in a shop on Columbus Avenue and had a long conversation with the owners. There's nothing like a good bout of shopping to make you feel at home.

I had rung all the writers, or at least left messages with their assistants or on their answering machines, to let them know I had arrived safely and to confirm the dates and times of their interviews. I knew, given their busy schedules, I only had one shot at this. Within a day of the appointed interview some of them were flying off to other continents on book tours, for writers' festivals and speaking engagements.

My aim was to capture them all at the same point in time, in the same city, to freeze-frame them. Like insects caught in amber. Then, at another time and on another continent, I could take them out, hold them up to the light and look at them from different angles. And I could listen to the different nuances in their voices on my tapes. No amount of note-taking or transcribing can take the place of the intimacy of the individual voice.

Being Australian, unknown and an outsider, was an advantage. Apart from my friendship with Marilyn French and two breakfast meetings with Gloria Steinem that Jane had arranged on previous visits, I knew none of these women. Nor had I lived in America, which meant I knew nothing of the power struggles, the hurts, the insults, the bitter feuds, the shifting alliances, the internecine wars for which feminism and all revolutionary movements are renowned. I was coming to it all fresh and would take them as I found them. As an outsider I had licence to ask the unspeakable questions and prod a few sacred cows, relegating any tactless blunders to cultural differences. I am not a cold, detached observer and my interviews will always be a genuine dialogue. No doubt some exchanges will be more relaxed than others and will vary according to the time available, the mood of the participant and the extent to which each woman is prepared to make herself vulnerable to the truth.

Of course the interview is a game. Even an art, in the best hands. These women are all skilled practitioners, having been interviewed hundreds or even thousands of times. It was a challenge. Oriana Fallaci, the celebrated Italian journalist whose interviews with world leaders were published internationally, once confessed that for her the interview is 'a love story'. 'It's a fight. It's a coitus.'

Marie Brenner, who wrote interview profiles for *New York* and *Vanity Fair* magazines, describes the interview as a seduction. Janet Malcolm, the microsurgeon of the interview, believes it to be a mutual game of seduction and betrayal.

I prefer to think of it as a journey, an adventure. You never quite know where it will lead you. And that's what makes it exciting. No different from life, really.

1
ERICA JONG

Day One, 2 pm: *Trump Palace, Upper East Side, New York City*

It was hot. Sticky, sweaty, sultry. Either that or I was having my first hot flush. They call them 'flashes' here. That's all I needed, for my hormones to start rock and rolling. I had taken my hormone replacement therapy tablet this morning. Perhaps I should have put an oestrogen patch on my bottom as well. Revenge of the menopause. Germaine Greer eat your heart out.

As I strode up Columbus Avenue looking for a cab, the front pages of all the tabloids were still headlining Connie Chung's removal. She was not going quietly. Good for her. Once inside the cab I started to panic. I checked the tape recorder, the batteries, the tapes. Again. Erica Jong was taking off for Finland tomorrow and wouldn't be back for three weeks. If I blew this, I'd had it.

The street crawled with wall-to-wall yellow cabs. People swarmed along the pavements like worker bees. Central Park was green, leafy, shimmering. I tried to dissolve into the spring day; live in the now, savour the present. I looked at my watch for the tenth time in five minutes. Surely I'm not going to be like this for the next two weeks. No. The first interview will be the toughest. Like the first kiss or lover or marriage, or fight.

Here it was. Trump Palace. Uniformed doorman. Marble foyer. Classy. I was early. I sat in the foyer talking to the doorman about how you can't believe anything you read in the paper. He thought there was definitely something else behind the Connie Chung story. The phone rang. 'You can go up now,' he said to me. Up in the lift, clutching my over-stuffed bag. Out of the lift.

Annette, my fax pal and Erica Jong's assistant, met me, shook hands and led me into the office. There was a table piled with letters, opened invitations. Stacks of other letters. Files from floor to ceiling. This was an industry.

Erica finally walked in, greeted me and took me into the adjoining room. She offered me a drink. I went for iced water. She was wearing a navy business suit, navy stockings and shoes to match. The corporate literary woman. The frames of her glasses were turquoise. She looked serious. As I started to tell her about the book she cocked one leg at a right angle over the other, leant forward and I saw a flash of cleavage between the string of pearls. The ultimate contradiction.

When I told her that to most people her name was synonymous with orgasm, she crinkled up her nose and laughed. 'Do you really think so?'

'Of course,' I said. 'After all, what is the zipless fuck all about?'

She looked a little sceptical but I don't think the thought displeased her. To be honest, I had always thought of her as a kind of Goldie Hawn character with brains. In the flesh, however, she was not scatty. Or overtly sexy. She did not flirt with the interviewer and it was not a seduction or a betrayal scenario. More of a collusion, I'd say. Sorry Janet Malcolm.

In the bookcase, just above her head, was a book of the collected poems of D.H. Lawrence. It was the romance of sex that she loved. Like Lawrence, they called Jong a pornographer. As she talked about her critics, I suddenly dredged up from my memory a book review that I had written on *How to Save Your Own Life*, the book that followed *Fear of Flying*.

It was smart-arsed. The review, not the book. I too had been a victim of the mind-set that went, 'so you think you're sexy and you know all about fucking. Huh!' I suspected reviews like that had bugged her all her writing life.

She was funny. She laughed a lot. I bet a lot of people missed the humour in Jong. They took it all too seriously and, in another sense, not seriously enough. After all, a woman writing about sex was a joke, wasn't it?

These and many other contradictory thoughts were galloping through my brain as I tried to focus on the game of the interview. The aims? Not to be distracted; to manage to engage the subject so thoroughly in the conversation that you get through the set pieces, the well-rehearsed lines, the little retorts that have always gone over so well; and, finally, to squeeze out enough time to actually get to what you considered is the truth.

I want you to feel as though you were there with me asking the questions, some of which were obvious and some of which you would probably have blushed at to hear me ask. I want you to hear each woman's individual voice with its own rhythms and eccentricities, I want you to hear the story of her life, not in a seamless narrative but more or less how it was told, without the questions or the interruptions. Sometimes, of course, I haven't been able to resist a comment or an aside, but these are for your ears only. So lie back and enjoy.

With Erica Jong the most obvious place to start was with the fact that she was and will always be best known for giving women the licence to have the sex and passion and romance of their choices, and lots of it.

'One of the hardest things for me is not being taken seriously. On my epitaph they will have "she invented the zipless fuck". But not long ago I was sent a book which was the first really serious scholarly consideration of my literary reputation taken in the context of feminism. It's truly fascinating because it places all the crazy things that have been said about me in the context of the denigration of women in our culture.

'I think this book is a turning point in my reputation. It's written by a feminist scholar in Indiana, not somebody I know. She's very interested in how literary reputations are made, what makes for a person's work reaching what she calls canonical status. She's found things written about me that I didn't even know about. They're so horrendous, I'm glad I didn't. But throughout the apprehension of my books there's this constant sniping at sexuality and a deep thread of anti-Semitism. It's really quite extraordinary.

'My reputation is turning because somebody is seeing through the bullshit and it may not have immediate results but I hope it will. I have fifty years still to live. I can wait. The first chapter is "Can it be good literature if it's funny, sexy and written by a woman?", which is really the central question. There has been a tendency to denigrate me based on the fact that I have written sexual things and said outrageous things and haven't been deferential to men. What is shocking to me is how little it's changed since the writers of the eighteenth and nineteenth centuries. The same things were said about them. I mean, Mary Wollstonecraft was called a "hyena in petticoats". I've been called "the mammoth pudenda". What's the difference?

'I think in many ways I'm very much a woman of my times, with all the ambivalence and contradictions, still wanting to be loved and nurtured. I don't think I could write about women accurately if I didn't know all these feelings.

'I'm an adventurous person, easily bored, hungry for experience and wanting to devour life. I guess that motivates me a lot. I want to know about everything and do everything and feel everything, experience everything, so that's why I have charged around the world, having lots of affairs.'

She certainly had. Affairs with both men and women, rich and poor, mad and sane, of all nationalities and temperaments and political and religious persuasions. The one that impressed me most was the affair conducted in the gondola. A fine sense of balance is clearly needed for this kind of research.

'I think restriction is a kind of pathology. It's pathetic that women consider restriction normal or fearfulness normal. I truly believe that both sexes are entitled to adventure and self-knowledge and self-expression. Male writers who have led highly sexual lives and written about them are taken seriously. There's a terrible double standard. But I think that's all the more reason to confront it head-on and change it.

'When my first book *Fear of Flying* took off as a best-seller, it certainly wasn't because of the publishers. They practically killed the book. But people read the book and said, "This is the way I feel" and handed it to their friends. When I go to a reading now and read from my work, people come up afterwards with dog-eared, battered copies of *Fear of Flying* with things underlined. The copies look like they've been read a hundred times. There are asterisks in the margins, you can see the book's been passed along and twelve different people have looked at it – and that, to me, is the greatest tribute you can make to an author.

'I think the reason it sold was people said, "Look at this, you've got to read this." They saw their own thoughts on paper for the first time, about sexuality and many other things. It was as if somebody had sliced open their heads and put the contents on the page, with great irreverence and humour, and it was fun to read. It was a very readable book, a sad book, a funny book, an entertaining book and a page-turner.

'What I always hear from readers is, "You validated me and you made me know I'm not alone, I'm not a freak, I'm not the only one who has felt that way." Yesterday I was at an Israeli Expo conference and all these Israeli women who had read my first book came up to me and said, "You liberated me. After I read your book I went out and slept with this one, this one, and this one." They read it in Hebrew twenty-two years ago, so there was a sense that women often feel very dirty about themselves and self-abnegating, as if they're the only ones who ever did this. It was a book that made you feel good about yourself and your sexuality and made you feel less lonely.

'That was not my intent. But books do reach out beyond the skin and make people feel joined in some way. There is a sense in which you should be changed by reading a book. Of course, most books don't change us at all, they're merely entertainment or they annoy us because they're too jejune or whatever, but a book should enter into your life and make you feel differently about yourself. If you go back to the eighteenth century and think about Rousseau's *La Nouvelle Héloïse* or *The Sorrows of Young Werther*, those were books that changed the way people felt about gender, about nature, about yearning, about romantic love – and they gave voice to a generation's longings. And I think *Fear of Flying* did the same thing.

'Even though my own father still asks, "How come they think you are a pornographer?", I don't think my books are "dirty" but I think that a woman merely writing about sex in an assertive way seems obscene to most people, because of our culture.

'Christianity, which has dominated our culture for the past 2000 years, is extremely sex-negative where women are concerned. Women have had to choose between marriage and celibacy, there is no other place for sexuality. They are either whores or Madonnas and, as one of the scholars who was speaking yesterday at the Israeli Expo said, this was not the previous view of women in the Jewish world or in the pagan world. In the pagan world, women were seen as great goddesses and in the Jewish world in the Old Testament writings, women were heroines who saved their country. You have people like Esther and Judith and it's only in the Christian era that you have the virgin mother and the whore. Basically, we're still labouring under that ugly division which is so harsh on women. It's a means of disempowering them. You can't have power if you are a virgin or a whore because you don't have any sexual power either way.

'We live in a sexist society and our mothers communicated to us the pain of living under sexism. Either they communicated it by being depressed and taking to their beds, or they communicated it by rage, or they communicated it by saying, "Don't wear your heart on your sleeve," or, "You'll catch more flies if you do this or that, be tricky, don't give up your virginity," but they communicated it with a great dose of anger.

'I think it's unrealistic to imagine, given the limitations put on women in our culture, that they wouldn't be angry. Maybe, in a weird way, their anger prepared us for our lives as women. I always felt my mother's anger made me a feminist. I don't know how much I'm doing it to my daughter, Molly. She's pretty smart and very psychologically acute and she'll say something like, "You know, Mummy, it's too bad that our relationship is constantly polluted by your rage at Daddy."

'That's a very wise thing for her to say, because there has been so much provocation from that quarter that sometimes it does play a role in our discussions. Once, when she had said that to me, I said, "Okay, I'm dropping the resentment, I'm dropping the anger, my former husband will never be the person I imagined I would like him to be, so be it. I accept it and I'll try to rise above it because I don't want to be full of anger."

'Psychologically, girls have a tremendous and powerful identification with their mothers. They become their first love object whereas boys have to separate from their first love object. This psychological task for girls would seem simpler, but in a way it's not because there's also a fear of engulfment. When you're a little girl you love your mother so much you want to be like her and then when you become an adolescent you're struggling to prove that you're different. That, I think, is built into the mother/daughter dynamic in any age. It's just that we live in a time when social conditions are changing so much with the sexes, that the rules have changed from decade to decade. Since we don't have a traditional society, it makes the mother/daughter thing more difficult to play out.

'If you think about the decades of this century, as I did when I was writing about my grandmother, my mother, myself and my daughter, I realised that my mother was a teenager in the 1920s wanting to be a flapper, admiring Edna St Vincent Millay and Dorothy Parker, never wanting to get married, feeling herself to be a free spirit. But then she had her babies in the 1930s and '40s and was a grown woman with three children in the '50s. She lost that independence because of the problems with raising children without child care, because of the sexism towards women artists in our society, because of having to accommodate to my father's work and all the things that I understand only too well now and empathise with now. But as a fifteen-year-old I said, "I will never do that."

'I think there's a basic psychological dynamic between mothers and daughters which is probably unchanged throughout the ages, but sexual roles have changed enormously in this century so we can't really pass along our role to our daughters. They have to change and be something different and that has made for tremendous bitterness, fear and guilt.

'There's that wonderful quote by Lou Andreas-Salome that I use in *Fear of Fifty*: "If you want to have a life, steal it." This is true for both men and women. Men mostly steal their lives from their fathers and women steal their lives from their mothers. Later on, when you're a mother yourself, you realise that your view of your mother was wrong. It was ungenerous, you didn't understand what she'd gone through, you had no idea what it meant to raise you, you didn't know the restrictions that her life contained and sometimes you make an incredible truce with your mother at a later age. But that adolescent breaking free was a necessary stage you had to go through. I think it is inevitable.

'I worry more about girls who never get angry at their mothers – they are the ones who are really in trouble, because some kind of belated anger comes out at the wrong time. You have to be secure in a relationship to be able to express anger – to rage and shout. Otherwise you can't have a relationship. You can't always be walking on egg shells, it doesn't work. You can't stay with a person you can't yell at. Anger is energy, anger can be very creative, it's not necessarily a bad thing. It can propel you to do things you wouldn't otherwise do.

'I have always had to make my own living but I never wrote only for money. I think I always put myself in a bind financially because that way it was easier for me to overcome the feeling that women really ought not to write. If I could put myself in a terrific bind, which I always managed to do because I'm terribly extravagant, then I could say, "Well, I'm doing this to support the baby," but in fact that's bullshit. I was doing this because I absolutely needed to write and I would have written whether or not I made money. It's an absolute visceral need in me, but there's always that guilt if you are of my generation that being a writer is not good for the kid and you should be home fussing over it all the time, which is ridiculous. So by always being in some kind of financial emergency, I would say, "Well, of course I've got to go out and give lectures and get book advances because otherwise the child will starve. How am I going to pay for the private school?"

'It's pretty funny when I look at it now. It's also a way of getting past your writer's block and there's something quite wonderful about being forced to do it from financial necessity. Writing is a strange life. On the one hand it's a solitary life and on the other you go running out and about to fill yourself up with ideas and experiences and stimulations. Or at least I do.

'George Sand, no matter how traumatic her life, always managed to write for four or five hours a day. I don't know how she did it, but life was much slower in the nineteenth century. It wasn't like she flew around in a jet. The travel was long and arduous, by donkey and boat. When she and Chopin went to Majorca for the winter, they settled in for six months. They didn't have the speed in their lives that we do. We cross continents and are totally jet-lagged, it's very different. That other, slower pace of life is very enviable. I think we've lost a lot with instantaneous travel. We've lost the dream time that we need so much.

'In the spring of 1971, while Greer was launching *The Female Eunuch*, I was in purple hot pants, purple shirt, purple granny glasses and high-heeled fuck-me sandals launching my first book of poetry, *Fruits and Vegetables*.

'We actually both did parts of the same television series for Channel 4 in the UK, but we have never actually met. I loved *The Female Eunuch*. I thought it was brilliant when I read it. I loved her public persona, it was so "Fuck you world!" Then I read *The Obstacle Race*, her book on women painters that was much neglected here. It is an absolutely seminal work on women painters. Since I come from a family of painters and I studied art history, I was fascinated. *The Change* I thought was terrific, very energetic, well written – everything she does is well written – but I disagreed with subsiding into "cronehood". I suspect she probably disagrees with it too. I'm not prepared to subside into cronehood at fifty, I'm sorry. I still want to look as nice as I can – although I'm not obsessed with looks, I don't want to become a crone.'

When she said this she looked to me for confirmation that cronehood was not something I saw lurking behind her in the shadows. I snorted in derision at the mere thought of such a thing, as was expected of me. But, in truth, there was no way the woman who sat opposite me would ever 'let herself go', as my mother's generation would say of somebody whose grooming and sense of dress had deteriorated. Those full cherry-like lips would never be reduced to a thinly stretched pencil line, the first sign of cronehood. Not at the rate she kissed people. Lots of passionate kissing is very important; it keeps the lips soft and supple and stops those lines that shrivel the top lip. I don't think Greer addressed kissing enough as an antidote to the ravages of menopause. Too concerned with the labia and not the lips. Jong never neglected one for the other.

'Even though I got married a lot I never married anybody who I thought would sit on my talent or keep me from doing what I needed to do. Sometimes it turned out that they did and, if that happened, I left the marriage. But I always entered into the marriage thinking it was an egalitarian situation and that it was going to be stabilising and good for my work. I always went into it assuming that the person I married would support my literary ambition, and mostly they did. Until things went wrong. Between my third and fourth marriage I w's single for almost a decade, raising my daughter. I was charging .:ound, I had a lot of different lovers but I was determined not to get married again.

'The reason I married my husband Ken finally, apart from the fact that he talked me into it, was that I came to feel that I was spending an awful lot of my energy fighting off involvements and commitments because I was so terrified of marriage. I also came to feel that it was a counterproductive thing to be doing. You can't get away from the fact that it is nice to have someone to come home to, who is your best friend and your pal, especially when you are going out into the world and taking it on the chin for saying rebellious things and getting a lot of flack for being who you are. It's nice to have somebody to go home to who believes in what you're doing and who cuddles you and says, "There, there, it's fine, I love you and I understand what you're about and these arseholes don't."

'It's very hard to do that all alone and for the most part I think people do want to live with one another. I'm a gregarious middle child, I'm not a solitary, so inevitably I would get involved with people. But I do know what it's like to live alone and to be totally responsible for myself.

'I'm not a beauty and I'm not somebody who ever attracted men or women because I was the best-looking in the room. If I attracted people it was through sheer force of personality and because I'm in love with life. That comes across. I've known an awful lot of women who are not beauties who have men following after them like they're the universal honey pot. It's not just about what you look like. It's true that immature men at a certain age want to show off to the other guys that they can have a model or whatever, but men who are a little bit more mature want a woman who makes them feel good about life and about themselves.

ERICA JONG
35

'I think that the fashion magazines have really sold us a bill of goods about how perfect you have to be to have a partner. Your attitude toward life is far more important than whether or not you look like a model. The pleasure in being alive is probably what has attracted men to me and that's part and parcel of everything that I am in my writing.

'It's energy more than looks. The whole question of sex and what is it, and life force and why some people communicate a connection with life force and other people don't, is really related to poetry and art.'

D.H. Lawrence has a lot to answer for. I too was influenced by this same theory of 'lifeforce'. I still think it's true. And I think it explains a lot of the energy in the books of all these women. Feminism itself was and is generated by sexual energy. Younger feminists often forget this, but then every generation probably thinks it invented sex.

'My sexuality made me crazy and there were many times in my life that I wished I was indifferent to men and not so much in the thrall of those tempestuous feelings. Probably the best thing about getting older is that you're not as vulnerable to those feelings as you were when you were younger.

'I think that Gloria Steinem said in one of her essays that she got sex mixed up with aerobics. She's absolutely charming. It was very interesting to me that I was smack in the middle of writing this memoir and suddenly Steinem comes out with the most autobiographical book she's ever written – *Revolution from Within*. Then Germaine Greer comes out with *The Change*, which is really a memoir of her ageing more than a book about menopause. It's really strange, why everybody is reflecting at this stage of their lives.

'The books that changed my life were *The Second Sex* by Simone de Beauvoir, which I read in high school, *Vagabond* by Collette, which I think is one of the greatest feminist novels ever written and a novel that could be written today. I remember reading *Memoirs of a Catholic Girl* by Mary McCarthy and thinking, "What a clever book – to write one chapter about what happened and in another chapter what fictionally happens."

'When you're writing autobiography you're constantly aware that autobiography is fiction and fiction is autobiography. I created the character of Erica in my autobiography *Fear of Fifty*. I like her. I think she has a saving grace, she can laugh at herself and she doesn't take herself terribly seriously. It's not like Kissinger's memoirs or Nixon's memoirs.

'If you don't reach a point in life where you can send up your own weaknesses then you shouldn't write a memoir, or an autobiography. Who wants to read about somebody taking themselves seriously? The greatest thing about reaching the age of fifty is you look back on your life and you see the stupid things you've done, but instead of beating yourself up for it you find it funny – you've come to that change in perspective.

'Probably the most consistently stupid thing I ever did was invent men and then fall in love with them. I would turn them into a combination of Robin Hood and Mr Darcy and Heathcliff and then later on when I ran into them I realised they weren't anything like the man I'd invented. That was a very prevalent mistake.

'The other thing was suing a movie studio when I was thirty years old. Now that was stupid. Who can win suing a movie studio? Everybody warned me against it and I persevered on my crusade, I was going to change the world. Now I think it was funny but it was extremely painful at the time. It's all grist for the mill. A writer's life should be interesting. There's almost nothing you can't make into a book.

'I think Naomi Wolf is far more comfortable with power than my generation was and that's great – but then she has a fabulous feminist mother. She was raised by parents who both worked, were intellectually radical, so she's further along in the process. Even so, I think that in *Fire with Fire* there is a tendency to be slightly complacent, but not as bad as some of the other members of that generation because she's very, very smart. For example, she launches into how, since the Anita Hill/Clarence Thomas hearings, the Congress of the United States will never be the same again, and I read it and I thought, "Gee, not so fast Naomi, this problem is cyclical. [In 1991, Anita Hill alleged that Clarence Thomas, President Bush's nominee for the Supreme Court, had sexually harassed her when they had worked together ten years earlier.]

'Gloria Steinem has resisted getting married. Good for her. But I know myself too well and I know that I have certain dependency needs that have to be met. For me to have a nurturing man in my life has been good for my creativity. You have to know yourself. What's right for one person is not necessarily right for another person. The older I get the more I see myself becoming my mother and my grandmother, snatching the plates off the table and putting them in the dishwasher. My husband does all the cooking and I do the cleaning up, which is a pretty good division of labour because I find cleaning up quite meditating, it lets me dream and think.

'When I look in the mirror now I see myself turning into all those forebears. I have a lot of empathy for them, they don't seem so old-fashioned and I'm fascinated with their lives. This is what I'm working on with my new book. I think of my grandfather, my mother's father, fourteen years old, walking across Europe, making his way to Paris to be a painter. I think of my grandmother coming to London, learning English, which she never really spoke very well. The way those people made new lives, and escaped from Europe. They were already in America a long, long time when the Holocaust happened. I'm fascinated with their strength, with their determination.

'Also, it's in your fifties that the first great harvesting begins of the friends. People your own age die and then it really gets serious. I've started to understand things that my grandparents told me when I was a little girl, things I had no understanding of then. My grandfather, who lived to be ninety-seven, used to say, "I don't want to be here any more, everybody I used to know is gone, people don't understand any more the world that I grew up in or the world that I lived in."

'I can see how if you outlive all your contemporaries, things could be very lonely. Just as when I was in my twenties, I always had friends who were in their eighties, like Louis Antermeyer the anthologist or Henry Miller. It fascinated me to know the older generation and since I was very close to my own grandparents, it felt natural to me. But as I get older, more and more I want to be in touch with people of different generations who are younger than me. I'm very involved with the lives of my nieces and nephews. I want to know how they think, what they think about. You have to be, you can't be stuck only in your own generation. That's a kind of prison.

'For the next hunk of my life I really want to write this big family novel that paints the whole world of the generations. I think I have the empathy now to do it. I don't think I did before. The novel I was always proudest of is *Fanny*, because I thought, "Now I have cut my teeth as a novelist, I've woven together all these stories and I've gotten them to the Caribbean and back to England."

'I would like to see my work intelligently adapted in other forms. I'm at work on a musical based on *Fanny*. There has been a lot of sniffing around about doing movies on my other books, but none have ever been made for a variety of reasons, including the fact that they were about assertive, uppity women and the film industry in America doesn't like assertive, uppity women. It's still totally male dominated, but suddenly I seem to have a lot of champions in the film business who are trying to find ways to make movies of my books.

'I love being an assertive, uppity woman. What's the alternative? The alternative is being depressed. There's no way to be a woman in this world and not be assertive and uppity unless you accept your oppression and just lie down and die or get into bed in the afternoon.'

How did she know what I did when I was depressed?

'You must be assertive and, in a way, I think it is very fortunate to be a woman in this sexist society. Just as it's fortunate in a way to be a Jew in an anti-Semitic world or a black in a racist world, because you're condemned to be the outsider and the outsider has a better vision of society than the insider.

'I've always felt like an outsider. But I think a writer must be an outsider. It gives you that specific angle of vision. If you are anointed by the system like some of the men I know with their sinecures and serving on the boards of corporations just because they are presentable white men of middle years, if you're cosseted that way by the system, there are things you never get a chance to see. It's in your interest not to see them. In a way it's fortunate to be a woman in a world that discriminates against women.

'Sure it would be easier to be a man, but I'm not interested in an easy life, or being famous. Fame is a sound bite. And mine was "the zipless fuck". Fame certainly accelerates the process of figuring out what you think of your life and what you want to do with it and what you respect. It dispenses very fast with the notion that the world's opinion of you matters. In a way that's fortunate because you understand that fame is always a misunderstanding of who you are. It's nice to have it but it doesn't give you any sense of your inner worth. Then you can get on with your sense of inner worth. Regardless of all that I have done and been, I have always hung onto my sense of self. I have it very strongly, now and always.

'I don't think anyone ever took away from me who I basically was at my centre. My parents communicated to me – how ever they did it I don't even know, and I don't think they even know – a tremendous sense of freedom. And they also communicated to me that it was okay to be an artist. How they did that I'm not sure because in some ways they didn't even give themselves permission to be that.

'It was an advantage that my father did not have a son. Tillie Olsen says, "How fortunate we are to be born in families without sons." I think that's a part of it. But there was a great emotional tyranny from my mother and my sister. I felt that growing up. I'm very much a second child and I know this from living with my husband, Ken. He is the first child of three and he expects to get his own way about certain things and he expects me to compromise. Sometimes I do and sometimes I don't, but the roles that you're allotted in the family at birth cling to you for the rest of your life. The second child has to do a lot to get attention. But you have to have something more than attention seeking propelling you to do all the sheer hard work I've done that's involved writing eighteen books. Certainly there's an element of anger and "I'll show them" and exhibitionism in it. Who can separate out all the parts – I'm just so happy when I'm writing. It takes me a long time to get to it but when I do it's just a wonderful thing.

'I'm still a bit of a daredevil, but you're never as bad when your daughter's becoming the daredevil. The last time we were in London together and she was invited on a radio show with me, she said, "Well, you know your parents have sex but you don't want to read about it. This is not an autobiography, it's a desperate cry for help."

'The joke of it all is that Molly never reads my books. If I've forced her to read the stuff about herself, which I have, that's a lot for her, but she completely insulates herself against me as a writer. She only wants me as a mother. So that's fine, so she doesn't read anything I write. It will be interesting to see how she deals with sex.

'Her generation has been brainwashed about AIDS and it's scared, which is good. But they're very late bloomers in this generation. They go out with gangs of kids, they don't get involved with one particular partner. Molly's only sixteen and a half, she's had a couple of boyfriends, but not serious ones; I think she'll come to it later. I married the first guy I slept with. It was a generational thing. In my college class a lot of people married their first lover. I gave in to it because it was a way for me to break from my family of origin, which I needed to break with and which was so overwhelming to me. There was my mother and my father and my grandfather, my grandmother, my two sisters. I was tremendously attached to them and I needed to get away. The reason I was drawn to marrying young, as my two sisters did too, was to break that spell.

'A lot of women get married to choose a second family and then work through their various neurotic feelings about their first family. Sometimes you have to go through various different stages in order to work it through, and I think I did that. My life was tremendously impacted by Michael going crazy. Having a first husband, a first lover and first best friend – a soul mate – who became psychotic and actually thought he was Jesus Christ – he had these raving paranoid fantasies – impacted on my life tremendously, and skewed it, in a way. I think that's why I married a psychiatrist next, who was unsuitable in many ways, but whom I clung to. I think that's also why I eventually left the psychiatrist. There are so many things that wouldn't have happened if I hadn't gone through that incredible trauma at the age of twenty-two.

'Humour was my device for dealing with the pain, but quite recently I've thought a lot more about the nervous breakdown Michael had and I've been able to transport myself in memory back to the person I was. It's terrifying. I buried the terror very deep under jokes but lately in therapy I've started to think about it and I realise what a huge thing that was.

'Therapy can be wonderful. It's been a very liberating force in my life but I was always attractive and attracted to people who had the potential to be psychotic. I'll tell you why. Psychotic people can jump into the metaphor in a way that a poet can. The difference between me and a psychotic person is that I could jump into the dream, jump into the fantasy, but I could come back and they couldn't. So I would fall in love with these people and then suddenly realise that I knew the way back to the world above ground and they didn't. I don't do that any more in my life. If I meet someone who's mad or incipiently mad, I turn on my heel and walk the other way. But when I was a very romantic adolescent, those were the people I found so appealing. I sought them out, especially if they were brilliant and fey.

'Falling in love is a surrender and in order to be a poet or a novelist you have to be able to surrender to the characters in the book, to your fantasy, to your dream life. It's literally true that you can't create anything if you can't surrender to the dream life. You have to be able to surrender there at the desk, let go of the conscious control and go into the images, or you can't write a thing.

'My honesty terrifies people. But what's the point of being an author if you're not going to be honest? I mean, there are certainly easier ways to make money. You could become a financial analyst and form a mutual fund. That doesn't take an enormous amount of brains, but you have to sit in front of the computer all day and worry whether the interest rates are going up or down, and you have to care a lot about that.

'I'm much better with money than I used to be. I finally figured out in the middle of my life that all the people I've paid to do that for me might as well have been throwing darts. I don't think it's such a big mystery. You diversify your assets, interest rates go up, the stock market generally goes down, it's not such a big deal. I've sort of stopped giving that power to other people, as if they knew something that I didn't know. I'd rather make my own mistakes.

'Women and wealth is the last taboo. Women feel that they are not allowed to have money and women often take their holdings and put them in the hands of some man, often the one they happen to be living with. Even women who know more about money than the men whose hands they put it in – it's very weird. I think that's also a kind of brainwashing. It took me a long time to get to the point where I was not afraid to do that. I discovered that I became pretty good at investing money for Molly. I had no conflict and so, since I didn't feel conflicted about it, I always did very well with it. And then I started to think to myself, "Well, why is it that I can do that with this little bit of money that I've put aside for Molly?" Because I don't have any ambivalence, I want Molly to have a little nest egg for her education. But it's been a big process of working through dealing with the money.

'I'm not a wealthy woman, but what is wealthy? I have enough money to write the next book without being in the thrall of publishers. I'm not living from advance to advance. My idea of wealth is having "fuck you" money, which is that you're able to say to publishers, "Forget it, I'll publish my own book, I don't need your advance." I don't have that kind of money. Very few women have that. Very few people have it – mostly people who have inherited it or been smart in investing it. But if I think about it, perhaps if I had "fuck you" money, I would get lazy. Maybe the great goddess has been wise by not giving it to me.

'One of the problems we have as women is extending sisterhood to a wide range of women. Joan Collins has become a friend and Molly's become friendly with her kids. Joan's really feisty, she's a terrific mother, and she's absolutely unstoppable and un-put-downable. I think that's great. I think she would call herself a feminist but many feminists would be aghast at that. Because she's an actress, she wears a ton of make-up and designer clothes and, although she doesn't admit it, I think she's had a face-lift a few times but I don't think you have a choice when you're an actress, that goes with the territory. You're not going to get parts if you've got saggy skin and lots of chin. If you're an actress or an anchorwoman, you don't have a choice but to have your face done.

'I think the situation of women is really in a bad place. First of all we haven't figured out how to be sisters yet and that's really critical. I have a tremendous belief in sisterhood but women journalists have to stop jumping on other women, and stop making it appear that Hillary Clinton is a bitch. I think they are much tougher on women than men because that's one way of making the transition, in our adversarial journalistic system. Also, all of the ambivalence about their mothers comes out when they interview older women. A cat fight always makes good journalism, so the male managing editor or the male publisher thinks, and the shots are finally called by men or by women who might as well be men because they've figured out how to act like men in the world.

'We're a long way from having a truly equal society where both genders have equal input intellectually, financially, politically, sexually; a long, long way. Sometimes I wonder whether we'll ever have it because what you see happening, if you can make a generalisation, is that there are fundamentalist movements emerging everywhere in the world, from the Arab world to the Christian world to the Jewish world. The greatest danger of our time is fundamentalist zealotry. The fundamentalists view women very much as chattels and we could easily have the biggest backlash in history. In the 1960s you went to the Arab world and you saw young women walking around in miniskirts, now you go to the Arab world and women in their twenties are back in chador.

'The Republican congress in the US is slashing funding for all medical research. Nobody's doing research on women's diseases.

Why do women get breast cancer? Why do women have thyroid disease overwhelmingly more than men? They're going to shut down birth control clinics, programmes that educate kids about contraception. These budget cuts impact on women and children worse than anybody. Since women and children are the poorest section of the population, they're the ones that stand to gain most from Medicare. I think that American women are in much greater danger than we even know. It makes me terribly angry, because I pay a lot of taxes and I find it appalling that the money that I earn with my pen, which is a difficult way to earn money, and send to Washington in great gobs, is being used for stuff that I utterly disapprove of. And I can't do anything about it. It makes me very angry and makes me feel very powerless. I find it appalling that national broadcasting may be cut, medical research may be cut, contraceptive research may be cut. I don't want to pay money for the shit heads who are buying armaments around the world. Every time a missile goes overhead I look up and think, "I bought the wing." Public universities in the US are being destroyed, libraries can't stay open, they've cut the hours, they don't have enough money to buy books. What is going on? Those are the things that I want to fund.

'I put the anger into my writing and hope that I change people's minds. I do believe that writing does change people's minds, it does filter into the system, it does have an impact. The United States under this Congress is going to make some disastrous moves. What generally happens in this country is that we swing one way and then we swing the other way. I don't think it's a very efficient way to run a country, but that seems to be the way we manage.

'I think women have to identify as a class or a caste, which they have not done through our history. We have mostly identified with our men – our sons or husbands or fathers. That was the hope that Naomi Wolf had in her book *Fire with Fire* – in 1992 we suddenly saw our position as a class and saw what power we could have. I hope that's true. I think we've a way to go.

'Sometimes conditions have to get worse in order for people to wake up. If abortion had been taken away two years ago when

ERICA JONG

45

everybody thought it was a distinct possibility, right before the Supreme Court reappraised the whole abortion issue, you would have seen a huge rallying of sisterhood because that's a real issue. That didn't happen. The Supreme Court, although it's quite conservative in its constitution, came down on the side of privacy, between a woman and her doctor. That was a very conservative rationale for maintaining the status quo. Now in states where abortion is legal it's threatened on the funding level and we'll see where that goes.

'Feminism has joined the mainstream in a way. Everybody believes in certain feminist things and there has been real substantive change in the ideology about what marriage is like, who raises the children, who stays home when the children are sick. There has been a lot of change in basic attitudes. What there hasn't been is legal change and financial change and change in the infrastructure.

'I always thought that writers could change the world and I believed in the power of the written word. But I never thought anybody would read *Fear of Flying*. I believed I was writing it for the desk drawer. I couldn't have written as clearly if I hadn't told myself that nobody would read it. At that point I was a poet who had published two volumes of poetry. Why would I think it would become a best-seller? I thought it would have sold a couple of thousand copies. I wrote it because I had to and yet I did feel these tiny pricklings in my fingers – you know, that it was possible, that it might go well out there, but I wouldn't consciously let myself believe it.

'When I was writing *Fear of Fifty* I had a wonderful sense of excitement at getting down a generation's point of view. I wrote it with tremendous passion and I felt that it was absolutely the book I had to be writing at that moment. I try always to write with that enthusiasm because I think that puts energy into prose. Poems are written that way, as an epiphany, and I try to write my fiction or nonfiction that way too.

'Of course not every book is going to be the amanuensis to the *Zeitgeist*. In a writer's life there might be certain books that stand out and that reach an audience, and other books that don't. Or certain books that reach a scholarly audience and other books that misfire completely. That goes with the territory of writing for a whole lifetime. What I find so upsetting about our culture is that we demand that everybody hit a home run every time. Art can't happen that way, that's terribly commercial. Artists can't create focus groups and find out what people want to hear like a politician or a television producer. Even if you could you wouldn't want to. It's not what you ought to be doing. You should not be giving people what they want, you should be giving people what they don't yet know they want. You should be plugged into the times, in a kind of mystical way, almost, and then you put into words the incoherent longings of your time. If you're lucky. Then people discover what it was that they needed to hear. But it can't be done the other way around. An artist or writer is a specimen human being who just goes about the world hoping to be a bundle of nerve endings that take in everything and transform it into a voice. You may do that a couple of times in your lifetime, you may do it in certain passages of a book, and never again. But you're not motivated by that, you're motivated by the need to do it.

'In *Fanny*, one of my characters – the ship's doctor who's then mowed down by cannon fire – says, "Fanny, the word can change the world." That's what I would put on my epitaph: "the word can change the world".'

'That's a good title,' I said. 'I might use it.'

'Have it,' she said, 'I'm good at titles.'

Annette, her assistant, was at the door. Time was up. As I was packing up, Erica gave me a hardback copy of her latest poems, new and selected, called *Becoming Light*. Inside it she wrote a generous inscription. The ink was purple.

As we walked to the door I said, 'Do you think Molly would call herself a feminist?'

'Oh, sure,' she said. 'But the image of the word is not so good – her generation thinks if you call yourself that you'll never get a man.'

'Perhaps it's time to make feminism sexy again,' I said. 'It sure didn't do you any harm in terms of getting men.'

She looked at me and laughed. 'That's for sure.'

ERICA JONG

47

Finally, after we shook hands, she said, almost as an afterthought, 'When you see Susan Faludi, tell her she was wrong to call me "not a feminist" in her book *Backlash*. It's a bad example of younger women attacking older women. It's not a good thing to do.'

Once out in the street I took a deep breath, hailed a cab, went straight back to the apartment, threw my things down, put the tapes in the little zip-up case I'd bought especially for this purpose (I'd heard too many horror stories about tapes being lost), poured a glass of Australian wine, arranged a plate of Zabar's food, went into the bedroom, took off all my clothes and lay down under the revolving ceiling fan. One down, nine to go. Would I last the distance? I'd heard of stress melt-down, but this heat was burning me up from the inside. Perhaps it was just all that talk of sex? At least I had a couple of hours to calm down, be cool and think about madness before I met Phyllis Chesler.

2
PHYLLIS CHESLER

Day One, 7.30 pm: Her house, Brooklyn, New York City

I had showered, dressed and joined the throbbing pulse of people on Columbus Avenue. They were all eating, drinking, chatting, shopping or just taking the air. It was still hot. I was scanning the traffic for a cab that looked like it had a driver who spoke English – I didn't know exactly where I was going and I couldn't afford to be driving around Brooklyn half the night. My appointment was for 7.30 pm and from the tone of Phyllis Chesler's voice on the phone, I knew she would be on time and waiting for me.

I had never met her before, but Phyllis Chesler's ground-breaking indictment of psychiatric theory and practice, *Women and Madness*, is still the benchmark for studies in this area. For every woman who had ever felt angry, aggressive, rebellious, depressed, suicidal or just 'off the airwaves' and who had been told by doctors that she was neurotic, mad or even psychotic, and who had been prescribed mind-numbing drugs or given electro-shock therapy, this was the book that first placed it all in a feminist context. This book gave women hope.

The car window was down and the air was blowing in my face and hair as we sped alongside the Hudson River. The light was clear, bright. The river was shining. We crossed the Brooklyn Bridge with its thousands of linked but crossing wires. A good image of the women's movement.

Once in Brooklyn, as the driver searched for the street, we travelled through great extremes of affluence and poverty. Sometimes they were only a few blocks from each other, just like the rest of New York. I scanned the houses until we finally stopped at the right number. It was in a leafy street with well-established trees, a tall stone house that appeared to have three levels. I climbed the wide stone steps to the door on the middle level, and knocked.

Phyllis answered my knock and led me into a passage and then into a very large white, book-lined room. At one end there was a living area, at the other a kitchen and dining table. She had thick dark hair, very bright eyes and was shorter than I expected. She looked healthy, despite her very nasty prolonged battle with Epstein-Barr virus. She offered me something to eat from the pots on the stove.

I was far too churned up to eat but accepted a coffee and followed her downstairs to a long, well-organised room with work benches along the walls. It was air-conditioned. I still seemed to be overheating.

'Young women often ask me how long it took to write *Women and Madness*. I say, "I think that one's first book requires one's entire life up until that point."

'I was very lucky that it was published in 1972 as opposed to 1952. Because in 1952 I would have written the book, it would have been as good as it is, but nobody would have read it and it wouldn't have caught the imagination of the critical mass of thinking people, mainly women.

'There may be women with great minds and hearts and genius throughout all of history but if you're born at the wrong moment, your works may die on the wind. Since I wrote *Women and Madness* I have read nineteenth-century first-person accounts by women who were just thrown in the loony bin because their husbands were crazy or wanted their money or wanted them out of the way or wanted to remarry or because these women had strong opinions of their own and they were punished for that. The greater the woman, the more dangerous is her situation. This is a problem because, on the other hand, heroism is our only alternative. There really is no alternative but to be heroic, and then you're really in danger because of the extent to which men and other women will judge themselves by your greater light – they will try to put your light out.

'I wrote in *Women and Madness* that we are all in today's world essentially motherless. If you think about the kind of mothering that creates a strong self, then few women have had that. Most of us have mothers who could have lived in the stone age or in Biblical times. Some would say, "My mother really loved me," or "She did the best she could," or "She wasn't cruel," or "She wasn't sadistic." Which is important, but it's not the same as saying, "My mother was, in her own right, a strong person who bequeathed to me a legacy of entitlement to that." Or "My mother was not a servant to men or to men's ideas and I therefore take it for granted and act accordingly."

'There are more young women whose mothers have been feminists in the second wave of feminism and as they begin to write and speak and act we realise they are gatekeepers. They're canny, crafty gatekeepers. They have seen the price that their mothers have paid and they don't want to pay it. Also, because they're young, they think that they can have it all. They really do.'

Phyllis said all this seemingly without taking a breath. She was like an engine revving up for a marathon journey. I thought I should try to take control.

'But didn't we also think we could have it all?' I said. 'Wasn't that part of the motivation? Didn't we want to have our cake while we still had our teeth?'

It was as if I had not spoken. The engine increased volume and tempo.

'I've seen daughters who are now in their twenties or thirties, really so privileged and in such an unreal world that, were reality to hit them, they would not be its match. They have not been trained to that. In the case of Naomi Wolf, I know her and I like her and she's a very earnest young person, but she's wrong, she's simply wrong.'

No messing about here. No equivocation. No holding back.

'I don't think her book has changed the world for anybody. Her first book, *The Beauty Myth*, is recycled stuff from early '70s revisited, but gutting the politics. What happened to her is that – at a very young age, with much skill and passion and colour and theatrical sense but with no political activist history, with a core inside that is weak rather than strong, with a desire to please more than a desire to change the world – she wrote *Fire with Fire*. There are things in it which I think are true and good but do not go far enough.

'She begins to correctly analyse the ways in which second-wave or third-wave feminists are very inhumane to other women. It's one of the subjects I've been grappling with. Erica Jong and I agree on this. Erica has an utterly sunny temperament and it belies the hard work and the long-distance running that she does. Erica's facade is a little bit Marilyn Monroe but she is utterly serious. For a long time I've been writing a book called *Women's Inhumanity to Women* and now I'm thinking I should just call it *Feminist Inhumanity to Women*. The sad thing is that we're not worse to women but we're not better and we experience it harder because we expect better and different from each other.'

She was right. And honest enough to say it. For too long we have expected all feminists to be saints or at least to want to achieve sainthood. The fact is that we expect too much. Being a feminist is not like joining an order of nuns. Feminism has to allow itself to encompass the full range of human behaviour from the best to the worst. We set ourselves impossible standards. I only thought this, there was no time to say it aloud.

'There are so many books out there by men that are really inferior brands. Not just inferior books but books filled with such misogyny and such vitriol towards women or such complete indifference to women's condition that regularly get touted and well reviewed and covered and make lots of money. You can get great works by women who can't find a publisher, can't stay in print – it's like we've overstayed our welcome. It's like they're saying, "Okay, you did a fantastic job the first time, Kate Millett (*Sexual Politics*), Phyllis Chesler (*Women and Madness*), Erica Jong (*Fear of Flying*). Now get the hell out of our faces! We want young, we want virgin." That very thing that makes a man and wine better as they age, is used against us. I think that the long-distance runners among us are better – we get better as we develop.

'The truth is, when people want to talk to me just about *Women and Madness*, I know a little despair because I've been developing the themes that I sounded in that book in six other books and many articles. I didn't know it at the time but I see, looking back, that everything I have written subsequent to that had its birth there and is there waiting, including *Women's Inhumanity to Women*.

PHYLLIS CHESLER

'Certainly, a woman's right to self-defence, which I've now been working on, is in there and the way in which I looked at the image of Amazon women: military, graceful, warriors in battle. The Amazons visited me in a dream. I didn't know anything about Amazons, and so there are so many things that, looking back at that book, I have no idea how I knew about. I must have been guided by angels galore.

'I was looking at what it means to be unmothered or to be improperly mothered. Not mothered in the sense of "fit in and preserve the status quo" but mothered to change the status quo.

'I think that not enough has changed in terms of the psychiatric treatment of women – the double standards, the way in which women flinch when we're told that we're probably crazy. It's almost as if it's the Inquisition and we hear the fires being lit in a pyre. Amazons and witches and crazy ladies. Joan of Arc was my Amazon archetype who was broken in Christian time.

'I was looking at the themes of freedom, what it means to be colonised. We can't afford to romanticise our "nice treats" that we've purchased with our fame and our dignity. So when you say women are so nice and so compassionate, the truth is, yes, they are, but not to each other and not to themselves; mainly to grown men and to maybe just their own small children but not to the children of women elsewhere. That doesn't mean that we're any better morally than men, who have the virtues they've purchased at our expense.

'When I wrote *Women and Madness* I was not a biological mother, I certainly never wanted to be. I never thought about becoming that. Looking back I see that I had a very particular kind of attitude about pregnancy and motherhood. I was agin it. I was more concerned, as so many were, with the right to have an abortion than with the right to choose to have a child and then to keep custody of the child you choose to have. During the writing of that book I had some affairs with men, not all at the same time and mainly in between meetings. It was a change from my earlier boy-crazy life – easy to heartbreak at the hands of men who didn't seem to love you back and couldn't be intimate the way you wanted but you still somehow needed them in some irrational way. When I wrote the book, I was married to myself and I was married, if anything, to a movement that was very heady and very sweet. I was dazzled, literally, by the movement that we quickly made. That was my mate or my inspiration or the atmosphere in which I created.

'Writing the book I got terribly punished. I was a full-time professor at a university and instead of being rewarded for doing the studies that I then published in the book, the other members of the faculty yelled at me. They didn't want me to use the secretaries to transcribe any of my interviews, although they did that and more for the men. A couple of my colleagues, as they became feminists, ganged up on me and said that if I published anything it should be published anonymously. And I said, "Well, that's really silly. Anonymous was a woman, she's already published under that name."

'But that was what I call the Chinese cultural revolution in American feminist times. It was down with the intellectuals. The writer Marge Piercy and I met in a consciousness-raising group and we were very attracted to each other's minds and work and talent, and most of the other women in that group found ways to keep us apart. We had to meet secretly because the women in that group did not appreciate the work Marge and I were doing. I remember once I was late to a meeting and they were yelling at me. This must have been 1970. And Marge suddenly became queenly and said, "Don't you understand that the work Phyllis is doing will change the world for women. If she's a little bit late, don't be so hard on her." I nearly wept because her not understanding was the unexpected miracle.'

In all this time I had barely said a word. Phyllis, on the other hand, had barely paused for breath. It was as if she had to expel as many words as possible in the shortest possible time. I suppose if you really believe you are going to change the world, you don't have any time to waste. She certainly had a sense of destiny that she took very seriously. She saw herself not so much as a saint but as a driving force for good.

PHYLLIS CHESLER

'How knowledge can be used for good has remained a theme in my work. I didn't really look at material reality, which is what my next book was about: women, money and power. I didn't really look at men, which is why I then wrote a book about men; I thought it would be a counterpoint to *Women and Madness*, but it was very different. Although I look at male uterus envy and the murder of the goddess and fratricide among men, which is pretty serious, it was a very different kind of book and I don't think the themes continued from *Women and Madness*.

'I went to Israel because I had been reckoning with anti-Semitism among feminists and I was just amazed and blown away by it. So I went to Israel for the first time and I met this man who didn't speak English very well and knew nothing about me. After *Women and Madness* came out, I got a front page on the *New York Times Book Review* and everybody was calling me. I didn't know what to do with this fame. I wasn't certain it was a good thing, I thought it's fine if you can use it for good and it's not so fine when you can't and when everyone thinks you can. And it's not so fine when you can't get enough cash flow to do your next work but everyone thinks that you must have a lot of money because you're exceedingly famous. So this man followed me back from Israel and he was always there. I would rush out to a meeting, come back and he'd still be there. So after a while I thought, "Well, all right," and then he needed a green card after the Yom Kippur War started. I think I wanted "tribe". I wanted a certain family that's not American, that would be more Mediterranean, more Middle Eastern, and I had done this before, I'd married somebody from Afghanistan.'

'Stop,' I cried. 'Slow down. It's all too much to take in. So the husband from Israel was number two. Where did number one come in?'

'Oh, yes, I have a history of marriage. But I'll never do it again. Only two husbands. I had a son, who's now seventeen, with the second one. Husband number two promised to be the mother, but he lied. He said he would be the perfect feminist father. He left me, the Amazon warrior, holding the baby. I was holding the baby thinking I was going to drop it. Then I watched how I couldn't drop the baby. I was thirty-seven and a half, I did natural childbirth and it took thirty-two and a half hours. This was my choice. I thought that this was a sacred kind of experience. Everyone had been predicting that I would give birth to some Amazon princess but "she" was a "he" and I thought that was nature's lesson to me and my comeuppence.

'So he left me holding the baby and I didn't let the baby drop and I think it has made life philosophically richer but economically so much harder, so much more difficult. It's being the mother and the father and the aunt and the uncle and the sister and the brother and the entire extended family. The father doesn't see him. The Israeli grandparents don't see him. My father's been dead a long time and my mother's old and not so well but she does see him. I have two brothers, one of whom we don't see and the other of whom we see occasionally. I mean, it's the typical nuclear family holocaust. I was jilted at the altar of motherhood. He lied, he basically couldn't follow through on it.

'Without my becoming a mother I certainly wouldn't have written *With Child* and I wouldn't have written *Mothers on Trial*. I don't know if it changed the world because it had a slightly unfortunate history in publishing but I have 10,000 letters from women who said they carried it around like their Bible through their divorce and custody battle. When I was pregnant women started finding me to tell me how they had lost custody of their children, so it was like a chill wind blowing across my grave. I launched into a six-year study of custody battles, what they mean legally and psychologically and ethically and throughout history, and it's certainly the fiercest face of the so-called backlash.

'I think Faludi's book on backlash was good. I was cheered that it was selling well. She's a sober, serious type, probably shy – that's the persona I get. I don't know her. I don't know if she's totally right because I really do think the backlash never stopped. Also the frontlash never stopped. Just as rapes may have been as frequent in a previous century but went unreported and unrecorded, I think that frontlash is enormously ferocious and we just didn't measure it. For a moment we believed our media clippings – that we had it made, that we were on the upswing, that we couldn't be defeated and that we would be united. But it's not true. It just took a little while for the forces in patriarchy to really begin to "disappear" our best works.

'It is a different world for some now, it is a world transformed, it is a world in which things that we didn't even whisper about behind closed doors are now utterly out there on the table. But that's not enough for me. You know why it's not enough? I'll tell you. Because look at what they're doing in Bosnia, and that's not even Rwanda. Everything we know makes the mass rapes and the forced pregnancies in camps more painful. And what is most painful of all is that we can't airlift those women out. We have no sovereign feminist space to take them to and we have no government in exile or on earth to rescue real women from awful disasters. It may be that bitterness and despair have set in because we can't do this in our lifetime or quickly enough.

'I usually can bear things as long as everyone is fully conscious about where we are. I have a hard time when people are in fugue states and they can't name things properly and they have no sense of where they want to go. One could argue that we have accomplished an extraordinary amount of change in a short time. More than we can even tell. But we can also argue that it's not going to be as easy as we once hoped and it won't be as fast as we wanted it to be and as individuals, even as writers, our work may not prevail in our own lifetime. It may be lost for a while. That's very painful.

'I write for eternity.'

You have to admire someone who not only says this but clearly believes it. There's no false modesty, no wishing and no hoping. Just a straight-eyed look and total belief in what she says.

'A lot of Kate Millett's books were out of print for a long time. Some of my books are out of print right now and previous books went in and out of print. I didn't pay attention because I was writing new ones and that means that generations came up behind us which do not really know the work of radical feminists. They really don't. They know Derrida, Lacan; they know all that deconstruction garbage. They don't know political activism. This is a problem. It did not come about because we as writers didn't do our job but because the universities wouldn't hire us and wouldn't teach us and the existing think-tanks wouldn't hire us or teach us.

'Women's Studies became a reactionary ghetto, an anti-activist ghetto and an anti-radical ghetto – with exceptions. And that's been a disappointment. Now you can't buy the *Female Eunuch*. I've looked for it in bookstores, I can't get it.

'I remember first reading an excerpt of Kate Millett's *Sexual Politics* when I was in a bookstore. I just stood there and didn't leave, I read the entire thing. In 1967 I was working in a lab in a medical college when somebody told me that the women were getting together to make a feminist revolution. I left the lab instantly looking for where this was. So I was ready for Kate's book and it was a wonderful book. It came out as I was already doing the research that would become *Women and Madness*. I had already made a public demand for a million dollars at an American Psychological Association meeting which was met with laughter and hysterics and viciousness, but I didn't care. It made world headlines and that meant when I got back from the meeting in Miami, publishers were calling me for this book. I would have written it and handed it out on the street corners myself or paid people to read it. I just had a sense of mission that was utterly sublime. I knew that I would have to do this book. I was looking at not just the myths, I was looking at all the National Institute of Mental Health statistics on where the bodies were buried. As I did it I was whirling like a dervish doing everything in ten different areas. I was part of a moment in history and a movement at that time in which all good feminists set out to effect change. I wasn't angry. I was just happy to be doing this work and to have other women near me doing similar work. I probably was in love with justice, with a notion of freedom.

'I always felt different from others and I never felt that I fitted into my family. I had the typical adoption fantasy. I don't even think I knew I had a gender. But I was very "girlie-girlie". I was always reading and always writing. I wrote poetry at a very young age and I was a very good student, but as a child I was very unhappy. Who can say why? Maybe because my mother was unhappy or resentful. I know she did her best and was exceedingly dutiful to the role. My mother is very traditional, very anti-feminist. She's eighty-three and I love her, but she still says, "What, another book against the men?"

'Like many women of her generation, she is a worshipper of all things male. She is submissive to it even though she herself has very great male animus. She worships her sons, although she criticises them as she does me. I think I was spared her worst; my brothers got the worst of it. I was first-born. They came after me and I resented it because I thought I really should have been quite enough for my mother. I probably have never gotten over how suddenly I lost her. Basically she's given me some very great virtues. She never stops working, she never lets go, she's relentless. But I have a much greater need for physical affection than she does. As I wrote in *Women and Madness*, a lot of mothers are phobic about their daughters' bodies, they're uptight about being easy-going, loving. I don't think my mother was more physically affectionate with my brothers. It's only that she lived through them and for that they are to be appeased and they are to be supported.

'I was different from the other kids; I was always reading, always thinking. Even though I wanted so much to be close and excited with people about ideas, I was dealing with girls who were happy to make the sorority groups, who were very passive. I grew up in the dreadful 1940s and '50s. My rebellion became running away with boys, always with a book in hand, always with Keats. I read Freud when I was thirteen. I thought I was special. And that means fated for some great thing, not that anyone around me told me so. I had an insight. My father had a very rough life and his mother was slaughtered by Cossacks in a part of Poland owned by Russia. I can't remember this but my mother said he would make up stories for me. I always wanted to hear stories. I always had a great love of stories, of fables, of tales. I studied acting. When I was a child my mother took me to the therapist because I developed very bad headaches and nightmares after my brother was born and the therapist told her that I was a genius and therefore I would never be happy, therefore my mother had nothing to blame herself for.'

My mouth dropped open at the word 'genius'. She meant it very seriously. It was not said with any sense of irony. She was totally serious.

'But it would be a good idea, they told her, to let me express myself creatively. So I studied painting, acting, piano, music and Hebrew. I probably had some more lessons that I forgot about. My parents made it possible because they understood I had to do it. But then I also ran away with boys – I was boy-crazy. I used to be the only girl in a boys' gang and I loved it. Then I developed breasts, like suddenly, overnight, and it was never the same. I didn't appreciate being treated differently. They started hitting on me. I didn't have sex until college but I did a lot of other things. I had a bad reputation. No-one quite knew what to do with me. I applied to one college out of town and said it was the only place I'd go. I wanted to be left alone to pursue my own course of study. My first husband was a prince from Afghanistan whom I met in college.'

At last we had come to husband number one. It had taken a while and I had made a few attempts to direct the conversation but there was no point. Her words were like speeding cars on a freeway. It was better just to let them pass you by than try and stop them or even slow them down. They were intent on their destination. And if I stood in their path they would simply run straight over me, and keep on going.

'I brought him home to impress my parents with how interesting the student population was at the college. They were hysterical and that threw us together; I didn't even want to marry him. I wanted to study the history of ideas at the Sorbonne in Paris and I also wanted to travel around the world. He was saying, "If you want to travel around the world, come and marry me. I can't introduce you to my family if we're not married." So I did it, but not with a romantic, girlish notion that this would turn out okay.

'We travelled through Europe in 1961, then through Iran to Afghanistan, where they took my passport away and where I became virtually locked up. Female, chattel, property, even if a foreign national. So I plotted my escape. It was very dramatic. I developed infectious hepatitis while I was there and nearly died. Every so often I still think to myself that I could be dead and buried in a Moslem cemetery in the side of a hill.

'It's a beautiful country and since then he's been in exile from there. He did remarry and has children. When I met them for the first time they wanted to know why I came to Afghanistan. I said I was in search of a missing tribe of Amazons. They thought that was as good an answer as any other. I may have been in search of Jerusalem but I was utterly confused. I like to put it this way: "I have once married the son of Hagar and once the son of Sarah and now I'm done with it." I'm Libra, I'm October 1st, so maybe I've asserted some balance in these two choices. My first husband had a problem because he was in boarding schools in Switzerland and then in America and he wanted his own little miniature Statue of Liberty to take back. His father had three wives and twenty-one children and was a very interesting man. I concocted an escape from Afghanistan with the wife of the mayor, who was German, and at the last minute my then father-in-law, to save face, got me an Afghan passport and everybody saw me off at the airport. I went to Tashkent and then to Moscow and then to Copenhagen and back to New York with $10 in my pocket. My parents had at some level disowned me. I called them and said, "Well, guess who's back." My husband wanted me to return but I was very adamant, never again. So we got an annulment. He fought it but I got an annulment granted. I concocted grounds, certainly not failure to consummate the marriage – although the first time we did it, I left his dorm and went back to my dorm and was puzzled because I wondered, "Had we done it?" I wasn't certain because we didn't know about clitorises or orgasms. So I went back and knocked on his door. I said, "Let us do this again so I will then know that it happened, because I'm not certain." There I am, a girl with a bad reputation and I haven't got a clue. When I got to college somebody had said, "Oh, here's a Tampax." I said, "Thank you," and then I said, "Well, where do you put it?" "Up," she said. I said, "Up where?" I just didn't know.'

I drifted off here to a vivid picture of myself at the same age having the same tampon torture. My mother's dire warnings about tampons – that they would cause me to lose my virginity, which would in turn ruin my prospects for a happily married life – meant that I simply had to try them out. My first unsuccessful attempts at insertion led me to believe that I would have to marry a man with a penis the size of a gramophone needle. I spent several days in agony with a succession of tampons partially inserted. I developed a very strange walk and was forced to lever myself slowly into chairs.

Phyllis stopped – she could see she had lost me. My flashback expression having gained her attention, she paused briefly, smiled and continued.

'I married him because he was the first man I slept with. But did we have what I would now describe as a fully passionate, consummated, knowledgeable, lover relationship? No! He was about ten years older and a dashing figure in his way. When he finally returned to Afghanistan he became the country's first minister of film and theatre, which went nowhere with a 99.9 per cent illiteracy rate. But he was a dreamer and he meant well.

'I have had many lovers and women are in my life now. I think that it's crazy for women not to be connected with each other, including in terms of making families. This doesn't mean that I hate men or I regret ever having been with men or would never recommend a woman to be with a man. On the contrary, it's just that to only lie in the arms of only one half of the human race in one's life is sort of silly. And to reject someone because they're the wrong gender, that's sillier still. It's a limitation. Politically, my head was certainly pro-lesbian. But in the early days it just simply didn't work. And if it doesn't work at a chemical, cellular level, what's the point? I made various attempts, I did little experiments, it just didn't work! So I never experienced going to conferences as a way of looking for a social life or cruising women. Then, in 1982,

I nearly died in a car accident and the next year I was at a party with a longtime friend who's a formerly married mother, a lesbian later in life. There were many beautiful women at this party and they were all desperately dancing to attract the few less-than-beautiful men present. I found myself sitting there looking at it all and I said to my friend, "Okay, that's it. Forty-three years, it's enough. I've done my time." And I said, "Tonight I will have a woman."'

'Very warrior queen,' I thought to myself as she continued.

'I said, "I'm going to a gay bar." My friend came along because she was worried and I remember it was a dive, it was dark. It was Saturday night, there was a collective IQ of eighteen. Everybody was fiercely, puritanically, coupled. I started dancing by myself and then pretty soon someone started dancing next to me, a very Italian-looking woman, with lots of curly ringlets, who looked as if she could be an old statue that I'd seen in places in Europe. She said to me, finally, "What's your name? Is that your lover over there? Where do you live?" And I said to this complete stranger, "My name is Phyllis, that is not my lover, I live in Brooklyn and would you like to come there now?" This stopped her in her tracks. She thought about it for a while and came home with me. Then we didn't get out of bed for quite a while. This time it was different. It probably would not have continued into a relationship had she not been totally open to co-parenting with me. My son was five and a half. She was a nurse and because she was not a feminist and not an intellectual, she was very helpful to me in certain areas of work where street smartness is required – such as helping mothers running away from bad marriages. We were together from 1983 to 1990.

'The truth is that I'm married to this revolution. Whoever I commit with, they ultimately feel that I'm cheating on them, that my mind is elsewhere in my work, that my work is my mate and my muse and my driver. One after the other they punish me and they feel themselves mightily punished. Men get away with wives who support them to write great books and forgive them their excesses and their failures and make their social path easy and not harder. But with women it's just the opposite.

'I love my son, he's wonderful. His name is Ariel and at seventeen he's begun to give me digs about my not being a traditional mother. He could never see me when he wanted to, so now I have to make an appointment to see him because that's what he learned to do from me. At every turn the world does not easily forgive my kind of dedication. But I also think that if I'd had a mentor, if I'd had any encouragement, that I would have indeed made a hundred-year plan, forget about a ten-year or a five-year plan. I knew that I had to get a PhD, I knew not to have a child before I was utterly identified and economically independent. I don't know how I knew because no-one had told me. But I also let fortune or fate, the way a girl or woman will, lead me by the nose. I regret that. I never planned how to be economically secure or never thought to accumulate savings or stocks or investments or real property and those are things that revolutionaries require. I acted as if somebody else would either rescue me or the situation. But no matter how they beat me down and beat me back, I keep coming back. It's as if I've got this sacred fire power that's in me, I'm at its service and I'm in its grip.

'Sometimes I'm angry on behalf of other women, the way mothers would be with children, but not on my own behalf. When I think that my work can be stopped, when I think that they will not allow me to continue birthing my works, then I get scared. Sometimes I'm bitter because I think we've lost these generations of younger women and men and I utterly despair of that because there's no way to get them back. I've been an artist and a Bohemian and a grass-roots activist and organiser, but now the times are economically perilous and harsh and I'm the sole supporter of a young man who's much taller than me. He's in junior year of high school and it's a very expensive little proposition to be a middle-class person and a revolutionary and an artist and a feminist. It's hard. I've never written for money. *Mothers on Trial* took six years to do and cost $250,000 to produce. I travelled everywhere, I interviewed, I studied, I had staff and the advance for it was $55,000 which spread out over six years; you see what writers earn. I earned from other means and I always put all my resources at the service of the book, thinking that somehow if I could pull it off this time that I'd then be allowed to pull it off next time.

'I'm a high-art junkie. I try to tell myself that I have to become a proper bourgeois and I have to think about myself first, I have to take care of my own tiny little garden, but it doesn't work. I was with the women in Jerusalem who prayed for the first time at the wailing wall. It was very exciting because it was a historic moment. I ended up being the one who opened the Torah for the women for the first time ever at that most holy site and it wedded me to the action, and I became very involved with fundamentalist feminists and a lawsuit and I was raising money for them. We did the equivalent of nuns taking over the Vatican and officiating at Mass. The women in this lawsuit were requesting religious rights equal to mine. Why was I wasting my time with a non-goddess, patriarchal religion? Because for these women to do this took enormous bravery and 5000 years to get there. I was very much at their service. It was a seven-year struggle and in order for me to work with such women I had to spend time with them. My partner then, who is not Jewish, misunderstood that this was my work. I was not going to take the veil. I was not going to become a fundamentalist woman. I was visiting the camps of my sisters briefly. The image I have of it is that I was flying through the desert and I heard the daughters of Jacob singing a song for their freedom while chained, and I went back to see how to help. It was a very righteous action but I think my devotion to it ultimately broke her heart. She couldn't be part of it and she felt totally left out.

'Our ending made me very sad. I became very sick with chronic fatigue and was utterly alone. I wrote my first analysis of this situation and I sent it up to the women on Kate Millett's farm, who I love very much. They got on the phone and said, "We're making our own short lists of who would be there to visit us if we suddenly fall ill." I said, "Well, are you going to come and see me or not?" And they said, "Well you're so far away, we wish we could but we can't." Kate Millett did come to see me, but the reality is that here are these other warriors who are career junkies and they don't slow down their lives in the fast lane because one of their comrades falls ill. They'll visit you in the hospital once. And if it's a thrillingly, dramatic illness they'll come a couple of times. If you have a lover who co-ordinates and choreographs a communal response to illness everyone will pitch in and do her little piece. But somebody's got to organise it. They're not going to see it on their own – without that choreographer there's nothing but chaos. If you're dying, that's different.'

There was a pause here and I jumped in with questions about the other writers.

'Gloria Steinem I love and have known since 1979. But she didn't write a book that changed the world until very recently. I don't know whether it changed the world so much as, to be fair, the extent to which it was experienced as one of these internal revolutions that gave permission for women to stop and look inwards. It followed on from Alice Miller's work on healing, recovery movements. It's not anti-political or reactionary but it could be absorbed with less threat.

'Betty Friedan's *The Feminine Mystique* is not a good book in terms of writing but it said something at the right time that led to great things. You have to judge the woman by her work, and you have to judge the work by what it does in the world. If you don't like her or her political philosophy, that doesn't matter – look at her work. That's very important for women to know. Instead of saying, "Do I like her, is she my friend?", look at her work and its effects. It's important as feminists for us to also see how the feminist leadership treats women. I want to know how interpersonally challenged they are as human beings.

'I'm thinking of how Betty Friedan lights up when men walk into the room and how she doesn't really love women or love being a woman. How can you make a revolution then, together? You can't.

'Why are women so hard on each other? We want women to be perfect, but women cannot be all things to all people. And if you're doing great works it's less possible, less likely. Now I'm with someone who's a lawyer and who really deeply appreciates my work and has her own work and her own career. She handles a lot of custody cases and has also been very helpful in terms of my interest in the case of our nation's so-called first female serial killer. I did several magazine articles and the book I'm writing about it is still in progress, unfinished. It's a true crime narrative with three different voices.

'I have eight books I'm working on, all in different stages. I have a PhD in psychology. I studied languages and comparative literature at college and I went into psychology to support the habit of writing. I was going to be a therapist, which I've done.

'It's important to have access to the elders of our tribe, to those who have some wisdom and perspective and have been where you are, who will sit with you for a while. I think it's tragic that we apparently have to pay for that. But if we can, there are times that it's needed.'

My head was reeling with the speed and the scope, cinemascope even, of the narrative. But there was one question that I was determined to ask. Now was the time. She had stated in her now familiar unequivocal style in *Women and Madness* that she considered there to be few genuinely or purely mad women. Did she still believe this?

'No, I take that back. I have now met every one of them.' [Raucous laughter.] 'Maybe what I meant to say is that there are not that many women who are psychotic. A lot of women are pretty crazy but that's different from psychotic. Maybe the sexual abuse did it, maybe the lack of support from other women coupled with the physical abuse has just driven them around the bend. If you add some genetic predisposition to some kind of mental illness, to no jobs and no dignity and shame and overwork and too many roles to play and never being rewarded, and add always being punished no matter how good you are and how you come through in all these different roles, and then add to that different illnesses and life crises and traumas that women endure; all of that doesn't mean that anyone should then go around diagnosing women punitively and locking them away or straitjacketing them or improperly medicating them.

'I've never felt that I've lost my grip, although menopause wasn't easy and being ill with Epstein-Barr syndrome wasn't wonderful. Actually, my sickness was funny and awful. I would get phone calls like, "Can you come to my art opening?" or "Can you come to my reading?" And I'd say, "I would love to but I am very, very sick." "Oh, does that mean you won't come?" I mean, forget about saying, "Well, can I do something for you?"

'Then I had a friend, I love this friend, she's from London and she makes films and she made a big show of coming to see what was going on with me. She came all the way out to Brooklyn and it was very funny because it took me all day to get ready for this one-hour visit. Then she comes in and has me wait on her: "Make me tea. I don't like that tea. Get me another tea." I was utterly speechless because she's a very good, nice woman. And then I thought maybe the especially good, nice women can't bear to see me sick. It is too terrifying for them to see me low. If it could happen to a strong woman then it means it'll happen to them.

'I wrote a column for the first time recently in which I begin to talk about feminist betrayal. You have to tell the truth if you're a writer. It depends how you tell it and then it's in the hands of the reader. Those who are looking for weapons to use against women will find them whether you give them to them or not.

'I'm not an outsider when I'm either carousing with like minds of women or teaching women who want to learn what I have to teach. Even though I'm still a whirling dervish, the illness and the poverty have thrown me a bit. I used to do four or five other paid jobs to maintain all my projects, but now I've been too ill to do that. I've now done some fundraising and I've borrowed heavily against this house. I have never been able to earn a solidly middle-class living merely as writer. I have to be a university professor, a lecturer, a therapist, a courtroom consultant, an expert witness to be able to manage the kind of activism that I've kept doing. Now the lecture fees are not what they once were for so many of us and there is a whole crop of anti-feminists and so-called feminists out there who get attention and some fees, but their day will pass. Like Camille Paglia. I tried reading her book *Social Personae*, I tried. Apparently Camille had told these television network folk that there was no feminist smart enough to come up against her and, besides which, none of them were attractive. So when they asked me I said, "Well, I think I have to do this." But Paglia backed out.

'William Buckley pulled together a bunch of women to yell at each other on television. Betty Friedan was one – she wasn't great but she wasn't bad. And then there was Ariana Huffington, who said very bad things about Gloria Steinem which were unquotable, but then Gloria pointed out to me that she had just helped raise money to defeat the campaign of Ariana's husband. I said, "Oh that explains it." But she was still bitchy, vicious in a female, traditional fashion. These kinds of women are collaborators. It's not just the men that we must look at, we must look at the collaborators. We always expect more from women. These so-called feminists use other women as target practice but they won't go up against the men. We need to go up against real power and never stop doing that. At the same time we have to become aware that each moment of conscious life is more precious and should become so.

'One of the things I've learned from my sickness is patience as a balance to all my frenetic activity. I can't travel as I once was able to but as I get a bit stronger I'm going to try and do it again because I get some pleasure from that. But I have never spent time looking for Mr or Ms Right. When I married the second time I explained it this way: I wanted to be left alone, I said, but by somebody. Now I think I need community. I may or may not be able to create it in a world that opposes it. That means community that will support women like me, not community that if you become dead in your head, you can then get a bed.

'I can't imagine myself stopping my life to go out on a street corner to find a date or a lover. It's inconceivable. One can sometimes get desperately lonely when one is utterly alone. I look at people as either "civilians" or "in the army". I'm in the army. The civilians, they come home, they quit work at five, they clock out and they tend to their rose gardens. I'm amazed, I don't get it. I'm an outsider from that. I look at it and I'm like the albatross. I don't know how to fly. I don't know how to do these ordinary things. I don't mind being near them, I wouldn't mind having them do a little bit of that for me, I wouldn't even mind myself learning how to garden in every sense of that word. But that's not me. There isn't enough time and as you get older there seems to be less and less of it and it passes by more speedily. I'll be a warrior to the end but I'm becoming more of a writer. I was always a closet literary writer and didn't tell anybody that I wrote poems or fiction, so when I say I'm more of a writer I mean I'm struggling more with finding the precise right words and not settling for less and polishing each word as if they were precious stones and I'm making a necklace of them. As I experience doing that and the joy of it, I really can't see how I could then organise grass-roots feminist activities at the same time. This may be a calling that I can't turn my back on and I may be forced to have a begging bowl.

'It takes a woman a lot of time, effort and energy to make her mark in history and to even get into the battle. But what a privilege to be on the stage of history battling there as opposed to being simply the orphan child on the outside, grey and poor with no education, grinding slowly upon the step. It's very unusual for large numbers of women to be out on the stage of history, in our own names and battling for ourselves. There have been token numbers of women writers in the past, women who have had great genius and perhaps married or were born into the right families and therefore their genius could be subsidised. They didn't have to work as chambermaids. But they have not always been in favour of women's freedom, or they have not always identified with it. A number of the women writers, myself included, who do poetry and fiction and journalism and academic studies and a number of different forms of writing and are probably very talented, have been, in my opinion, including myself, cut down at the beginning. There was backlash for 10,000 years of patriarchy; enormous, horrifying backlash which has not ended. And with the very first of our second-wave breaths, they cut us down, and they kept cutting us down. The story is that we have persevered at great cost. The story is that we've created fragile confederations of sensibilities, organic roots that are not part of hierarchical structures. I do consider myself blessed.'

The word 'blessed' had a strongly biblical ring to it. And indeed I felt that I had just spent the past few hours living in the Old Testament as told by MGM with its colourful stories of good and evil, trial and error, crime and punishment. This woman was the female equivalent of Charlton Heston. It was a story full of strange passions, a tale told by a woman full of sound and fury, signifying everything.

I hoped she had not drained herself of too much energy, given her recent illness, but she said that wasn't so and was still wanting to feed me.

I refused but insisted that she should eat, joining her at the dining room table with a glass of red wine. While she ate I answered her questions about my life, my books and my work. She was genuinely interested, not merely pretending. We were heavily into an animated conversation when her partner, the lawyer, arrived home from work. She joined us in a glass of wine and we all laughed and raved on like old friends.

At about 11.30 pm Phyllis rang me a car and packaged me up a selection of her current writing, photocopied me a couple of articles she thought would be relevant and signed copies of her books for me that are out of print. There was such an intensity and a warmth about the way she did this that I felt like a bright child who was being given all the best material to take to school. I bet she's a great teacher. Even though I had talked in patches during the interview, her answers were at times long, uninterrupted monologues, not pre-rehearsed, but thought through in a way that I knew she had really given me her best in order to be a part of my book. Whatever project she took on, she would give it her best shot.

Nearly midnight. Alone. Sitting in the back seat of the limo, the breeze from the river still warm as I crossed back over the bridge. The lights of Manhattan sparkled and twinkled at me. God, it was so beautiful. So very beautiful and strange and exciting. Perhaps it was time that I, too, began to consider myself blessed. To be here in New York, talking to women who had created history and, in that act of talking, to be myself recording and interpreting the history of our times, was definitely to be blessed. It was also, judging from today, going to be more than a little exhausting.

3
ROBIN MORGAN
PART I

Day Two, 2 pm: Her apartment, Greenwich Village,
New York City

Robin is a small, neat woman with a quiet demeanour and a large presence. I had interviewed her briefly a year ago for my television program when she had been launching the new Ms magazine (subscription only, no ads) in Australia.

Now she was back to being a full-time writer again; she told me she had given up smoking, exercised regularly at the gym and had taken up gardening. In fact her garden, now her passion, inhabits almost as much space as her entire apartment. Her living room is also her work room. While the apartment is small, neat and well organised, like its owner, it is also comfortable. Work happens at the benches overlooked by a wall of books and relaxing occurs in the same room on comfortable chairs and couches. We sat opposite each other and chatted. But, like everything Robin does, the chat had a purpose. She asked me about the book and who else was in it. I told her about Greer's refusal and also about her then recent public savaging of Suzanne Moore, a fellow journalist in Britain, and how Greer had made particular reference to Moore's three-inch cleavage and her 'fuck-me' shoes.

Robin said, 'She can talk. When we were trying to talk about rape in the '70s, Greer was here talking about being sexually free and running around with no underpants. When we refused to debate Norman Mailer because it just gave him publicity, she took him on.'

I knew she was in the middle of writing the first part of her memoirs so after two hours of interviewing, as agreed, I stopped. Polite and warm and forthcoming as she had been, I sensed that she was itching to get back to her own work. She told me she was having Marilyn French to dinner that night and wanted to get a couple of hours writing done before she started cooking.

I thanked her, entered the surge of eccentric life that is Greenwich Village and did some browsing. And some shopping. Well, quite a lot of shopping.

When I got back to 'my' apartment – even though I knew it was Bob's I had already come to think of it as mine – I realised it certainly resembled something I had lived in for some time. I was glad that I hadn't been knocked down by a bus or a cab because Bob would eventually have returned to find my clothes and shopping bags, empty food cartons and unwashed wine glasses on every available surface. He was such a methodical, meticulous housekeeper. Everything had its perfect place. Housework had not been my top priority; after all, I was writing a feminist book, so I was exempt. Oh well, I didn't have time to tidy it up now. Nancy Grossman and Arlene Raven were picking me up at 7.00 pm.

I always checked the tapes before I tucked them safely away, like babies in their bassinette. It was a practice I had developed over the years. Not that I had ever had a disaster, but you can't be too careful. I remembered an incident that Oriana Fallaci had described in one of her books, where someone stole the precious tapes of her interview with Golda Meir. She was devastated, utterly. She had sent the then seventy-four-year-old leader a telegram saying, 'Everything stolen – repeat everything stop. Try to see me again please.' So distressed was Golda Meir for her that she agreed to do it all over again.

I ran a quick check on the first tape. It was fine. Then I tried the other side. It sounded peculiar. Words were being cut off at the end of sentences. Robin's voice was disappearing. I rewound it and played it again. Sweat was breaking out on my brow but this time it was not my hormones. It was panic. How could this have happened? It hadn't happened with any of the other interviews. I had bought this new little tape recorder especially for this trip. I had tested and retested it. What had gone wrong? I sat on the edge of the bed with my head in my hands. It was 6.45 pm. I had to get ready. I played that side of the tape again. It was useless. Sometimes every other word was missing. What would I do? Nobody sent telegrams any more. And a fax was an everyday event with none of the urgency of the delivered telegram. Robin would be cooking and getting everything organised for her dinner with Marilyn. This was no time to be ringing her. I stared at the small black tape recorder as if it were a bomb that I needed to defuse. I clicked away at all the buttons. Nothing seemed to be wrong. Anyone who has ever done an interview will understand my panic. Now I was sweating everywhere but my hands. I was going to throw up. I looked at my watch, realised I didn't have time, grabbed my bag, went down in the lift in a daze and stood outside the building on West 69th waiting for a battered Cadillac to turn the corner.

Nancy was waving and beeping as the Caddy came into view. It always cracked me up to see her sitting behind the wheel of this huge car because she was so tiny she had to sit on a cushion. In the time it took for me to run across the road and leap into the back seat, the cars behind were already banking up and the drivers honking their horns.

Arlene leant across from the front seat to kiss me hello in that cool Lauren Bacall style that was hers.

'You're so hot. Are you sick?'

Never one to hold anything back, with tears pricking my eyes I poured out the gory details.

'Don't worry about it,' said Nancy, weaving this huge vehicle, needle-like, through the tapestry of traffic.

'We'll sort it out, over dinner,' reassured Arlene. 'At least she's not taking off in a plane tomorrow. You still have time to do it again.'

And I must admit that once inside the restaurant, Café Loup, to which they had first taken me and a friend nine years ago, sitting at my favourite table in the 'Nancy Grossman alcove', as I liked to call it, with one of Nancy's famous collage paintings overlooking us, I did begin to calm down. The bottle of Australian red that they ordered, just to make me feel more at home, helped too. They reminded me of my birthday the year before when I had taken them to the first night of a preview of the play *Vita and Virginia* starring Vanessa Redgrave and Eileen Atkins. Afterwards, high on the performance, we had come here to this table where Mississippi mud cake had been ordered with candles that when lit played 'Happy Birthday'. Hilarious kitsch. Would I ever be so happy again, I wondered. I couldn't possibly write this book without including the author of *Sisterhood is Powerful*; the New York Public Library had just named it one of the books of the century.

By the end of the meal, with the help of Nancy and Arlene, I had determined that I would simply explain it clearly and calmly.

They were sure Robin would understand and allow me some more time. After all, she's been a journalist herself. She knew how these things happened. I only wished I did. To reassure me, Arlene got out her tarot cards which she only read on special occasions for close friends.

'What if I get the hanged man?' I wailed. Ever the Australian pessimist. Fortunately the cards were good. Very good. There was harmony in the house of the book, my hopes and fears were in balance and the outcome was the high priestess. All I had to do, Arlene said, was make the magic and the rest would follow. I had never really been sure whether I really believed in goddesses or tarot cards or clairvoyants but tonight was no time for cynicism.

The back seat of the Cadillac was like a huge travelling leather lounge and Arlene sprawled there next to me. We had both eaten so much we had to undo the top buttons on our trousers. Nancy sat up front on her cushion chauffeuring us on a little tour of New York to cheer me up. As I sprawled back in the seat watching the lights flash by, I remembered being just a little girl lying like this in the back of my parents' car watching the trees like dark lace in the sky. Just the three of us. Nancy Grossman was one of America's most respected and acclaimed artists, a woman whose work was chosen in the Bicentennial Celebration of American Art. Arlene Raven was a founder of the Los Angeles Woman's Building, Womanspace (the first feminist art gallery), an art critic for the *Village Voice* and many other art publications, and the author of seven books on feminist art. I knew they both had work waiting to be done back in their loft in SoHo. They didn't need to be tooling around the streets of New York. This was indeed sisterhood. This was family.

'Look at these,' said Nancy, and I sat up and stared out of the window at several women in hot pants, very good-looking, very good legs, standing on a street corner.

'So?' I said.

'They're the latest craze,' said Arlene

'Chicks with dicks. That's what they call them.'

That's what they've called all the women in my book, I thought. They got it wrong of course. The women in my book didn't actually want real dicks (at least I don't think so), they just wanted the freedom and the power that went with having one.

'Let's go around the block and have another look,' I said.

And so we did. We cruised past in our old Caddy looking at the chicks with dicks smiling back at us. Probably very ideologically unsound. But it was crazy and it was fun . . .

Around eight o'clock the next morning I hovered over the phone, trying to get the courage to call Robin. When I did, finally, I gabbled out my dilemma and threw myself on her mercy.

She sighed. I could tell the prospect of going over it again did not thrill her, but she agreed to take a precious hour out of her own tight writing schedule on another day. I hung up. And thanked the goddess. Well, what the hell.

4

MARILYN FRENCH

PART I

Day Three, 4 pm: Her apartment, TriBeCa, New York City
Marilyn French was thinner and more frail than when I had last seen her but the body in no way reflected the spirit. When I told her about the problems with my tape recorder (which, by the way, the bloke in the electrical shop told me were due to my inadvertently flicking the switch to the voice-activated recorder which cuts out at the end of every sentence), she fixed me with a steely eye like the Ancient Mariner and said, 'It's just as well it didn't happen with me. I wouldn't have done it all over again.'

'I know,' I said, believing her. You only had to be with Marilyn for a short time to know that she was not a person to mess with. She would never suffer fools, gladly or otherwise, and having been diagnosed with a terminal illness she had none of her precious time to waste.

Her modern, beautifully decorated apartment was on the forty-eighth floor and took in a 180-degree view of New York City. I stood at the full-length window in her living room and drank it all in. It was mesmerising. No wonder people loved helicopter rides over this city. If I lived in this apartment, I would just sit at the window all day and watch the view change.

It was just as well we moved into her study where the window was higher and I could concentrate on the task. She settled herself as comfortably as she could on her couch. I sat on the chair opposite. Her focus was total. But her voice betrayed the fact that she was not feeling strong today.

'If you feel exhausted at any stage just stop me and we can finish another time,' I said, knowing that she would push herself to the outer limits before giving up. Marilyn is not someone who ever gives up. Well, only if she is forced to. Her will is tangible. Partly, one suspects, such determination is genetic but mostly it has been forged out of the life she has led.

'Let's begin,' she said. Impatient as ever with small talk.

'When I was a child I thought of myself as asexual. Of being beyond sex. I was well trained in the worst kind of western thought. I don't know if I had read Aristotle but I had certainly read enough people who suggested that body and mind were two separate entities and that mind transcended body. And I was mind, not body. I felt that right up until the time I gave birth to my daughter.

'I remember the first time I read by myself. I was not yet four. It was a Sunday and I wanted my father to read the funny papers to me and he wouldn't do it. I was very angry, I asked him over and over again, he just kept putting me off, so I said, "All right, I'll do it myself," and I did. I was so shocked that I could do it. I read "Tiny Tim" and I understood what I was reading and after that I always read the cartoons myself. I needed my father or my mother for a word here or there, which sometimes got me in trouble because I would read the newspaper at night. I remember there was a murder case and I was reading about it and I called out to my parents who were in the kitchen, "What does the word tunic mean?" And my father said, "What are you reading?" I said, "I'm reading the paper," and then he of course would have liked to have kept me from reading about this but my mother wouldn't let him do that. I was rather frightened by the way he barked at me, and shocked that there were things I wasn't supposed to read.

'Both my parents were born in this country, in Brooklyn. But their parents, all four, came from Poland. My mother's father was a very successful tailor but he wasn't good to his wife; he was a heavy drinker and he died, leaving debts, before my mother was born. My grandmother's life was a story of destitution and as a result she lost her children. My father's family was more stable. His father was quite a brute but I don't think he beat his wife, he beat his sons, which is a major reason my mother married him. The beatings turned my father into a man she could control; his sister's not like that at all.

'My father went to college briefly but he was very dyslexic. My mother's great need was to be a member of the middle class. I think she thought once you're in the middle class you're safe, none of these humiliating things will happen to you again. She was a child of a mother who never spoke English well but who could read English and she could read and speak German as well as Polish and Russian. She was not an unaccomplished woman but she dressed like a Polish woman – with her hair back in a little bun and wearing little old cotton housedresses and tie shoes. My mother felt ashamed of her and more than anything wanted to be American and a Wasp. My mother out-Wasped any Wasp I ever met. Her tastes in food and clothing and house decorations were so Wasp – everything beige, muted and understated. No spices or garlic in the house. She made it into the middle class but it didn't make her any happier. My father, I don't know what he wanted out of life. He wanted my mother, he wanted sex.

'My mother thought I was a genius. She said I drew a perfect banana when I was less than two years old and I never talked until I was a year old but then, when I did, I used full sentences. I don't know that in my household that meant a great deal. My mother had no education herself but she revered it. She was a woman of great sensitivity more than commonsense. She was a thoughtful person and she had examined the way other people raised children. Most women of her generation did not think about it, they just did it. And if they'd been yelled at and spanked and beaten that's what they did to their kids.

'All the kids on my block were treated that way. Not us. She had great ambition for me. She went to work when I was quite young to save money so I could go to college. As it turned out she couldn't help me in the end, when I did go, but she tried. She wanted to, she foresaw, but she didn't ever push me. In some households if a mother thought a child was bright and didn't have much ambition for herself, if she planted her hopes in the child, which my mother did in me, she would have pushed that child or put pressure on her in some way, but my mother never did that.

'My father didn't ever exist as a presence in my life. There's no point in even talking about it. He didn't care about us, he never had anything to say about anything. He just was there; the moneymaker to whatever degree there was money. We were very poor. He read meters for the electric company. My mother pushed him to get out of that when the war started and he ended up doing quite difficult work. When he retired they hired five men to take over what he did. He worked as an engineer without an engineering degree. He was a bright man in certain ways but he had no self-push or confidence. Both my sister and I inherited our mother's spirit.

'At school I kept getting skipped up a grade, which made my life miserable because I ended up being very tiny compared with the older children and much too young for them and very unhappy. I didn't put much about myself, or at least I didn't feel I was putting much about myself, in *Her Mother's Daughter* because I wanted to concentrate on the mother, but I think that I modelled the character Anastasia largely on myself up to a point, until she goes to college and becomes a totally different person.

'I was unhappy in school and I was unhappy at home because it was a very unhappy household. My father had no relation to us except we occasionally felt the breadth of his hatred. My mother was in a state of depression and sometimes would go weeks without speaking to us. My sister would run outdoors to play all the time and my mother would get very angry about it. I didn't, I stayed home. I retreated inside my head. I had my place on the couch in the living room and I read, I drew, I wrote novels, I played the piano, I composed music, I made paper dolls. Creativity was everything to me. I lived totally in that world.

'I begged my mother for stories of her family and the past. I loved my mother talking to me. That she was talking at all was a good thing. It was the only way I could ever feel close to her because she was so disconnected and so depressed. She was on drugs from the day I was conceived, or that she knew about me, until the day she decided to get pregnant with my sister, which was four years after I was born. She was on everything short of morphine and the only reason she decided to have my sister was that the doctor said the only other thing he could do, because she was still crying all the time, was to give her morphine. She said that she didn't really want to become that serious a drug addict. She either had to stay on the drug she was on, or just stop. She decided that the thing to do would be to have the childbirth experience again and that's what she did. She got pregnant, willingly this time, and welcomed my sister, Isabel, into the world. That made me jealous because I had not been similarly welcomed, but there was never any question that I was my mother's favourite child and that my sister came in a very poor second, which she's never gotten over.

'Isabel had opposite ways of dealing with our home. She blotted out the unpleasant. She ran outdoors and found playmates and really had a very happy childhood outside of the house, which my mother had tremendous contempt for because she would play with anyone and my mother looked down her nose at that. That made her like my father's family, who were outgoing, social and high-spirited, and so she was one of them. Whereas I was like my mother: inward, depressed. I just burrowed more and more inward, I manufactured a life, I lived almost totally in daydreams until a couple of times I got caught up in them. I would make up stories to tell my mother about my triumphs at school and once she mentioned one of these triumphs to a little friend of mine and of course it had not happened. The friend didn't say anything, she didn't even know what my mother was talking about, but I realised what had happened and I was horrified. And then one time I found myself blurting out something to my mother that hadn't happened at all without knowing it, to make me seem popular and happy, and those things frightened me. They pulled me up short and made me realise what I was doing. They didn't stop me from living in daydreams but I did stop pretending that they were real.

'I grew up into a person who felt that the truth of the experience, of any experience, was the sorrow of it and that I had to find the sorrow within everything if I expected to know anything about anything. I grew up with tremendous ambitions, all kinds of ambitions. I wanted to be a writer, I wanted to be famous, I wanted to be beautiful. Even though I did not know anything about sex, I knew I wanted a very wide sex experience. When I first heard the facts of life I nearly died and I was at least twelve before that happened. You know how you know and you don't know at the same time. I wanted to have everything, to try everything. I wanted to travel. I wanted to know about art and music and philosophy. I wanted to know about the street. I wanted to know everything that was possible to know and that was what I set out in life to do, to learn in every area that I could.

'I learned a lot. Obviously nobody knows everything and naturally I know now that I have had a smattering of knowledge. I consider myself very knowledgeable about music but compared to a professional musicologist I know nothing about. I know a great deal about art but not compared to a professional art historian. I could have a conversation with a musicologist or a conversation with an art historian but finally I'm an amateur in all these things. Literature is my field, literature I do know.

'I got a reputation as a writer very late. I was almost fifty. It was too late, it was too long, the joy would have been having it young and I didn't. I spent years up until fifty in some despair, not sure that I would ever get published. I'd had some short stories published but that was all. I had no reputation. The fame was too late for it to give me much pleasure. I had a terrible marriage and that lasted way too long and I couldn't get out of it.

'My discovery of my body didn't happen until I was fourteen or fifteen because I didn't even start to menstruate until I was fourteen, which was something I was very ashamed of and my mother told me nothing about it. In those days nobody did. In fact I think I took my own virginity. I woke my mother up one night, I was very upset because I had been masturbating and I'd gotten blood on my finger, and I made her come in the bathroom with me and I showed her this little bit of blood on my finger and she said, "Oh, Marilyn, what did you wake me up for that for? For heaven's sake, it's nothing," and went back to bed. I don't know if she knew what I'd done. I have no idea. That was very funny.

'I didn't act as though I cared about boys. I wouldn't let on. I was deeply ashamed of caring about boys, of finding them attractive, and I pretended it wasn't happening. It never occurred to me to take the opposite tack, which most girls did. If they were interested in boys they looked at them and flirted with them. Not me, never. Never in my life. To this day I don't flirt. Anybody that got involved with me had to really be very keen. There was a boy I was really in love with in college but he was bad news and I knew it. He had no respect for women. He drank too much. He was irresponsible in a lot of ways. He was really happier if he was with the guys. I didn't sleep with him, I wouldn't, but it was the first time I felt desire.

'I couldn't envisage a life because no-one had the kind of life I wanted. I wanted to be independent. Where was I to escape? Girls didn't do that. Nobody did that. Boys didn't do that. There was one young woman on our block who didn't live at home and who wasn't married and was the source of great gossip on the block. I couldn't imagine how to live. What I wanted more than anything was to be sexual. I was filled with desire but I was terrified of being sexual. My mother had filled me with terror because she said, "I only did it once and it didn't even go in all the way and it ruined my life forever. I had to marry your father. Look at me, look at my life."

'My mother's life was not enviable at all. So I was terrified of sex. I had very strong desire but very strong terrors and the only way that I could deal with them was to get married. I got married to have sex. My husband, Bud, got through to me; he was persistent, he didn't let go. I felt safe with him because he seemed like a person who would always adore me and do whatever I said. I did have power over him most of the time. Actually, although I would have been horrified at the thought at the time, what I wanted was someone like my father who just adored my mother and obeyed her, always, and got pleasure from that. They didn't have terrible fights. I married a man who was not quite like that. He only seemed to be like that. My sister did too. She later got involved with a man who wasn't like that at all but she turned him into that. Most men are like that, they want to be dominated.

'I don't think my mother made my father a doormat. It wasn't that she was mean or domineering, it's just that it was the only way she could feel safe with a man, because of her own father. But she was very thoughtful of him. She gave him the things that he needed, like dinner on the table the minute he walked in the door, and she attended to the state of his digestion so that when she noticed that he was belching a lot she would get him things with cream in them because she had decided he had ulcers. She thought about him in the same way that she thought about us. She gave thought to the way she cared for her family. I wanted anything but that, I wanted to avoid that, I did not want to marry my father and I thought I was doing something very different. But in fact, when I look back on it, the qualities in Bud that probably made me trust him were very much like my father's. But he had another side that wasn't like my father. He was very much his own person, but in a sick way. The only way he knew how to assert himself was in rage.

'I was twenty when I married, still in college. I finished the next year. He became a lawyer later but he was never very successful. My mother didn't stand in my way. She thought he was very submissive to me and I guess she thought that was okay. The sex was terrible. And it never got better despite some effort on my part. I think he had a lot of hang-ups about it. I don't think he was any better or worse than anyone else. I think it was common with men in those days.

'I still thought I'd be a writer and I thought in terms of money a lot. As a child, part of my dream of being a writer was to own a townhouse with a black door and a brass doorknob. My husband was writing comedy sketches with another guy and they were always on the verge of success for three years. He earned his living in various ways. He had many different jobs and eventually he didn't like any of them. The writing didn't pan out and he went back to law school, but that was after we'd been married quite some time. In fact I was pregnant while he was doing it. I had my children while he was still in law school. He had a job in the daytime.

'We lived with his mother. That was the worst time of my life. She was a bitch. I ended up spending most of my married life with her because soon after we moved out her husband died and she came to live with us. By then I had learned that the person who pays the bills has the control, and I paid the bills. I was good at money, except that my husband would go out and buy things and get us in debt and I couldn't control him. I'm not so good now because I don't even know what I have.

'The children were not particularly a joy to me. I don't think there was any joy in my life. When he passed the Bar, got a job and we moved into our own place, life immediately became a great deal better and I could enjoy the children a little more. I'm not saying I didn't take any pleasure in them, but I didn't take much. I started to write and the writing kept me going even though I didn't publish anything. After maybe a year of writing I began to send things off. The novel that I remember most was called *Myersville* and, actually, if you take the opening part of *The Women's Room*, that's what I was writing. But I couldn't finish it because it was too sad. It was about my neighbours. I didn't realise I was interviewing them but that's what I was doing. I was trying to find out what it was to be a woman, what women's lives were supposed to be. I had no idea.

'There was no time that I stopped expecting to be a great writer and to have great success. It wasn't a belief. It was a conviction. An agent did ring up and say she loved something I wrote, so I did have a few little moments of hope. But mostly I hoped because of what I wrote, because I'm not a stupid person. When I had studied literature in college, I had not taken college courses the way other kids do. If I took a college course and we read a novel by Hawthorne and a novel by Melville and a novel by Henry James, I read all of Hawthorne, all of Melville, all of Henry James. If I took a course in drama and we read Ibsen and O'Neil, I read all of them. I really immersed myself in literature while I was in school and I knew that what I was writing was good. I didn't know why I didn't get published. I know now that it was because I was writing feminist books in a time when there was no feminism. But I knew that what I was doing was of good quality. That's why I never doubted my work, although I had no real reason from the outside world not to.

'Little by little I worked my way into independence and the more independent I grew, the happier I grew. I went back to school, I got a Masters degree, I got a job teaching. I can't tell you the fights this involved at home – the terrible battle I had just to have the car one night a week to go out and play bridge with my women friends. Any move towards independence threatened my husband unbelievably. He thought the sex was good, he had a great time. He thought we were happy. That's what he always said. I didn't talk to him too much about my unhappiness. I talked to him mainly about the way he treated the children, which upset me terribly. He would listen, he would weep, we'd spend Saturday morning just sitting around the kitchen and he'd say, "Oh, do I really do that? I don't mean to do that, I mean, it's terrible," and he'd start to cry. Then the kids would come in the house and he'd be screaming at them. It was as if I had not said a word. It was very frustrating.

'There was a great deal of love between us, but it got killed over the years. Although I have to say I probably never have loved anyone as much as I loved him. That kept us together despite my misery and despite his increasingly erratic behaviour. But it finally became a matter of life and death. I knew I couldn't go on living if I stayed there. I couldn't stand it.

'It was very hard for me to leave him, that's why it took seventeen years. He claimed that he needed me. He did have five automobile accidents the year after I left. He just cried and cried and then he would ultimately curse me out. He was a Jekyll-and-Hyde figure. I don't know how else to describe him. Obviously I needed him too or I wouldn't have let his crying get to me the way it did.

'I had two affairs while I was married. I didn't like it. I didn't like sneaking. But I had far more sexual pleasure in those affairs than I had with my husband. All of his claiming that I was frigid, I thought was really suspect. I was not economically independent. I didn't earn enough to support myself and the children but just earning something gave me strength. He threatened to take the children away from me when I'd had a lover, but I just laughed. I sent them to live with him later on. He complained how much they cost. He'd been sending me $140 a month. I was on a fellowship. We got by. I had become happier over the years because I started to teach. I loved having a job, I loved teaching, I loved my colleagues. I had a different social life and a different level of friends. Bud had pressured me to drop all my friends, and they were all male anyway, when I left college. So I didn't have any friends of my own. The people we knew were not people you could talk to about ideas or literature, so when I started to teach I made friends of my own and they were great people and I could have great conversations with them.

'My life improved in every way. In the first place I had more money. In the second place I got out of the house and did something that was intellectually stimulating. I had more self-esteem so I think I was probably a better mother, although I think I was always a very good mother. Mothering didn't make me particularly happy when I was really miserable in the early years but I mothered in the same way my mother had, which was thoughtfully. I always asked myself what was best for these children and what would make these children happier. I didn't put much pressure on them, I didn't hold them up to standards. I let them have as much freedom as possible, which is how my mother had raised me. But I didn't tell my daughter sad stories and I was very physically affectionate because I had missed it so much as a child. I think I must have gotten physical affection from my grandmother in my earliest years because I don't think I would have been able to be physically affectionate if I hadn't gotten some affection.

'I think that's why I had a nervous breakdown when I was four, because we moved away from my family and into a silent house with just my mother and my father. I had been very fat, as my grandmother fed me constantly, but I weighed less when I was four than I did when I was one. I stopped eating, I became very depressed. My mother took me to a doctor who said it was jealousy of the new baby, but she knew that it had begun before the new baby was born. I can remember the depression of sitting in that apartment, the silence of it. I'm sure that it was a result of leaving my grandmother's house and losing love. I was as affectionate with my children as they would allow me to be. My daughter never wanted affection very much. She pulled away from me. My son was very affectionate. They are still like that today.

'I didn't teach every day, so I could write. I was watching myself grow and knowing that it was happening. I was very happy. The only thing that made me unhappy was my marriage and the way Bud treated the children. I left when they were thirteen. I sneaked a divorce. I never would have been able to get it if he'd known. I went down to Mexico, it didn't take a long time. But it took a long time to wean him away from me; he just kept stalking me. We didn't have that word then and I wouldn't have known how to use it because it didn't exist, but that's what he was doing. For years. Imagine a situation that wherever you go you turn around and there is this man, staring at you with this hatred. It was the same old Dr Jekyll and Mr Hyde. It was, "Honey, sweetheart, I love you, I've changed, I'll change, I'll be different . . . What do you mean, you bitch, you whore, you cunt." The same old stuff. It never was any different. It was so repetitious I'd laugh after a while. It was a joke but he was not a joke, he was very frightening.

'He came with a rifle once to where we were eating with my parents. I saw him with the gun. I didn't know what to do, I didn't tell anybody else at the dinner table, nobody else could see him but me. I thought if I saw him raise the gun I'd say to everybody, "Get down!" He went home promptly. But it was terrifying. Someone who gets angry in that way, when their eyes pop out of their head and their face turns red, it's terrifying.

'I really didn't get away until I went up to Harvard, but even then he followed me. The children would come in on a Friday afternoon and say, "Did you know Daddy is sitting downstairs in a car?" He worked on Long Island, so it was a four to five hour drive to where I lived and he would come up on a Friday night, over and over and over again. Once I invited him in. The children said, "Could Daddy come in?" and I said, "Wait a minute," and I called up all my friends and asked them to come over, and then I said, "Now you can ask him to come in." I never let him come in again. There wasn't any point. I wouldn't speak to him, I didn't see him, I wouldn't let him in the house.

'He got involved with other women. The children would see him occasionally and they would tell me what was going on in his life, so I knew that there was this possibility that he might marry someone else, which made me feel really off the hook. I figured if he got married he couldn't keep calling me. By the time he did get married, it was many years later. He called me up and asked me to come back to him. I said, "Bud, how can you be saying this to me when you're getting married next week?" He said, "How do you know that?" I said, "The kids told me." "How did they know?" I said, "You know, not everybody doesn't tell their children anything the way you do. Your bride told her children and they told your children and they told me." "You bitch, you whore, you cunt." And he slammed down the phone. That was my last telephone call from him.

'I'd had a long-term affair with a young guy, lasted five years. It was a nice affair, Joe was nice, I felt he was good for the children. I don't think I ever really put him in a book. I may have put bits and pieces of him. He didn't live with me, he lived on Long Island. He would come up every other weekend for about four days. It was perfect. But my daughter got raped and she turned against him. I don't know why. Maybe she just turned against males. But she didn't act that way, she went out with guys. He did not know how to deal with the rape and tried to jolly her out of whatever state she was in, which was not the right thing to do. But he never did anything bad, he was too young to understand how to deal with it. But she made such a to-do about it. She was in very bad shape. So I broke up with him. It was really time, anyway. You shouldn't be with someone that young for too long. He was fifteen years younger and was staying a child. He had me, why did he need to grow up? I needed a man.

'I had lots of affairs after that, which weren't really important. I didn't have another serious affair until I got involved with a woman many years later. I did not take any of the other affairs seriously, I don't know that the guys didn't, but I didn't. I wasn't looking for love that would endure, that was going to be for my whole life. I enjoyed these people, I loved them within some limits. I had sexual pleasure of varying degrees with them, I had companionship, and none of them did I let get too close. I kept them very much at a distance. They had to call before they came, they couldn't just walk into the house.

'Truthfully, I can't imagine having any other kind of relationship and I don't think that's what most people want. I have been a wife and mother for too many years. I didn't even have a door on my study, everybody could interrupt me any time and they did. I had to have the right to close my door and the only way I could get it was this way because men do not respect a woman's boundaries. They think if they come over you're going to cook dinner for them and you do. Apart from Joe, I never cooked for anyone again after my marriage, but I had to keep a very firm hold of all my relationships. When I was teaching, the students would just come over any time they felt like it. I would draw the curtains on my bedroom and turn out all the lights in the house at night just to get some privacy.

'I don't have friendships of convenience. The people that I'm close to are people who I love and I love them because there's something beautiful and divine in them. Now I assume that everyone has that, but I can't see it in everyone.

'I had written a Masters essay on Shakespeare at Hofstra College and I had a Renaissance project which nobody wanted to deal with so it eventually became the Shakespeare book. I had to find someone who was willing to work with me on Joyce. I only had another year in which to finish my PhD at Harvard University. I was living on fellowships and I had two teenage kids so I didn't have time to fool around the way maybe other people did. So I did the Joyce in a year and my adviser thought highly of it and urged Harvard Press to publish it. That was my PhD. When I finished it I got a job teaching at Holy Cross College but I had no money that summer, my fellowships had run out and my job didn't start until September, so I had to get through from June to September. Aspen University was giving fellowships so I applied and got one. It saved my life, and it was there that I started the first draft of a novel.

'I had written about 150 to 200 pages and I threw it all away. It was the first draft of The Women's Room. The murders at Kent State were the central image and involved an older woman who's gone back to study. Initially, Kent State had offered me a fabulous scholarship and it would have made my life very easy if I'd gone there but I couldn't have passed up Harvard for Kent State. But I could very easily have been on that campus in 1968 during the time that the National Guard killed the students. I imagined a woman, who would become Val, getting herself killed in a similar kind of massacre and that was the first seed of the novel. I knew that how I told it was everything and that if I wrote this story from the perspective of the woman it would not have a very good chance of being published. So I chose to tell it through a young man, a young reporter who gets sent out to cover the story in this little town.

'I tossed it all in the garbage because he was just too callow and I couldn't tell enough through his eyes. Then I started to teach and got caught up in turning the dissertation into a book for Harvard Press, so that took me a year or so. Finally I went back to the novel and I wrote it again from the perspective of a housewife who was a friend of this woman who gets killed. I had the same problem – the housewife couldn't see enough, just didn't know enough, wasn't sensitive enough, wasn't aware enough. And then I read one of Margaret Drabble's novels in which she alternates narration from first person to third person. I just read it and didn't think anything more of it. A while later I woke up in the middle of the night and thought, "That's how I can do it. I can have the housewife, the ordinary woman, with whom my reader will relate, tell the story, but have her tell it as an older, wiser person who comes back and looks at the events of the past, and alternate the narrational line between this housewife, Mira, as an older, wiser person with political understanding and insight and the younger person that she was who didn't know all those things." That was how I could get the reader in and yet provide the additional line of insight that I needed.

'Once I came up with that I started to work on it the next day and it just took off. I had huge trouble getting it published. I got some of the most furious letters I've ever received when I tried to get it published . . .

'I'm sorry,' she said. 'I'm afraid we will have to stop now. I'm not feeling too well.'

'Of course,' I said. It wasn't just the pain in her face but the pain that had been her life that had drained the colour from my own cheeks. The sheer grit and determination that had carried her through was still there in the intensity with which she told her story. She was an amazing woman. But I could see that dredging it all up again had taken its toll. Her normally husky voice had been gradually fading to a whisper.

I packed up my recorder (which I had checked was on the right setting at least ten times), said goodnight and left.

5
ROBIN MORGAN
PART II

Day Four, 4 pm: Her apartment, Greenwich Village,
New York City

No chitchat this time. We sat in exactly the same places and started talking as if we had never finished. Robin was the consummate professional and there was no need for me to apologise for the inconvenience or thank her once again.

At the end of this second interview we relaxed with a glass of wine and a stroll in the garden. Like a matron in a maternity ward she bent down and touched and described each bed of flowers to me as if they were miracles of birth. And in the middle of New York City, they undoubtedly were.

What follows is a combination of both interviews and is, I believe, the stronger for it. Having been a child actor, Robin is confident in her dramatic expression and says her lines as if having learned them thoroughly. Once she is set on a course it is difficult to jump her off the rails. At times her tempo, flow and rhythms were almost like that of a prepared audition. It is easy to understand why she is described as one of the women's movement's most renowned and articulate voices.

Poet, political theorist, writer and activist, for the past twenty years she and Gloria Steinem have often been called the patron saints of feminism. They have both been involved in the movement from the beginning, have been unswerving in their devotion and dedication, and unstinting in what they have given to it. For them, being a feminist was not so much a political act as a calling.

I was prepared to confer sainthood on her just for giving me another interview.

'In 1970 when *Sisterhood is Powerful* was published, if anyone at that point had told me that a quarter of a century on it would still be selling, I would have been touched. I am grateful to have produced something that has lasted but also a little depressed because I would have thought that surely by now we should be way beyond this basic primer.

'My activism came out of the male Left that had been the civil rights movement, which is where I cut my political teeth. But by the late 1960s the Left had become apocalyptic and violent, very boys' style. There was not a long-distance runner sensibility, and partly that's US politics and insurgent movements, and partly it was because the "revolution" was supposed to be imminent. When I look at what has happened to that Left, which has fizzled and gone nowhere, its male leaders selling out, and compare that with what has happened to the feminist movement, it is bloody amazing. We have come a very long way, but obviously nowhere near enough. We control 20 per cent of state legislatures now but we're still 52 per cent of the population. Everyone danced on rooftops when we doubled our numbers in the Senate and in the House but it's still only six out of a hundred. So there's an enormous distance to go yet and that's just in terms of electoral, visible, traditional politics.

'The real changes have occurred in consciousness, in lifestyle, in the labour force, in consciousness about work, in consciousness about violence against women, about sexuality, about recognising different kinds of families. There has been an extraordinary shift in consciousness in what is historically a very short period of time. When it's your life it seems like a damned long period of time and you think, "Let's get on with this, I've only got one life here, I'd like to see a little progress." When you pan back, to use camera terms, and look at it historically and look at how the language itself has changed, you see the reflection of real changes in consciousness.

'I haven't read *Sisterhood is Powerful* recently, but for years whenever I did I would almost get cramps from thinking, "Oh, why didn't I add such and such and why didn't I do this?" But by and large I'm proud of the young woman who put that together. I started it in 1968, just after I'd organised the first Miss America Pageant protest in Atlantic City, which was the first mass demonstration of the women's movement of this wave in this country. After Atlantic City there were a lot of requests for the few of us who had organised the protest to come and speak on different councils. We took different friends in rattletrap Volkswagens and station wagons filled with shopping bags full of mimeographed copies of papers that different groups had written.

'I earned my living as a book editor and it seemed to me this was crazy. I thought we ought to put together a book that would reflect this tremendous diversity, so we wouldn't have to be getting bursitis cranking up all the mimeograph machines. So *Sisterhood is Powerful* has a piece on ageing women, three pieces by African-American women, a strong lesbian presence, a Chicana piece and, foreshadowing *Sisterhood is Global*, there's even a piece on China, pieces on secretaries and executives, women in the military and, this was the anti-Vietnam period, pieces on psychology and economics. Then there is this hilarious deliberately eclectic mix of poetry and leaflets because I wanted to give the flavour, the insouciance, the excitement, the defiance and the fun of that moment in time. We were terrified and euphoric at the same time. I still am. I never mellowed.

'My mother and I, like many mothers and daughters, have had a love/hate relationship for all of my life. I was born in 1941 and we had been very close at different times and then very estranged. As I became involved with this nascent women's movement I had tried to talk to my mother about it. Later on we would all realise that the last person in the world that you can ever organise is your mother, because even though you may have suddenly realised that she's really your sister and not just your mother, she still thinks she's your mother. Sometimes we can happily infect with feminism each other's mothers but it's very difficult when it's your own. Finally my mother and I reached a moment of mutual understanding, where there had been enough glimpses of each other as female human beings that I was grateful.

'She was an extremely brilliant, high energy and extraordinarily talented woman. She wanted to write and of course was never permitted that. She had one year of college and then had to drop out and even then she'd put herself through so there was all this energy and raw intelligence and a tremendous anger in her that had never had anywhere to go. All of her hopes and dreams and visions and fantasies and will were poured into me, her only child, which was very flattering on the one hand and on the other hand was a bit suffocating. I was a working child actor and she wanted me to continue with that. "I Remember Mama" was an award-winning seven-year-long live television series; it was only one of those that I did. I was working from the time I was two. I was a child model and then a child actor, with all the pressures that entailed. But I always knew from age four I really wanted to be a writer.

'It wasn't until I was about sixteen that I could manage to get myself out of the acting business. My family were working-class, first-generation immigrant folks and the path to the American Dream seemed very difficult. My father and mother were divorced before I was born so my father was a basic cipher of a presence. I was raised in a house of women and my acting work supported the entire family. One positive outcome was that I was never given the feeling that there was anything I couldn't do. It's a good thing for any child to feel that, and in particular for a little female person.

'I was a very hard-working child. I was an A student, there were piano lessons and it was a half-hour show from age seven to fourteen every week. At the time I knew no other life so I would have said I was happy. In retrospect I was not happy in the slightest. I can't claim that it was a melodramatically, ghastly childhood. Given that context, which I would have preferred not to be given, I was probably fortunate in that I wasn't schlepped from audition to audition. There were always steady jobs and I had the feeling of continually being in work. I haven't ended up an alcoholic or drug addict, the usual things that ex-child stars seem to become, so that's nice.

'I was bringing in enough money to support my mother and my aunts. That meant that there were certain normal childhood activities I never engaged in because they might be dangerous. I never did sports and any time I wanted to it was always, "My God, you could fall down and you could hurt yourself or you could scar your face and the family would starve." Those words, "the family would starve," were very powerful. So I read books instead. This was safe, permissible and, thank the goddess, there were books at home and they became a lifeline in what was, I now realise in retrospect, quite a lonely childhood.

'I was reading at four and I began to scribble immediately. My mother and my aunts had a real Eastern European Jewish reverence for education so that they never stopped that aspect of me. It's when I wanted to read and write rather than act that we tended to conflict. When I was eighteen I managed to move out and get a job as a secretary in a literary agency. I was writing poetry nonstop. My mother was very unhappy with me. I moved from Sutton Place, which is a rather posh section of Manhattan, to the Lower East Side. Usually people do it the other way round. But I was delighted. I just wanted to be with poets, writers and artists. What I definitely got from my mother is a refrain in my poem which is simply, "There is nothing you cannot be." So, rest her soul, that is inscribed on her tombstone.

'I never had the feeling that I was not loved and cherished. But would that have been true if I hadn't worked? I don't know. My mother worked as a saleswoman in a shop but stopped when I was around seven. She invested well the money I earned. I never saw any of it. And when I said that I wanted to leave the business and get my own apartment and move out from her, she said I never would see any of it. And I didn't. Not a penny. She was able to buy herself a co-op apartment on Upper Fifth Avenue and live quite well off my childhood earnings. She did her stocks and bonds obsessively on the phone with her brokers all the time and I came to loathe that so much. I'm the complete opposite, hopeless with money. My pattern has been: you live your way through debt, and then there's another advance, and then you pay off the debt, and then the cycle begins again. And somehow through all of this I managed to support the marriage, so I must have done okay. It's just the chronic stress that is attendant on that. But it's a tremendous privilege to be able to work at what you love doing, which for me is writing.

'Kate Millett was the smart one who bought a farm and now all these years later it is finally clear of debt and is earning its keep. I set up the first feminist fund and all the monies from *Sisterhood is Powerful* have gone back to the movement. It was never listed as such in the *New York Times*, because anthologies aren't listed as best-sellers, but it became a best-seller. God knows how many millions of copies it sold over twenty-five years. But it seemed to me that it was a collective book and the profits belonged to the women's movement.

'My mother would not have approved. My then husband did not approve. Nobody approved. Kate Millett said to me, "You're absolutely out of your mind. You paid all those contributors and you're the one who spent years of your life doing this. Since when do you think you're independently wealthy?" "Well I'm not, Kate," I said, "they just turned my gas and electricity off." She said, "Well keep this money." I said, "No, I can't." Retrospectively, I have been foolish; it certainly would have saved me some grief. On the other hand, most of the feminist media, the feminist bookstores, the battered women's shelters, started in the United States with seed money from the *Sisterhood is Powerful* fund. The only requirement was that the money couldn't go to individuals, it had to be autonomous women's groups. Emily Goodman was the attorney who helped me and the fund went along quite nicely for four and a half to five years and gave out over $250,000.

'And then a woman sued us, claiming that we had plagiarised the bibliography. Yea verily over the years I have been asked how the hell can you plagiarise a bibliography? It's like plagiarising the alphabet. But this woman had her heart set on this. We tried to go to feminist arbitration. I felt like I'd staggered into the twilight zone of horror. I couldn't believe it. And she sued the publisher, Random House, as well. But three and a half years later the Random House corporate lawyers had cost so much that the royalties were indemnified to pay them back their fees. She had hired her lawyer on the basis of a percentage of her gains. So that was a real tragedy. The royalties, believe it or not, have only cleared a year ago and now they're largely going to the Sisterhood is Global Institute.

'I've had a chequered existence with finances. At a conference once a woman said to me, "I've heard that you have a chalet in Switzerland," and I almost fell off the stage laughing. I said, "My dear sister, I tell you what. If you can send me the address and the keys and the airfare I will go there very gladly, but I cannot afford even the airfare and I certainly don't know the address and I have no keys. However, if you know something I don't, pass it on."

'When I was an adolescent I envisioned somehow for myself something that I would have called laughingly "the life of the mind". Now God knows what I meant by that. Perhaps being an academic somewhere, but I didn't imagine what happened in most of the '70s and a great large chunk of the '80s, which was giving three to four to five speeches a week.

'I wanted something to represent literary criticism in *Sisterhood is Powerful*. I said to Kate, whom I knew, "I want a piece of your doctoral thesis." She said, "Oh, don't be silly, what could be less interesting to anybody than a doctoral dissertation?" I said, "This is a very good section." Well, that little extract grew to become the book *Sexual Politics*, which was a major pillar of the women's movement.

'Gloria Steinem and I are similar to the extent of trying to juggle public presence, organising, travelling and writing. But the real me is the writer and if I go too long without writing I get very crazy and very cranky. Somehow I've managed to write fifteen books. How I live now is in relative peace and a major adjustment from having to write in the corners of my life as I always have. I can do journalism and essays that way, even poetry usually comes when it wants to, but fiction needs long, uninterrupted spaces of time. Which I now have.

'I spent the '70s and most of the '80s producing as many books as possible – fiction, nonfiction, poetry – and beginning the thirteen-year project that became *Sisterhood is Global*, which meant travelling all over the world, which I loved.

'My marriage ended in 1983, not surprisingly right around the same time that my mother died. Yes, funny that. It was a very rough period. But I was consoled by my extended family of sisters around the world and then I fell in love for the first time with a woman. God knows I had tried through the years to do this. There was a period in the '70s where I was the only radical feminist, a nationally known spokesperson, who was married. Much less a mother. Any other radical feminist was either a lesbian feminist or was heterosexual but single. When I fell in love with a woman everything seemed to come together finally – the politics, the emotion, the sexuality – and the relationship lasted for almost three years.

'Others have defined me as a lesbian or as bisexual. Some would say, "She's a feminist," some would say, "She's a theorist," but I would define myself as a poet; a hopeless, unsalvageable poet.

'One should never say never, but I think it would be unlikely that I might be involved with a man again, but you never know. I mean, women aren't perfect either. At the ripe old age of fifty-four, which sounds very grown up, I am living alone. I always miss it when I'm not in love, it's a very nice state in which to be. But I have my work, my friends and my twenty-year-old son, Blake, who chooses to live next to me. I love to be able to have friends in for dinner and in my garden, which has become this mad passion of mine. It is slowly escalating into an obsession and I'm very proud of it because in the middle of New York City it is not usual that you have grapes and tomatoes and twelve different roses growing.

'When Lang Communications bought Ms they suspended it for six months and then asked me to come on board as editor for an ad-free magazine. There were a lot of people who ran around saying, "She's going to bring back fiction, she's going to put poetry in, she's going to make it international. And no advertisements. Forget it! It will die." Well it took off like a rocket. Which I think shows that if you offer real quality food people are hungry for it. It sells by subscription. I had told Gloria [Steinem] I would do it for a year and it stretched to three and a half years. I was in the office at seven every morning and didn't leave until eleven every night. Every eight weeks we were producing a hundred-page book at a very high standard, with major writers, not only US but international, and we treated them well. It became obvious to me that I couldn't continue doing this so I brought Marcia Gillespie on board and I was very proud to be succeeded by the first woman editor of colour for Ms. I became contributing editor and took off for a protracted period of travel to strip off some of my executive toxicity.

'I never became burned out, just an old radical, which is better. When I'm asked, "How come you haven't mellowed?" I don't know what to answer them. All I can think to say is, "Have I blinked? Has it been won? Are women safe everywhere, are they all earning plenty of money, are we not being raped, is there world peace, is the environment not in danger?" All of these issues are feminist to me and I don't see that stopping. It's not as though I was in the shower when the revolution happened and therefore I can afford to burn out. After you rant and rave and have a cry and so forth, what is there to do but roll up your sleeves and get on with it?

'If I had to sum up my tactics or my strategies in one word I would say "audacity". At one point I would have said, "You couldn't make the revolution without women." This was when I was trying to convince the boys. And at a later point I would have said, "There is no revolution without women." Later on I would have said, "The revolution is women." Later on I would have said, "Women are the revolution" and after a certain point you begin to think revolution is actually a pretty small word for the big stuff that we're really talking about, which is transformation of the entire sentient life on this planet, and that's where I slip into metaphysics.

'I'm very fortunate to be female and literate at this particular point in history and to be empowered with a talent for communication that I can put both in the service of art and in the service of the politics that I believe is really capable of saving the planet. I identify as an international feminist and not as American. For a period in the '70s and the '80s the women's movement even became my mother. Literally. I sang for it, I tap danced for it, I worked for it, I gave money back to it. And no matter how much I tried, I couldn't get it to love me enough. I couldn't win its approval enough, I couldn't be professional enough for it, I couldn't kill myself enough for it. It's taken me all this time to finally see the women's movement not as my mother but as my sister, and sometimes as my daughter, which is nice, and not let it totally tyrannise me and not let it bring out the fascist in me either, which erupts whenever I overwork too much. But always underpinning and overarching all of this, there's the writing and, in particular, the poetry. I have a novel in the works, I am writing the first volume of my memoirs, I have a number of short stories that are percolating, I have a book of feminist theory that keeps knocking on the doors of my brain, but poetry is my foundation, my rock.'

So who does she see now when she looks in the mirror?

'A woman I really like. I see a woman whose hair has gradually gone from light brown to grey and is now going silver. I'm healthier at this point, after a period of ill health, than I've ever been. I don't quite know what I'll do with it all yet, except I'll write. Nobody is ever an ex-feminist, have you noticed that? You get people who may have resisted it to their dying day but nobody ever says, "Well, I was a feminist, but that's before I learned that it really felt great to be battered by my husband." That's because freedom is contagious and it feels good to be capable, to be competent, to be your own woman. It feels wonderful to love, to sacrifice, to lay aside your own powers for someone you love for a while but not for too long and not when that's expected of you your whole life through. So I don't want to sacrifice for another any more and I don't want to be sacrificed for. I'm tired of over-giving, which tends to be my sin. It's a fairly common womanly sort of sin; we tend to be the earth mothers. Ironically, I was least like that with my son because I was afraid of suffocating him in the way I had been, so that's probably one of the healthier relationships I have. But certainly with my husband and with other women, I couldn't ever give enough.

'Less than a year after *Sisterhood is Powerful* came out, *Monster* came out, which was my first published book of poems. It created quite a sensation, much to my shock and my ecstasy. It seemed to tap into a vein of women's rage that I certainly felt but that I had thought was unique. You think you are the only one who could possibly be so crazy as to think or feel these things and six different women in the room turn around and say, "Oh, you too?" And that moment is an amazing epiphany. That happened with many of the poems in *Monster*, especially the title poem which was about feeling that one was so surrounded with misogyny that one was in effect a monster. It became a kind of movement rallying cry. Sections of *Monster* began to appear on bumper stickers and greeting cards and T-shirts. It was like the poem took off on a life of its own.

'The first time that I became really aware that there was a growing international women's group and the concept of its solidarity was because of the Sylvia Plath poem in *Monster*. It began, "I accuse Ted Hughes of the murder of Sylvia Plath." Nothing if not radical. I didn't say that he actually shoved her head in an oven but I did say that because he'd been having an affair with another woman, because he was a womaniser and a batterer and so forth, she didn't really suicide. I pointed out that the next wife had also done the same thing but in fact had taken her two children with her rather than have him raise them. This was already scuttlebutt in literary circles, in the English-speaking poetry world, but the poem was quite powerful. Six weeks before bound books were due to come from Random House I was informed that Hughes had heard there was such a poem, had demanded to see it, and that he and Random House were stopping production. We then entered into a nightmare period of six months of trying to get the book published. Me and my one lone woman lawyer against the Random House corporate boys, with their grey faces, grey suits, grey brains, and their lawyers and Hughes and his sister, Olwyn Hughes, who were Plath's literary executors. It became a cause célèbre. Various Plath scholars rallied to my side and said that there were unpublished journals, some snippets of which had been sent to me, in which she herself accused him of rape, accused him of trying to kill her, accused him of driving her to despair, etc. I was given the choice of not publishing my first book of poems, which was rather important to me as a young poet, or withdrawing the poem. I would do neither. I tend to be a "both/and" not an "either/or" girl, so I will always try to look for the third way. In this case it turned out to be a way of rewriting the poem so that the point got across but it legally "scaped hanging", as Shakespeare would have said. And that was to phrase it as a rhetorical question, as in, "How can I accuse Ted Hughes of the murder of Sylvia Plath?" And then I expanded the rest of the poem in fact to add in, "How can I accuse a cabal of lawyers, of attorneys, of etc, of censorship?" It passed the letter of the law and Random House published it. Once the book was out it sold so well and so fast that Random House themselves were quite astonished. It was selling at the rate that W.H. Auden's work usually sells and not in his case for feminist reasons.

'It got very good reviews in the poetry world, so that was all very surprising, and then suddenly about six months after it had been published by Random House US and Random House Canada, I heard from Canadian feminists that the book had suddenly disappeared in Canada. Some of the early women's studies courses were using it as a text about women's culture. So I rang up Random House to find out why there were no books in Canada. And only then was I told that they'd reached a gentlemen's agreement with Ted Hughes that he would not sue for libel or slander if all books were withdrawn in the Commonwealth. Nothing would be published in Britain, in Australia, New Zealand or Canada and, to my shock, Random House had agreed without ever checking with me.

'But they had not counted on the women's movement. Starting with Australian feminists and then spreading to New Zealand, Canada and Britain, were so-called pirated editions. The women actually wrote to me with tremendous grace and asked my permission. I of course gave it and with tremendous courage they published. In Britain and many of the Commonwealth countries the penalties for libel or slander are much more severe than they are in the United States. They even extend to those distributing and selling the book and the penalties are severe prison sentences, not just fines. That was the first time, to my amazement, that the women's movement came through internationally. They picketed Hughes, carrying signs with the poem on it, wherever he went for about four or five years in the United Kingdom or in Australia or Canada or New Zealand. It was amazing to me as a writer to think that a poem could have that kind of impact and be such a tool in women's hands.

'By the mid-'70s the poems continued no matter what and *Lady of the Beasts* came out with more struggle poems about marriage. On that front my husband, Kenneth Pitchford, was enormously supportive and he was a really wonderful father to Blake. He was also a fine poet. We were both deeply political people, Kenneth was strongly a pro-feminist man. The eventual toll on the marriage was due to a number of different reasons, including the stress of both writing careers. He taught and he also worked as a freelancer. We both did. I'd done individual semesters but I'd never taught as a career. Kenneth was a founder of a GLF, of gay liberation – he counted himself as a gay man. One would obviously categorise him as bisexual but Kenneth was gay when I married him. His former lover was our best man. So it was never your traditional-variety nuclear family. Kenneth was the first person I went to bed with and then I married him. I'd been a working child in the theatre and therefore grown up with gay people, so it never seemed different or unusual to me.

'The writing was paramount and we loved each other as writers as much or more than we did as people. So there was this Bloomsbury-cum-Beatrice and Sydney Webb mixture. We were very much in love then. Intellectually he encouraged me to explore my own sexuality but emotionally it was a very different cup of tea and it was more double-standard than either of us would have anticipated. He did have male lovers now and then but there were whole vast periods when he did not. I discovered to my amazement that I really was not cut out to be a swinger; it bored me, made me slightly nauseous. We were married in 1961 and Blake was born in 1969. We were both very intent on co-parenting. But I was getting published and Kenneth was not. Women did not want to read men, and men didn't want to read men with pro-feminist politics. They wanted to read Norman Mailer, they wanted to read attacks on these crazy women. So poor Kenneth fell twixt cup and lip. That was very painful for both of us.

'We did still manage for twenty years to survive that and together produced a wonderful person, Blake, our son, and a hell of a lot of good poems and some very good memories. No marriage dies of any one thing. I very much needed time and space to myself and I think Kenneth did too. Another factor was the change in my own sexuality. Now he lives alone and he continues to write. We're not close but we are certainly friends. We always show up at Blake's concerts and have good and animated discussions, usually about poetry and politics. We didn't have Blake to save the marriage but I do think that it would have ended earlier without a child. If it had not been for my mother's rather dramatic response to my relationship with Kenneth, we probably wouldn't have married at all. We wanted just to live together. In a sense she drove us into the legality.

'There are interviews of me as a child star being asked, "What do you want to be when you grow up?" And my saying, "No, I don't want to be an actress, I want to write." The fact that I took my writing very seriously was in no small part due to one woman, Jean Tafti, who when I was thirteen came on the scene as my private tutor and gave me my first taste of the poet Yeats. She said, "Write me something," and I did, and from that time on she never doubted me. I think that I was burning with such a hard gem-like flame that I would have written anyway. But there is no way for me to know how much harder it would have been without the passionate reflection that woman had the courage to give me back of myself as a young writer. Later on there were other teachers who took me seriously enough to tear my poems apart and say, "This isn't acceptable, you can do better."

'Of the fifteen books I've written, seven are now in print and that's very unusual. By the late 1970s I was embarked on *Sisterhood is Global*, which would come out in 1984, and that took a good thirteen years really to assemble from conception through to publication. But *Anatomy of Freedom* had been published by then, which was the explication of my falling in love with advanced theoretical physics – which sounds hilarious when you consider that I had math anxiety but of course advanced theoretical physics has nothing to do with mathematics. It has to do with wonderful ideas and metaphors and images and the way the universe really works, which is witty and insouciant and very much like a woman. I made up my mind that I was going to demystify physics for myself and other women and in the process use physics as a metaphor for feminism. It's a strange book and it's all over the map: personal writings, journalism, reporting, there's a full-length play in it, poetry, dream journals. It is a defiantly eclectic mix and I have a fondness for that book to this very day.

'Once I had participated in the making of *Sisterhood is Global* I knew I'd been forever changed. I can no longer write about only the United States because things fired in my brain. Little synapses go off all the time saying, "Oh, yes, but remember there was that group in Peru. Oh, but remember that extraordinary woman in Sri Lanka." There's a real longing in me for community; on the other hand, writing is the best contribution I can make to community and writing is a solitary activity. It is still where I feel most alive, most happy, most me and least self-conscious.

'I have given a great deal to the women's movement and it's given a great deal to me. It's a hell of a wonderful exchange. It's also been exhausting, crotchety-making, exploitative and a million other things to me. But it's been worth it. If you seriously believe, as I do, that sentient life on the planet is endangered at this point and that the majority of the people on the planet who are women are at a historical moment where we are placed so that we can change that, then the importance of feminist politics is rather crucial. I don't feel worthy of feminist canonisation, I think being called a saint is pretty hilarious. I do take the politics really seriously and I have tried to live them. There is no off-stage for me. And that's made real problems for me at times in personal relationships, in trying to find out where I exist as a writer independently of my politics and then finally realising there is no divide. The women's movement gave me my own voice as a poet. *Monster* came from a freed-up voice; that is a glad debt I owe the women's movement.

'I'm not a missionary. A missionary takes the word and inflicts it on locals. What I see as one of my very real tasks in the international women's movement is being a form of access for women around the world to speak to each other. It's not my feminism that I'm bringing to them, it's discovering theirs and learning from theirs and that's really very different. And as for being called a saint? Sainthood is simply a synonym for the longevity of one's politics. If you don't burn out, if you don't fall by the wayside, if you don't turn reactionary, if you don't go bananas, if you don't become conservative or moderative or mellow, then you must be a saint. I haven't done any of those things, that's true, but that's also true of a great many other women. I can't really take such titles seriously.

'I'm pleased that my own writing has been useful and sometimes I think rather good. I'm also pleased that in that other capacity which I would call access, in other words as an editor, that I've been able to make space for, give voice to, widen audiences for other women's voices – some of whom I've disagreed with, but that's not the point. The point is that when you're talking about a majority of the human species they're not all going to be, thank God, a cookie pattern replica of each other. Phrases like "diversity is our strength" I really believe to be true. Now that I'm in my early fifties I do want to have more time for myself and more time for my own writing, but whatever I write will be feminist. The women's movement is now strong enough that I can tell whatever truths that I individually as a woman and a writer need to be able to tell.

'My path to this point is absolutely littered with errors and mistakes and I'm sure in a year or five years or ten years I'll look back at this moment and say, "Oh my God!" It hasn't been a pure path where I just saw one way and immediately trod it. No angel descended. On the contrary, many demons have accompanied me every step of the way. There's a consistent crankiness within me. Whatever I'm doing I feel I should be doing something else. If I'm at my computer I think, "I really ought to be out on the hustings, I ought to be organising, I ought to have said yes to that press conference," but whenever I'm there I think, "I really shouldn't be here, they don't really need me, I am most assuredly not indispensable, I should be doing the one thing that only I can do, which is being at home with my computer." The only thing you can say about crotchetiness is that after a certain age it's almost expected of you and that's kind of a relief.

'I'm a workaholic and I'm a control freak; obsessive-compulsive, anal-retentive. If it's midnight and we have a demonstration tomorrow and the magic markers are there and the cardboard's there but the signs aren't made and the rest of the women in the group say they're exhausted and they've got to go and lie down and go back to their families I will either say, "Tough, you're staying," or else I will be the one to stay there until four o'clock in the morning like a martyr and do the signs. At certain points during my editorship of Ms, because of my perfectionist standards I would wind up editing two-thirds of an issue and then be wiped out in terms of health.

'Perfectionism has really been a problem my whole life. The one place where I have a right and a responsibility to it is on my own page as a writer, but it spills over. One of the nicknames that the staff had for me at Sisterhood is Global was Attila the Hon because on the one hand they loved me, I don't doubt that, but there was also this Attila aspect to me under certain circumstances, and particularly as the stress grew. As I had to be fundraising to meet the payroll every week, I'm sure I could be very unpleasant in those circumstances. My only defence would be that I'm as hard or harder on myself as I would be on anyone I was working with.

'Emotionally I do believe in the perfectibility of humanity. That pertains to personal relationships and to one's art and to one's politics and the way one lives one's daily life. I am the crazy lady who coined the phrase "the personal is political". We came up with it together in a group in the late '60s. The New York radical women in 1968 were being hit from the boys in the Left with the line, "This is all very well to talk about politics but it's not political." At some point I said, "But the personal is political." Then The Red Stockings made it their slogan, which was quite wonderful, and it grew from there. I really believe it. I think that there is no atom of humanity that is not in that sense political.

'And it's true that the sisterhood has not always been kind to me. After the destruction of the *Sisterhood is Powerful* fund, my major fight was to not be extremely bitter. That was a real vision I had that was destroyed and it hurt the movement, more even than it hurt me. I have endured many individual trashings caused by envy or by lies. I don't do personal anger well – I do political anger well, but I have trouble articulating personal rage. One thing that has helped me deal with all that is to see things politically. I'm dead serious. I can't think of a woman who I would say is my enemy. There are a hell of a lot of women I don't like. Here's how it works in my gut. The language person in me would say, "Well, an enemy is more than an adversary, an enemy is really somebody unredeemable, somebody that you're willing to fight against for the rest of your life, somebody that you have to defeat or they're going to defeat you." Then I look at the power that women do or don't have, and I'm not denying that women have power over each other in many work situations, personal situations, whole political situations, etc, but these things are relative. If you pan back enough and change the frame, then you see it in the context of male power and of patriarchal power, and no woman has the power over any other woman that most men have over women. If I'm going to think in terms of "enemy" or "adversary", somebody who really has heavy-duty power over my own life or really wants me out of the way or wants me powerless, I tend to think of the Vatican, the fundamentalists of any religions, the Right-Wing fascists and Congress. Serious, bad and male patriarchal power. If I disagree with a woman it doesn't mean I don't like her, doesn't mean that I wouldn't argue with her, doesn't mean I wouldn't combat her positions but it means that I get to have the chance to examine what the political overlap is, where the similarities are, where the differences are. But she is not my enemy. Take Margaret Thatcher, for example. Every feminist has been beaten over the head by patriarchalists who say, "Is this what you mean by power?" We're so tired of answering the Margaret Thatcher question we could throw up. One answer is, "Well, if you take a man and you put him in an institution for thirty years in which he's totally surrounded by women and women's values, he's going to come out a pretty different and unusual man." Well that's what happened to her, in reverse. I recall a particular interview Thatcher gave after Indira Gandhi was assassinated and I remember her expression and her voice and it really moved me. She spoke of mourning this death not only because Gandhi was a great leader, etc, etc, but because now she felt totally alone. And I thought, "Oh yes, of course. Were we so naive as to think that the first one who was going to be prime minister on that level of a major world power would be one of ours?" No, of course she would be one of the boys. But again, if you have a historical perspective, it is not surprising. Her having been there, much as I profoundly disagree with the policies that she articulated and put into action, makes it more possible for one of ours eventually to be there.

'All of which is a way of saying that looking at things politically, and I mean politically in the deepest sense of the term, obviously not just electoral politics, gives one a chance to see more depth, to have more of a colour range, to see more intricacies and complexities as opposed to less. So in that sense, no, I don't have women enemies. I am not doing a Pollyanna. Women are just people and we've been raised in these cultures. What is amazing to me is that we have different values at all from the dominant culture. And we do. We tend more cross-culturally toward consensus in problem solving, toward distaste for violence, toward altruism. That is not just culturally conditioned because it's cross-cultural.

'The saddest time in my life was 1994. It was the ending of a ten-year relationship, a time of dealing with my mortality and real difficulty for the first time in my life in actually writing. It was a bit of a black hole. Friends have teased me and said, "If that was a black hole, you sure functioned better than some people nowhere near black holes." I continued my political activity and I lived on automatic pilot. I didn't just crawl into a corner and babble to myself, although I came closer to it than I ever have before. I have a small but intense circle of remarkably supportive friends. We do for each other. It is all women except for Blake. He is the one male friend, and an extraordinary one. Also, my sense of humour is a blessing, and mostly it didn't desert me. I remember thinking to myself, "There's got to be a way to use this because I've never felt so powerless before." The parts of me that have been very judgemental both of myself and others for years have been wisely humbled in the process. In the past year I've been brought to my knees and I've now reached a moment where I'm grateful for that. Hubris is still careening around and that's been both a strength and a problem. The motto for Sisterhood is Global is "Only she who attempts the absurd can achieve the impossible". And there is a real audacity, a real risk-taker that I admire in me.

'There's a pattern of making up my mind that I'm going to attempt the absurd, achieve the impossible. This was also true of making Ms magazine ad-free, you see. You just fling yourself out on a limb and you say, "Well, with sheer force of will, hard work, audacity, a little sense of humour and a lot of trust in women, we're just going to make this happen." That's all there is to it. And you say it with enough confidence that you almost cast a spell on yourself and make it happen. You don't let yourself look out of the corner of your eye at the enormous impediments. Every time something you've risked works there's a tremendous exhilaration. That doesn't mean it's any the less nervous-making the next time you face it and that may be when your terrors assail you. The only problem is that attendant with the risk there has sometimes been an arrogance that is unfair to others who don't wish to take the risk or who can't do it or for whom it isn't their right time to do it or isn't their choice to do it or isn't their thing. It's as if so much is invested in the risk one is taking oneself, that one feels one has to impose it on others. I don't think I need to do that any more. And if I've really learned that, it's been worth this black period.

'I don't really look on anything in life as a failure. My question is always, "Can it be used constructively?" For example, I carry a universal donor card. If they can use the corneas and someone can see from my corneas or live from my kidneys, my God, how fantastic that is. I have just realised, now at this moment, that emotionally, politically, spiritually I also carry a universal donor card. Now that's a new insight. Whew! It was worth doing this second interview just for that new insight.'

Her eyes were shining and she grinned at me with real delight. She was genuinely excited by this new insight into herself. I was delighted to have been of service.

'I don't mean this in a Disneyesque, happy, "isn't it wonderful how everything always works to some great and terrific pattern" way. Because I don't romanticise suffering. Suffering is extremely distasteful. But if an experience can be alchemised, turned into something that's useful, if the personal suffering of the past year or so has really taught me more compassion as a human being, and on the page as a writer, if it gives more depth to how I will depict other people, other situations, and if I couldn't have learned it any other way, then it's a gain.

'At the end of 1994 I thought there must be one thing in this year that I'm really proud of, and I found it. I had been to Nepal at the invitation of the Nepali women's movement and the Asian Foundation funded that for me to try and help build coalitions in this baby women's movement. In India Gandhi had renamed untouchables "children of God" but these women thought that it was patronising; now they use the name "Dalit", which means oppressed or held back or suppressed.

'I said, "Are there any Dalit feminist groups?" Because these women were fighting caste oppression as well as sexist oppression. They weren't permitted in the other meetings and they weren't within the Brahman feminists. So we became joined at the heart and everywhere I went, they went. If the Brahman women wanted to meet with the foreign lady they had to meet with the untouchable women. And at the end of my stay they said, "We've just formed a feminist group and will you be our patron and help us and be our godmother?" So I thought to myself, "Well, you got to midwife the first movement of so-called untouchable women calling themselves feminists on the planet." Whatever else happened in 1994 or didn't happen, that made it a very good year.

'When women say to me that something I wrote changed their lives or that they were at a meeting or a speech or a lecture and something I said made a huge difference in their life, it really does make it all worth it. So do all the letters I still get. They are amazing.

'Now I am interested in trying to leave behind a body of work that is good and solid, writing that I hope will be lasting.

'It has been an incredible honour to have been part of it all. And I hope I go on earning it.'

6
INTERLUDE I

11 am: *Grand Central Station, New York City*

After a week of schlepping around New York I understood why the locals take off for the country on the weekend. Like an over-demanding lover, it's a city you do need some respite from.

Deirdre Bair, who had been constantly on the phone giving support and helpful advice when needed, had invited me to spend the weekend in her country house with her husband, Von, and her two English bulldogs, Bonzer and Molly.

I arrived at Grand Central early because it is the closest thing to a cathedral masquerading as a railway station that I have ever seen. I could sit down and weep at the sheer beauty of it all. I didn't of course. I dutifully purchased my ticket – round trip off-peak to Connecticut – then my doughnuts and coffee, and hung about waiting to see the platform number come up on the rolling board. It was like bingo.

I chose a seat on the train facing all the other passengers. I hate to miss anything. My companion on the other side of the aisle was a skinny little mouse of a woman in her late thirties. She clearly had a cold and was red around the nose and mouth from too much nose-blowing. She was travelling with her bike; from the number of gears it looked like a mountain bike. I couldn't believe those little lolly legs could push such a big machine, but she secured the cycle safely before taking off what seemed like seven different coloured layers of cotton tops. She then opened one of the many bags she was carrying and extracted a drinking bottle, a muffin and a banana. After placing them next to her on the seat, she took off her Reeboks to reveal little pink cotton socks. She sat there nibbling at the banana and the muffin for the next thirty minutes, after which she lay down on the seat with her legs in the air and went to sleep for ten minutes. She then suddenly sat up, straight-backed, and crossed her legs in the lotus position. Holding her hands out in front in a meditation position, she fixed her eyes in the middle distance and started reciting her mantra, quietly and obsessively, to herself.

Three seats back a young, well-dressed yuppie woman, mid-twenties, took out a mobile phone from a Brooks Brothers bag on the seat next to her. She punched in a number.

'Hi. I've just rung to say that I don't know whether I'll make your party tomorrow. I'm on a train on my way to the country. My mother is having an impromptu lunch tomorrow and I don't know what time I'll get back. Yes. Fine. Bye.'

Then she punched in another number.

'Hi, Greg, did I wake you? I'm on a train.'

At this point a man two seats behind her, grey-haired, bespectacled, early fifties, whom I'd assumed to be asleep, shouted out, 'No, you mightn't have woken him, but you've woken me.'

She turned around and said to him, in a peremptory tone, 'Don't be so rude,' and continued her phone conversation.

Meanwhile the man had gotten up from his seat and was approaching her from behind. He poked her in the arm with his finger and shouted, 'How dare you make phone calls on a train. This is a public place.'

She did not even turn around to face him but merely said into the phone, 'I'm sorry, there's a very rude man on this train. I'll ring you when I get to Mother's.'

She put the phone back in the Brooks Brothers bag and stared into the middle distance.

Miss Mouse came out of her meditation bubble, her red nose twitching, and whispered to me, 'What a grump.'

I was really not sure what to make of this little vignette. In Australia no-one would have gotten away with telling someone not to do something. A feminist woman of my generation would have told the middle-aged bloke that it was a free country, that this was indeed a public place and if he didn't like it he could get stuffed. I wondered if this was cultural or if women of my generation were more used to arguing in public with men who disapproved of us. Miss Yuppie's rather smug composure was in some sense to be envied – such was her confidence and her self-regard that she was not prepared to let this man disturb her. She simply dismissed him. He on the other hand no doubt felt he had won because she had put the phone away.

And poor Miss Mouse was caught somewhere in a limbo between the two of us, uncertain of what to do, although disapproving of the male behaviour.

I thought all this while watching her put on her riding shoes, pull all her layers of clothing back over her head, ending up with a jacket with many different compartments into which she put a variety of objects including her water bottle. When she finally zipped up her jacket it looked as if she was carrying the kitchen sink on what would have been her chest. She sat like this for the rest of the journey as if she was going up into Space. We all alighted at Fairfield: Miss Mouse with her cumbersome bike, Miss Yuppie with her Brooks Brothers bag and very pursed lips and Mr Grump with his Lord & Taylor bag, emphasis on the Lord.

'Have a good trip?' asked Deirdre.

'Wouldn't have missed it for quids,' I said.

And while I sat around in her beautiful garden drinking gin and tonics under an arbour of wisteria I thought about Mr Grump and the patriarchal poke of the finger. I knew that people talking on mobile phones could be very tiresome but I wondered if he'd have poked her so aggressively if she'd been a young virile man. I doubt it. Had the past twenty-five years of feminist struggle left young women afraid or unable to express the anger of a previous generation at such an action. Or was it in fact because the legacy of the women's movement was such that she just assumed power and didn't feel she had to fight for it, that she was able to ignore him with such aplomb. Or was it a question of class, not gender. And what of poor Miss Mouse, no doubt by now puffing her way up endless hills on her bike, trying so hard to do everything right.

I had no chance to come to any conclusion because the dog called Bonzer – Australian slang for something really good – named by Deirdre because of her affection for my country, seemed intent, like a heat-seeking missile, on aiming his nose between my legs, which was most disconcerting. I wished I'd had him with me on the train. That would have livened things up. Given Mr Finger Poke a run for his money.

Later on that night, after I had been royally wined and dined and just before I nodded off with all that country air in a big soft bed in this three-hundred-year-old heritage house, I wondered where poor Miss Mouse was resting her weary little legs.

11 am: Deirdre Bair's country house, Connecticut

Sunday morning I got up late and sat at the long wooden table in the dining room drinking coffee while Deirdre and Von made fresh waffles with maple syrup brewed from the trees on their property. Afterwards we went for a long walk in an idyllic landscape which made me feel I was in the film *On Golden Pond*. I kept expecting Katharine Hepburn to pop out from behind a tree. Instead it was old Molly, the bulldog, who had insisted on coming with us, who claimed centre stage. Her legs simply didn't want to take her any further, so Deirdre carried her back home while I sang, 'She ain't heavy she's my sister.' I should have offered to carry Miss Mouse's bike.

Later that afternoon I returned to my Upper West Side apartment, totally refreshed, my only worry being that despite leaving at least seven phone messages for Betty Friedan to ring me in order to finalise a time, she had failed to do so. Every time I rang either her New York or her Washington number her recorded voice said she was sorry she was not there but gave another number where she could be reached. She was definitely moving around because the messages changed, which meant she must have received mine. This weekend, for example, she was spending at Sag Harbour so I left a message at the number there. By nine o'clock that night I knew I was running out of time and was at a loss to know what to do. I rang Deirdre. As a biographer she had faced every possible crisis of this kind.

'Persist,' she said. So I did.

At ten o'clock I rang Hildie, one of Betty Friedan's assistants, who had written to me in Australia to say that Ms Friedan could not possibly make a fixed appointment but suggested that when I arrived in New York I should leave a message on her machine. I now attempted to contact Hildie, again, and left another message on her answering machine.

Did anyone in this country ever speak except through machines?

7
GLORIA STEINEM

Day Five, 10 am: Her apartment, Upper East Side, New York City

It was Memorial Day in America and the morning streets looked forlorn and empty as the taxi deposited me opposite the small brownstone building where Gloria Steinem lived. Upper East Side. Park Avenue was just around the corner. A slight mist of rain had started to fall. I stood under a tree on the opposite side of the street to her apartment and looked up at the first floor windows, trying to picture what she would be doing. I had met her before, both times with Jane Galvin-Lewis in a coffee shop.

I had asked Jane to organise a meeting the year before in order to ask Gloria to be in this book. In spite of the fact that I knew her public persona was warm and accessible, after an hour of swapping anecdotes and observations about feminism and politics I could feel Jane's foot crushing mine under the table. Why was I so nervous? Because of all the women in this book, Gloria Steinem had been the most photographed, the most interviewed, the most discussed in the media, the most celebrated 'celebrity' both in the women's movement and the mainstream press; her every movement had been documented, her lovers had been cross-examined, her body weight envied and her beauty both admired and despised. Why would she want to take precious time out of her life to be interviewed, yet again, by a virtually unknown Australian?

When the pressure on my foot matched the glare in Jane's eyes, I had stammered out my request. The generous mouth smiled, even though the deep brown eyes retained their sadness, and she said, 'I'd be honoured to be in your book.'

And herein lies the dilemma. Was this genuine humility or just part of the charm for which she was famous? Was this the beginning of the seduction of the interviewer or was this woman truly the saint of the women's movement? Deirdre Bair's longtime friend Mary Perot-Nicols, a former editor of the *Village Voice*, had told me she was still convinced that Gloria had been very closely connected with the CIA. In 1976 she had written an article headed 'Ms Steinem, Are You Now, Or Have You Ever . . . ?' But the most damaging and prolonged attack on her had come from a radical feminist group called The Red Stockings who in 1975 accused Steinem not only of having a ten-year association with the CIA but claimed that Ms magazine, founded and edited by her, was 'hurting the women's liberation movement'. Betty Friedan brought these accusations out into the open in the *Daily News* and the Mexico City International Women's Conference, and a long article had followed in the *New York Times*. All the work she had done for Ms magazine, all the trips she had taken to the four corners of America and the world to spread the word and meet the people, all would be eclipsed if these accusations were believed.

It was five minutes to ten as I walked up the stone steps and rang the bell. The most famous feminist of our time welcomed me into her apartment, introduced me to Magritte, her cat, and asked me if I'd like tea or coffee.

'Come down with me into the kitchen,' she said. Six years before she had bought the apartment below the one she had owned for years, and connected the two by a tiny circular iron staircase. Tiny was the word.

'This is definitely designed for thin people,' I exclaimed. 'I hope I don't get stuck.' She laughed. But I was serious. 'How did your interview with Gloria Steinem go?' my friends would ask. 'Well, actually, it never happened. I got stuck halfway down her circular staircase. She had to call the fire brigade to come and cut me out.'

Once safely upstairs again, sinking cosily into one of the velvet couches while she settled next to me on another, calm descended. Heavy damask curtains draped the windows and the light was golden and diffused. The effect was timeless. A sensuality and warmth filled the room which she said a friend of hers had decorated. When she was writing *Revolution from Within* she had looked around at the space she had been occupying for years and decided to do something about the overflowing boxes, the piles of papers, the general debris of a lifetime's work and the sense of impermanence. The little girl who had inhabited the now infamous rat-infested house on the edge of a freeway while caring for her mentally ill mother finally decided to create a proper home for herself, fifty years later.

So where did I begin an interview about her life with the most interviewed feminist in America? Not only had it been documented in magazines, articles and a biography but she had written about it herself in Ms magazine and in her own books.

'Perhaps,' I asked her, 'we could start with you at five years of age and then focus on every decade after that.'

'Well that's different,' she said. 'The problem is remembering all the details. Remembering something at first try is now as good as an orgasm as far as I am concerned.'

'We'll get to the orgasms later,' I said. 'Paint a picture for me of you as a child of five.'

'Well I haven't combed my hair in weeks. I have on a red bathing suit because my mother, who couldn't get around that much, insisted I wear red so she could see me. We lived in Michigan at a little rural lake called Clark Lake. I was probably catching minnows and turtles with a tea towel sewn to a hanger and putting them in a tub in the backyard and releasing them at the end of the summer. I think of that period of my life as the wild child. I must have been reading already but I don't remember when I started. It was an isolated life so I'm not sure what my response to other people at that age would have been. I was quite capable of being shy. I probably retreated into fantasy a bit too much. I always had dolls, they were not necessarily "doll" dolls but were like little international figures and I'd always make up stories about them. I certainly lived in a fantasy world even before I could read and I was always going to the movies with my father. I had one girlfriend by then who was older and the daughter of a farmer. We also used to play paper dolls and make up stories. I was chubby with a round face.

'My mother was depressed and spent a lot of time in bed. When I'm depressed I may sleep longer, but I certainly don't stay in bed during the day precisely because I have that image of my mother. I try consciously to get out and not to put myself in the situation where I associate myself with my mother. Certain landscapes that I'm sure are very beautiful but I find remind me of the midwest make me very depressed. New York for me means freedom. Once you figure out where the depression comes from it does help, it does subside gradually. I'm not introspective. So if I was depressed by something for a long time I always assumed it was objectively depressing.

'If I had been a male writer and written a novel, which young men have the chutzpah to do and women don't, it would have been called *Getting Out*. My early life was all about this fierce desire to get out. I was thinking about it yesterday because there was one large fly in my kitchen. The stillness and the sound of that fly just overwhelmed me and I recognised it for what it was. I'm enough out of it now so that it didn't have a lasting impact but for years that would have just put me into a spin. The sound of a radio in an empty house used to trigger terrible feelings of despair.

'When I wrote *Ruth's Song* about my mother, I felt that it was self-indulgent and wasn't going to mean anything to anyone. I think it had been writing itself in my head for years but I couldn't do anything while my mother was alive because any reminder of the past sent her into another depression. More than any piece I've ever written it just wrote itself and then to my surprise it got more response than anything else. There are so many people, women and men, with crazy mothers because our mothers have been driven crazy. There was a man in Denver or Seattle, I can't remember which, who was a fifty-year-old television anchorman, quite conservative and quite stuffy. We had this incredible coming together because he had a mother like mine. In his case she had a frontal lobotomy in the 1950s and was still alive. It's a very powerful shared experience, not so different from people who have had alcoholic parents. Ironically, I didn't think I was writing about myself, I thought I was writing about my mother. It took me a while to figure it out.

'At five I had tons of puppies. We always had these mongrel dogs and I would never be able to bear to give up the puppies. Finally I would have to give them away and I'd keep the runt of the litter. When I was five my sister was fourteen, living in a local YWCA and going to high school, but she was around somewhere and so was my father.

'By the time I was fifteen I was living alone with my mother in Toledo in this rat-infested ramshackle house my mother inherited. It wouldn't be a slum by New York standards, only by Toledo standards. She was by that time mostly in bed and I was feeding her and looking after her. She was physically okay but the house was very difficult. We had the upstairs. It had a long hall and a couple of bedrooms, no central rooms and no central heating. There was a furnace but it had been condemned by the department of health so I would occasionally break the seal and go down and stoke it up a bit. Otherwise the pipes would freeze, which sometimes they did. It was very, very depressing. I would be getting up in the morning and wearing something that I had washed and ironed maybe that morning. I used to wash things and iron them dry. I didn't have any organised way of living and there was no washing machine. I would wash my hands and face and look to see if there was a mark on my arm from the water in which case I knew where I had to wash up to. I was always a little late and running to get to school.

'I went to Waite High School in Toledo. It seemed then like a huge school in which there was really only one rule: you had to stop playing football when you were twenty-two. The football team was the pride and joy of every one of those people. Boys went to work in the factories, girls got married when they left high school. At fifteen I was probably pretending to be eighteen in order to work as a dancer both after school and in the summers. I had started out taking tap lessons; by that time I was taking ballet too and my dancing school teacher put together shows for nightclubs. Sometimes I answered ads on my own. I was kind of stocky compared to "dancer" dancers, who are usually skinny. I was waiting until I was sixteen to work as a salesgirl after school. Sometimes I also taught dancing to younger students in order to pay for my lessons.

'My father was living in California at that time. He didn't ring up but I would get letters from him and saw him maybe once or twice a year when he came back. I was certainly obsessed with having boyfriends, we were all totally obsessed. I had very close girlfriends and we did nothing but talk about boyfriends. I envied my best girlfriend because she was little and cute and I felt big and galumphing. She had boyfriends much earlier than I did so she fixed me up. My first boyfriend was a packer at the local supermarket and he'd already graduated from high school. My second boyfriend worked in the factories. No sex. Definitely not. There were only two kinds of girls in this neighbourhood. Good girls and bad girls. At least that's what we thought and it was really horrendous if you got to be a bad girl in other people's eyes. Bad could even be, although almost everyone did, getting pregnant too soon. People were always counting the months after you got married. Lots of people dropped out of high school. If you were known to sleep with somebody you didn't eventually marry, that was really bad. I do remember stories of girls getting locked up in someone's garage and getting banged by the entire football team and it was viewed as their fault. Then their families would have to move away.

'Any conversations I had with my mother about sex were only of the most oblique and unuseful sort. For many years of my life I would think to myself that no matter how bad things were, it could be worse – I could be pregnant. It was like a little litany. Even though we were the neighbourhood crazies and had less money than people who were working in the factories, we also had books, so I had a view into the world. A lot of my friends didn't have books in their houses, because although their parents spoke English they didn't read it. They were Polish and Hungarian. I always had a lot of books in the house and I always lived in the worlds of books and that provided an idea of escape. I used to go to the little local library branch and get three books a week for many years without any discrimination whatsoever, I just chose alphabetically.

'I made up things in order to pretend that we weren't different. I pretended I had a curfew, that I had to be home at a certain time. I didn't invite people into my house. But I could get away with that because a lot of my friends were sufficiently poor or had sufficiently crazy families or raging alcoholic fathers, so that it was kind of a code of honour that you didn't ever ask to go to a friend's house; we met on the corner. I devoted a lot of energy to pretending that everything was fine at home, that my life was like everybody else's.

'I always felt detached, like I was just passing through. In literature there is a notion that kids fear having been adopted and that's because parents don't want to think that their children wanted to have been adopted. Actually there are probably as many of us who hoped we were adopted. I didn't really believe it but it was a little private fantasy. I was a wanted child and I knew that my parents were trying to do their best. I think that makes a big difference.

'My mother had given birth to a baby who was stillborn between my sister and me, a boy, and I always wanted to have a big family. I used to listen to a radio soap opera called "One Man's Family", which was mother and father, grandparents and all their offspring, and I'd think what if this boy had lived? Tom, his name was. And then I'd think it was really good that he hadn't because he would not have been able to survive this upbringing. He would have ended up crazy or criminal. So I had this perception, wrongly, that men are fragile and can't survive the same things that women can.

'At twenty-five – what year was that? My math is terrible. It was 1959, I was living in Cambridge, Massachusetts, in a little basement apartment. I had come back from India in 1958 full of idealism and activism and "how can the world continue to survive with this terrible imbalance of rich and poor?" I started to work in what there was of student politics. There was no civil rights movement and no understanding of poverty. A group of students or former students were trying to encourage people to go to a Communist youth festival to be held in Vienna. So I acquired this weird job of raising money for it. I was still being very straight, trying to look older, dignified, responsible, something I abandoned soon after. I never got to pearls, it was more skirts and blouses; worthy clothes. I always had a man in my life. Always. I was completely, as I was for many years after that, into a cycle in which there was a pleasurable six months to a year of romance, with all the adrenaline that engenders. Then a plateau of a year or two, then a beginning to look around again and the men always overlapped. I was always seeing someone new while not telling the truth to the one before, I'm sorry to say. I think men were my family, in a sense. Long after I'd stopped seeing the man in question I was still seeing his family.

'I was clearly looking for a family – it couldn't have been more obvious. I always thought my family was crazier than all the others I met. Sometimes I would adopt and be adopted by, as I did in college, the families of my young women friends. I was always the poor one being taken on vacation by generous parents so that the girl could have her friend along. Which was very nice of them, but it had a certain set of tensions that went with it. And obligations. In my first year of college there was a young woman whom I regarded as a phenomenon because she never seemed to have any problems and she seemed to lead this entirely charmed life. She got married after her first year in college and I was her bridesmaid and her family adopted me. Now in retrospect I realise that her family was quite crazy in a different way from mine but they were very glamorous. She was someone who'd had a French nanny and I was taking French with disastrous results because of my high school.

'My father was still living in California and we would hear from each other at Christmas and I'd see him again once or twice a year. After I was in college and could no longer care for my mother, my sister couldn't handle it either because she was going off to work and would come home and find my mother wandering around on the street. So she researched and found a good mental hospital and my mother spent two years there and then another year or so in a Quaker halfway house.

'I didn't think of myself as Jewish. The one thing my mother had told me was that being Jewish was a religion, it was something you chose not something you were born into. She had tried to give me some sense of Jewishness. My father was the Jewish one but he didn't care about it at all. But my mother and her Jewish mother-in-law were theosophists. When I got to college the local Jewish student group tried to claim me and I was not about to be claimed by anybody. I suspect I only became Jewish among Wasps. I was always the outsider. So I was Jewish among non-Jews and non-Jewish among Jews.

'By thirty-five I was living in New York. I had become a freelance writer here, making a precarious living. That was 1969 so the great cosmic light bulb of feminism was just beginning to go on in my brain. I moved here in 1960 and I loved it. Absolutely loved it. I hadn't been successful in writing about my interests very much because women didn't really write politics. Perhaps I just didn't try hard enough. I thought of myself as a writer even if I didn't admit it. I wasn't trained as a journalist but no journalist I knew was either. The idea of going to journalism school inspired a lot of contempt among many journalists then. Before I went to India I had tried to work for *Time* magazine but then women were only researchers and not writers. When I came back from India I tried unsuccessfully to get a job with the *New York Times* and other places so I became what was much better suited for my temperament, a freelance writer. I still think of writing as my total identity, even though I've spent most of my life in activism.

'Writing is the only thing that when I'm doing it I don't think I should be doing something else. But I only get a feeling of satisfaction after I've finished, not while I'm doing it. Especially in the beginning, I was writing things that I didn't care about or persuading myself I did care. I did actually manage to make a living but I didn't have anyone to support but myself. I was certainly well equipped and trained to live that hand to mouth life by my father. He'd taught me very well that it was fine to be in debt or it was fine to be always escaping from money worries.

'I always thought I would definitely marry. Then I would go through my little cycle of one man to another. I wasn't impelled in any way toward having children but I don't think I had said to myself, "I'm not going to have children." I like to keep all doors open. I wasn't very fond of babies. By that time my sister had probably had all six of her children, so they were around. She had married at thirty but that didn't make any difference to me. It didn't strike me as something I wanted to do.

'I always wanted to go to school like other kids and have a neighbourhood and walk to school. The compulsion or the desire was to be like other people but I didn't consciously feel lonely. If anything, I wanted to be more alone because my family felt like a shame and a restriction. My version of a family would have been to be the child in it, not to be the adult. If you've become an adult too soon I think you displace your childhood, you know you're not ready to become responsible. Even though I cared and looked after my mother, that bore very little resemblance to having a child. It's very, very different to be a small parent with a big child than to be a small child with a dependent parent but I thought I'd done that already. I didn't want to be responsible for anyone else and I didn't want to end up like my mother.

'The 1968 Democratic Convention was a great watershed for me because of the violence of the police and the National Guard against the anti-war protesters. That was the last time I ever really tried to dress and act in a conventional or a semi-ladylike way. At that point miniskirts and boots were what everyone was wearing. But as feminism came along one of the wonderful things it did was to release me from any feeling that I had to be conventional. I acquired this uniform of corduroy jeans and a leotard and boots and I just never got out of it. It was a great purging to get rid of the Toledo working-class worry about dyeing your shoes to match your Easter outfit.

'I was very different from when I was twenty-five. I didn't start to become myself until feminism came along. I realise that you're always the same person inside but I used to feel I had to pretend to be someone else. By 1969 I was just beginning to become myself. *New York* magazine had started in 1968. A small group of writers had helped to raise money and started it. The editor, Clay Felker, was really unbiased in that all he wanted was a good idea; also, because it didn't pay that much, there were more women working there. We were allowed to do pretty much anything we wanted. For the first time my writing life, my professional make-a-living life and my interests had come together. And it was in 1969 that I wrote my first feminist article on abortion law reform.

'I read *Sexual Politics* and I read *The Female Eunuch* and they certainly got to me as Simone de Beauvoir did not at that point. Her writing seemed distant to me, it didn't connect with my own life. What most got to me were two things. One: those short articles of early feminism that were like epiphanies, "The Myth of the Female Orgasm" and "The Politics of Housework", but there were just so many. These articles were being published not in the mainstream but by feminists or left-wing thinkers in underground places. They just totally bowled me over. And then in 1968 or 1969 I was sitting in that room, which was then my office, watching four women talking about sex on a PBS programme. They were all sitting in tall deck chairs in front of a brick wall. It was the first time I'd ever seen women telling the truth about sex in public and I remember just being riveted. I called up the television station afterwards. I was so drawn by these wonderful, smart, honest women and I said, "Who are these women? Tell me their names, I just tuned in." They were just talking about sex in public as if they had a right to it. They were not afraid of being bad girls or trying to be ladies or trying to be conventional or to be nice. They were very smart about sex as a political institution. I just couldn't believe it.

'*Sexual Politics* was Kate Millett's PhD thesis and was so rooted in literary criticism. I've always been put off by books that make you feel you have to read other books in order to understand them. I felt the rightness of what Kate was saying about Freud. She analysed everything in a very feminist way, very early. But it was more these brief articles that were specifically coming out of "the personal is political" where women were talking much more about ordinary real life that blew my mind.

'When I was in college it was the McCarthy era and that made me a Marxist. Nothing was more clear than if Joseph McCarthy was against Marxists then I should be a Marxist. I didn't think I was a Communist because I could see that there was not individual freedom in those countries. Then when I lived in India I discovered the Communists and the Marxists had a very bad name because they had betrayed the independence movement by supporting the British during World War II. They were rather duplicitous in the sense that they were not really being anti-colonial, they were obeying the orders that came from Moscow headquarters. So I ironically became anti-Communist because the Communists supported the British. I identified with the independence struggle. I didn't think of myself by that time as a Marxist or a Communist but as Left. I think I thought of myself as an anarchist, really, but I despaired of ever saying that because anarchism was so misunderstood and so intertwined with violence.

'By the time I was forty-five Ms magazine, which we started in 1971/'72, was well under way and an all-consuming, totally absorbing occupation. I loved working there, I loved this diverse group of women who shared the same values and I loved being in the office. I was by that time travelling and speaking a lot, which had just barely begun. Ten years before I didn't speak in public very often, I was too scared and nervous. Even before the magazine and the experience of going out to speak in our black and white women pairs, I had become a kind of travelling organiser. Between that and the magazine I was absolutely consumed.

'Also by 1979 the magazine was in financial trouble. It had become quite clear that we could not survive given the biases of advertisers so I was constantly raising money to make up the deficit. I was making two- or three-day forays and coming back to the office, which was my "home". The office wasn't safe. It was very dangerous. We were always getting threats. We all laughed and made jokes but we were embattled. It was definitely not the womb; it was more like the bunker. We were constantly under attack, constantly worrying and, by that time, financially terrifically stretched. I mean in huge debt. The worst part of that stress is not so much the stress, as not being able to talk about it. We absolutely couldn't because then the few advertisers we had would have left, so we had to keep saying, "Everything's fine." But we were always conscious of being lucky because we were some of the very few women who could get any salaries at all from doing feminist work.

'Money was not important personally, yet I was always worried that I would end up as a bag lady. That's only gone away in the last five years or so. It was a real fear. If you've come a long distance in your life you always think that you'll go back to where you started. I thought I would end up in some hovel by a railroad track or with no home at all. In order to deal with that I used to just say to myself, "Well then, if I'm a bag lady I'll organise the other bag ladies. It's a life like any other." It was such a big fear that I had to embrace it. But it never occurred to me that I could stave it off by saving money or by behaving in a financially responsible way. Or by marrying a rich man; that seemed too high a price to pay because then you lost freedom. I don't think I ever had enough money to last more than a couple of weeks. Sometimes I was not taking a salary as my partner Pat Carbine wasn't, because of the magazine's money situation. I could make money from lecturing but I gave that away too. Pat and I were probably personally on the line for all of the magazine's debts but we didn't like to think about that. Meanwhile I was fundraising for the caucus for Voters' Choice, for the Ms Foundation and for Ms magazine. I was constantly raising money. I was always tired but with enough enthusiasm to carry me through. I was still in the same pattern of relationships with men.

'In 1979 I was seeing the man who was my Olympic record in terms of length of relationship. Stan Pottinger was then the head of the civil rights division of the justice department. I liked men who had a dream, who were doing what they believed in. I am not attracted to someone who just wants to have a good life. I did spend a couple of years with two people who were like that. One was Blair Chotzinoff. I was engaged to him in college but that had more to do with sex and kindness. The other one was Tom Guinzburg, one of only a couple of well-to-do men I've ever gone out with. His father had a publishing house, Viking Press, and he inherited it so I thought he cared about books because he was a publisher. It took me a while to figure out he did not care about books, he should have been a sports writer. That's what he loved and I used to say to him, "Well then, do it." He would get furious with me because he was so convinced he had to do what his father had done.

'I've never had a sexual relationship with a woman. I'm the last non-lesbian, non-bisexual person in the western world I think. Monosexual. It sounds so boring. I don't know how to explain it except I'm sure it's socialisation. I really believe that we are all bisexual and probably we're socialised one way or the other. It's wonderful now to see young women and some young men too who really do fall in love with the person not the sex. I don't think I even understood what homosexual or lesbian was until after I was out of college. Even though one of my most beloved teachers, Esther Cloudman-Dunne, whose course I took in the literature of

Shakespeare's England, was living with another woman, a theologian. They were the most clear lesbian couple you could possibly imagine but I still didn't get it. When I was in junior high school another beloved teacher was half of a lesbian couple too and I didn't think about it. I always have loved women and had close women friends. They were like family so there was a sense in which thinking sexually about women was like incest. Looking back at it I think I must have been socialised to think that sexuality is about difference. Sex is about leaping over that, it's the most intense form of curiosity about someone different from you. Sameness for me wasn't sexualised. I've tried to think about it and be open to it. I used to have a button that said "Don't die wondering". One of the women I travelled with as a speaking partner is a lesbian and Rita May-Brown was the only assertive lesbian I knew who really courted me. Only once or twice in my life did I go to bed with a man I didn't want to go to bed with. It was so awful that I learned that either your juices are turned on or they're not. You can't talk yourself into it. So I figured it was best I left it alone.

'Around the age of fifty I stopped wearing the corduroys. I got tired of it. By fifty-five we had been forced to sell the magazine. Finding a feminist buyer was really good luck because it would have been awful to have to close our doors. It would have been a great defeat for the women's movement here because the press would not have said, "Oh, weren't the advertisers terrible not to support you." They would have said, "Well you see, nobody wants to read a feminist magazine." We've been able to prove now that wasn't the case but at the time that's what they would have said. So we were very lucky to have someone come along with their bags of money. At fifty-five, for the first time in at least fifteen years, I was no longer waking up in the middle of the night with sweaty palms, at least when it came to the magazine. I still had other obligations like the Ms Foundation but the magazine was by far the biggest one. I was sitting here at home trying to write my book *Revolution from Within*. Before the magazine was sold I had auctioned off the rights to two books because I was quite broke from not taking a salary and I was trying to make myself write. I thought, "Well if I have a contract, I will do it." I don't have an agent. Bob Levine, who's my lawyer and the husband of our managing editor, Suzanne Leane, conducted an auction for me and then gave the 10 per cent that would have been the agent's fee to the Ms Foundation.

'Fifty-five was a time of great momentous change for me. I had hit the bottom of the swimming pool some time in my early fifties, and I was just beginning to come back up again. When you've been under great pressure you only realise it hurts when you stop. There were lots of causes. The pressure of the magazine, losing the magazine, breast cancer, age, exhaustion. All those things came together. It was very tough. There were a lot of months when the world for me was no longer in colour, it was black and white. But I've always thought of myself as a survivor. I have always had the belief that if there were only a few people left in the concentration camp I want to be one of them. But I really had lost my optimism and my energy and my ability to look forward. I was a very non-introspective person. I had really neglected my own version of "the personal is political". Like many of us, I looked at the politics of my present life but not at the politics of my growing up. I had to get rid of the brick wall with which I had sealed off my early years. I didn't realise that they were continuing to influence my life. Writing the book helped a lot.

'By the time I'm sixty-five I want to have written another book. I want to have travelled more internationally. I'm drawn towards indigenous cultures, towards the last remaining remnants of pre-patriarchal pre-racist cultures. I don't mean to romanticise how many are left but I would love to travel the world visiting them. And I really think we ought to just declare the last 5000 to 10,000 years an experiment that failed. After all, it's only less than 5 per cent of history.'

The whole time she had been talking in her soft, even voice she had looked at me with total focus and concentration, as if she genuinely cared that we were communicating. It was very seductive. I had been warned about this by many people. She is known for charming everyone who meets her into total submission and adoration. As the most glamorous and famous celebrity of the women's movement it was so easy to fall totally under her spell, to drown in those big, sad, brown eyes. I fought those urges and pulled back to a question-and-answer mode. After all, as the interviewer I was meant to be the seducer, not the seduced. It was time to ask a few tough questions.

'Why are you so intent on staying so thin when you say in one of your poems that you love "the fat woman in a red miniskirt because she loves her woman's body"?'

'Alice Walker was saying to me one day that she felt she was metamorphosing into a big mama. I said, "Alice, you know that's great to have that tradition. I don't feel as a white woman that I have that tradition." It wasn't part of my growing up; the powerful, sexual, sensual older woman who took up space and was proud of it. My "feel good" weight is even thinner than I am now, a few pounds and then I really feel better, I feel free, like I can move through space. I feel pleasure in moving. I think it has to do with androgyny too. Because of my mother and the culture I associate hips and breasts with victimhood. To this day I worry about big-breasted women. I see them in the street and think they're vulnerable and want to protect them. I've never been anorexic. Even though I'm afraid of being obese like my father I would rather have a cold for a week than throw up. I just don't have food in the house, except fruit and vegetables. Because it's New York I can call up the Korean Deli and order anything that I fancy. Since I had breast cancer I've become a vegetarian and I try to eat healthy. But I fall off the wagon and have a pint of ice cream from time to time. Sugar is my undoing. I don't miss meat at all. I love to eat. I'm just on such a funny schedule that I've always eaten a little bit a lot of the time. I have a hard time getting myself hungry enough to enjoy going to dinner.'

'Why are you dressed totally in black if in the same poem you prayed for the courage to wear red and purple?'

'I'm sure I'm going to be wearing unacceptable clothes in my sixties and seventies. Now I wear purple and red a lot as well as black and brown. I have a short red satin skirt in my closet. I'd be glad to show you to prove it.'

'So where's the outrage?'

'I would prefer to be outrageous in a way that is on behalf of other people. If you're a naysayer and you can't say "yes" or you're only always being perverse for the sake of it then you're stuck. That's just as much a prison as conformity. Narcissism is a culturally male disease and depression is the culturally female disease. We only know what other people are feeling and men only know what they are feeling. It's so delightful in some sense to find a woman who's a narcissist because it's so rare. But it's a problem not to be able to empathise with other people, not to know what they're feeling. I have the opposite problem and I'm working on it, I'm trying not to be empathy sick and co-dependent with the world. The goal in both cases is balance. It's not either/or.

'I don't think I'm outrageous for the sake of it. Well sometimes I am. In speeches I always swear or say sexual things I'm not supposed to say but that's so that the barrier will be broken and so the audience can say those things. You have to be as free or honest as you want other people to be. It depends on who you talk to whether I strike them as outrageous or not outrageous. Probably more in image than in reality because I'm constantly confronted by people who say, "Gee, you're not as bad as everybody said." '

'What do you do for fun?'

'I love to go dancing. I pick up men as dancing partners but I've never brought them home. I have too much sense of Toledo working-class self-protection to bring home strange men. I went to a bar here which was this dump part of Tenth Avenue and people were doing the tango. There was this one guy in jeans, cowboy boots and a cowboy hat who was the greatest dancer I have ever seen. He was so wonderful. I asked him to dance and dancing with him was like being in a movie and suddenly being able to do things that you didn't know you could. He turned out to be a tango teacher so I took tango lessons for awhile. This is after the magazine sold when I was in my fifty-five era. Now I'm more likely to go to some disco place because to do the tango you have to find a partner. I love to dance. You have to get past the first twenty minutes of feeling a fool but after that's over you really enjoy it.'

'What about those people who have attacked you?'

'I've been around for so long I've been discovered to be a nice person, to be a terrible person, to be okay, to be lousy. You have to go through those cycles. Unfortunately the notion of news is what's different. There was a very bananas woman in the beginning of the life of Ms magazine who just arrived and said she could raise money. We all thought, "Well we don't like her but that's because she knows about money." Sounds crazy but we all suspended our judgement. She was always calling press conferences and saying we had stolen the magazine from her and it was her idea. That went on for a long time and was on the front page of the *Washington Post*.'

The only time I saw her become agitated and start pulling at the neck of her sweater was when I mentioned the CIA charges.

'Remember when I was telling you about my job raising money for the youth festivals. Well the idea that US students should go to Communist youth festivals was not a popular idea in the McCarthy era, as you can understand. So the only people who would support it were the CIA. They were giving money to the non-Communist Left through foundations. I knew perfectly well where the money came from and at that time thought it was great. I thought we were ripping off the government. When later on a reporter said to me, "Did you know about this?" I said, "Oh yes, certainly." The result was that in the mid-'70s a group of women accused me of being a CIA agent inside the women's movement, and that was very painful. It really wiped me out for a while because it's what we call here "being trashed". It's painful to be criticised for the mistakes you've made but it's tolerable; but to be criticised for what you've done right or think you've done right totally wipes you out. You just think you might as well not get up in the morning. I continued to function, I had to because of the magazine, but it really hurt. If I hadn't responded to the claims it wouldn't have gone from the feminist press into the mainstream press but people kept telling me I had to respond to it. So I did, which was a huge mistake. It's part of a larger stream of criticism that happens to many women and many people involved in social justice or anybody in a movement of previously marginalised folk. If you are doing well or have any degree of success then it can't be your own, you must be being told to do it. Some organisation or someone else must be behind it. Or sometimes it takes the form of criticism that you're in the control of some man. I think I'm too old for this now, maybe not. For years it took the form of people saying I was only doing x or y because I had slept with this man I was working for and getting assignments from. It's the same as the CIA charge. The idea is that if you are doing something that the rest of your group isn't doing or that is non-traditional for your group, you must be in the control of the dominant group. That's very painful and it takes lots of different forms. There is a river of accusation that's very painful. Another common criticism is attributing everything to how I look. That's very depressing. Sometimes I think that no matter how hard I work it'll be attributed to how I look.'

'What's the major contradiction in your life?'

'The fact that I feel so keenly the sex and race power system when I have actually been treated by it, as a white person and a woman, better than most. I have been treated well by men. Some of it is accidental because you know if one in eight men is violent then statistically you may end up with one of these men. It can happen to anyone. I have no illusions that I can control this. But to the extent that one can control it I think because I had a gentle, nurturing father I was never attracted to distant, cold, controlling or violent men. I see very strong feminist women who are still drawn to destructive men but I never was. Also, the neighbourhood I grew up in has something to do with it because I saw destructive, violent men all the time. Many of my friends' mothers were getting beaten up on Saturday night. There was a very large degree of fear in that neighbourhood and I got good at spotting danger. I've never been totally dependent on anyone and I think that's part of guarding against that. But I do beat myself up over other things. Like how slow I am as a writer. Forests have been sacrificed to my rewriting. For example, I have to finish something today. I'm convinced I will be able to finish it but I don't know. This is something I've been writing for three months that should have been finished long ago. I'm always stretching my deadlines, I always wait until the last minute, I underestimate how much time something will take to do. I beat up on myself about not doing it and being slow. Endlessly. After every speech I beat up on myself for what I didn't say, what I should have said or what I did say, which is sometimes worse than what I didn't say. I often walk round talking to myself.

'I'm happy with *Revolution from Within* and I'm also happy with the short pieces in *Moving Beyond Words*. For a long time I thought that only one subject was a real book, but I've decided that's maybe not true. I would rather be Alice Walker than Simone de Beauvoir. I think de Beauvoir was not always so close to herself. I only met her once but I think that when she wrote *The Second Sex* she still thought that someone else's class was more important than her sex. She was still putting traditional male concepts of class first. It was only later that she began to see sex as something that class had actually imitated and created artificially. I don't think that her inner and outer life were meshed in the way that Alice's are. Alice is just so totally vast and wise and together.

'I'd like to write poems. I took a poetry writing course at the YWCA because I'd had this sign on my wall that said "Express don't persuade". An errant idea for a novel came into my head the other day. I used to start short stories but when I was doing that I still thought I had to make up a childhood suitable for a *New Yorker* story. I didn't understand you could really write about your own life and I didn't think my life was worthy of fiction.'

'So who are the bravest women?'

'I think Bella Azbug is certainly high up there. She is amazing. She will plunge into the most forbidden territory, the guarded, powerful inner sanctum of places and subjects and put a different frame around reality. People who are really brave have the strength to be themselves and that comes from spontaneity. You don't stop and think, "I'm doing something brave," you just do it. The Good Samaritans, the people who helped Jews during World War II who were not themselves Jewish and who risked death, all say similar things. They say, "I didn't think about it, I just did it." Was it education, was it family stability, was it religion, what was it? The only shared characteristic seems to be that they were not abused as children. Abuse interrupts, cuts off your ability to empathise with someone else. Alice Walker is brave. Even though she had a difficult growing-up, somehow she managed to preserve that.

'Before the civil rights movement Bella Azbug was a lawyer for black defendants in the South that no-one else would take. She had to sleep in the bus station because no-one would let her sleep in their houses. At the same age I wouldn't have been that brave. Of course Bella always had a mother who thought she should be president. Many women don't have that and they're unknown, obscure people who are having to face opposition within their own families. That's very great.

'Last weekend I went back to give the commencement address at Smith where I went to college. When I was doing a book signing in the little local bookstore a woman who was there because one of her daughters was graduating came up to talk to me. She's a public school teacher in California who has raised two girls totally alone and put them through college. This is very great. This woman deserves a national medal. It's the ordinary women without recognition and support that I really admire.'

'How did you learn to move among the rich and the powerful?'

'I identified with Blanche Dubois when she said, "I've always depended on the kindness of strangers." I've always felt that most people were fundamentally good if they could be and if I appealed to them that they would respond. That's been my security. I can remember painfully learning table manners by watching and copying. If you ever wondered how socialisation happens you know when you're in an insecure situation you just pick it up.'

'But what about class-based distinctions?'

'Sylvia Plath talked about going to have lunch with her benefactor. Do you remember that? This woman had given her money for a fellowship which Sylvia had earned and Sylvia didn't know the woman. She was having lunch with her and the woman had finger bowls after lunch with little petals floating in them. Sylvia drank the finger bowl and so the woman did too.

'I remember discovering ordinary things with the feeling that they were somehow great secrets, like taking a knife or scissors and scoring the bottom of new shoes so you don't slip. Or taking naps. After a year and a half or more in India, I was in Burma at Rangoon airport and I met a wonderful Chinese woman, very elegant, who'd gone to Vassar. She introduced me to her husband who was going to Hong Kong, as I was. After a couple of nights staying in the YWCA because I was being independent and it was cheaper, I was being totally bitten by bedbugs. By the third night I followed up their invitation to stay in their apartment. He was a very cultured man and he could see that I didn't know shit, so he taught me what to do with a hard-boiled egg, how to eat a grapefruit. He was a very kind man. Now that need to conform or do the right thing is gone. I used to be very depressed walking along the street when other people were riding past in cars because I remembered being depressed about walking by the swarming highway outside my ramshackle house in Toledo. That's gone. Now I take pleasure in being on the bus or on the subway or walking. I want to do what ordinary people are doing, it gives me pleasure. But the anxiety from when I was growing up, desperate to distinguish myself, was still with me for a lot of years.'

'Your "icon" status?'

'None of that happened to me until I was in my middle or late thirties. I'm grateful for this because if it happens to you too young, you may believe it and get dependent on it. It was very clear to me that some people treated me better than when I was unknown and some people treated me worse than when I was unknown. In both cases it wasn't a response to me, it was a response to their feelings about fame. Sometimes I feel trapped by it. I think that even if I died or went to live in Africa or totally disappeared, that there would still be this person with my name on, that would be like a balloon on a string up there with people shooting at it even though I was long gone. Sometimes I feel victimised by it. The bad part never goes away but the good part is when I'm walking in the street and somebody comes up to me to tell me what happened to them or the flight attendant tells me what's happening with the union or sneaks me into first class. All those things happen, which is the result of my being accidentally recognisable as a symbol of a movement that means very much to me. Now if I was a physicist instead of a cultural worker, as we used to say in the Left, nobody would know what I looked like. So I recognise it's an accident of my occupation. I'm in the media, that's what I do.

'I'm certainly more angry now than I used to be. I've progressed. As a socialised woman and a mid-westerner expressing anger is hard. Mid-westerners are very even and not very expressive, unlike New Yorkers who are much more Mediterranean. I'm still not as good at anger as I would like to be. Before I would instantaneously turn anger into depression. So I wouldn't even recognise it. With people I love and care about I'm less good about fighting because I still have this fear that if I fight, I'll lose them.'

'What will they say when you die?'

'I don't know. Maybe nothing. Think about the women of the last wave. I didn't know them when I was growing up. The single characteristic of women's history is that it's lost and rediscovered, lost again and rediscovered again. That's true of any marginalised group. I said once I wanted to have a benefit for my funeral in order to make money with it for the Ms Foundation. But friends and history are two different things. I would hope to be remembered as a kind and empathetic person – this all sounds corny – but as somebody who tried to leave the world a slightly more diverse, capacious, just, compassionate place than it was when I got here; as someone who nurtures and treasures diversity. I suppose the most common image for this country is a melting pot. It shouldn't be a melting pot, it should be more like a Waldorf salad, you know, where everybody's allowed to be the tomato, the avocado, the thing that they really are, but together it makes something it could never have made separately.'

'What about being thought of as a saint?'

'I don't want to be self-sacrificing. The very word is a problem. Saints are by and large women who have failed to challenge the patriarchy, like Mother Teresa. That's how they got to be saints.

'Contentment or productivity or happiness, I don't even know what you want to call it, is feeling that you can be yourself and contribute something uniquely to the world. You don't have to pretend, you don't have to be someone else. And the women's movement has given me that. It is about choice and about giving each other the power to make the choice. I don't think there's anything that I could be that would be a disgrace to the women's movement, except maybe a masochist and since I'm not a masochist, it's fine. It is about empowering you to be yourself and to trust this unique person that was born into the baby in the first place.'

'Is it tougher now than ten years ago for women?'

'It's not tougher in the mainstream in the sense of getting a job, doing what you want, working. It still needs to go a very long distance because men are not raising children as much as they should. Those things we know have to change. In a political sense it's tougher because the backlash has organised and solidified and made it acceptable to be prejudiced. That started in the Reagan administration but it has continued. So now something like "take our daughters to work day" got a lot of pickets and flack because they said it was discriminating against boys. It's like the backlash against affirmative action. This was summed up by Eleanor Holmes-Norton, who is a black congresswoman in the district of Columbia. Somebody said to her, "Why aren't the boys getting this attention?" and she said, "For the same reason there's not a white history month, that's why."

'Also, there are more bombings of abortion clinics, of cold-blooded murders of doctors and staff for the first time.'

'Are you optimistic for the future?'

'I'm always optimistic because it's a form of planning. Why would I be pessimistic? Then they would have won. I would say I'm optimistic but sceptical. Because I came of age in the 1950s I know exactly what my life was supposed to be like. I'm supposed to have married a professor or a corporate executive and stayed home and raised children. I didn't know what I wanted but I knew what I didn't want. I do think of roads not taken. If I had married my college fiancé I probably would have been in a loony bin by now, not because he wasn't a really nice person but because it wasn't my life. My father was always worried about me because he thought I was over-educated. When I came back from my junior years he had two suggestions. He took me to meet a guy who was selling the first aerosol cans. He thought I could sell those. Then he sent me a clipping from *Variety* where one of the hotels in Las Vegas was looking for a chorus line of women who were under twenty-five, five foot seven and over and had a Phi Beta Kappa degree. What would my life have been if I'd done either of those things? Hard to know. I'm just very grateful I didn't. It's hard to imagine how I could have survived, which is why I have such admiration for women who did those things and who survived.

'I'm not without regret but it doesn't have to do with the broad outlines of my life, it has more to do with the time spent wasted or repeating things I already knew how to do. Part of being a survivor, part of being able to function is that I'm too easily influenced by the atmosphere around me. I have taken on things that I shouldn't, whole jobs and projects just because I was in a group that was worrying about this. Planning ahead is the most reliable measure of class. Rich people plan for four generations forward and poor people plan for Saturday night. You don't think you have control of your own life and that measure of power or powerlessness has always interested me. The sense of time and planning. Now I plan to live until I'm at least a hundred.'

Even though she never once made me feel that time was an issue by sighing a lot or looking at her watch, I did not want to overstay my welcome as I knew she had a writing deadline and I know about the kind of internal anxiety that produces.

Never once had she made me feel that she was going over answers to questions she had covered so many times before. Even if she had. I had talked a lot about my life, my mother, my childhood, my writing, and her eyes never strayed from mine. Not once. She did appear to be genuinely interested. The point is, why? Why should she care what kind of life I've led? This chapter is about her, not me. Somehow she made me feel that I wanted to share these feelings and thoughts with her.

The sceptic may say, 'Come on, she's been practising this art of listening and caring and sharing for decades, she should be good at it. You have just fallen under her spell, like hundreds of other men and women. The seducer has become the seduced.' Perhaps. There is, however, the possibility that in this age of cynicism, indifference and disillusionment with heroes and heroines, she may be the genuine article. Sincere. Dedicated. Committed. Whatever the personal cost, the cause of women's liberation and equality is for Gloria Steinem a lifetime passion. In short, is she a modern saint? She's got my vote.

Emerging from the amber lamplight of her living room into the gritty glare of the street I realised I had no idea of the time. Hours had passed. Crowds were starting to gather for the veterans' march; rain was still hovering. I hoped one day all the old feminists would march together again, veterans of another war, of battles won. Perhaps Gloria could lead the march when she turned a hundred. And I'd be there to interview her. It's a good plan.

8
INTERLUDE II

Evening: 'My' apartment, West 69th Street, New York City

When I returned home to the answering machine there were many messages. But not from Betty Friedan. Damn. Damn. Damn. 'Persist,' I thought. I tried her assistant Hildie again and left another message.

At 7 pm Hildie finally rang me back. I was overjoyed. Her news, however, was not good. Betty Friedan was going to China at the end of the week and did not think it was going to be possible for me to do the interview. She was too busy. There was no time. I was not going to give up now. I explained to Hildie the urgent necessity for her to find me a space, even an hour would suffice. I would fly to meet her wherever she was. Except China, of course. 'Please Hildie,' I said. 'Please plead my case. I have come all the way from Australia. I'm totally reliant on you.' From her voice, Hildie was a woman of mature years and I knew she would do her best, as promised.

At 10 pm she phoned me: 'I'm sorry, Ms Mitchell, I have spoken with Ms Friedan and she has no time. All I can suggest is that you catch the shuttle to Washington very early on the morning of the 31st. She has to speak at a conference and if you met her at 8.30 am she would have some time before the conference starts.'

She gave me the address and I said, 'Tell her I'll be there.'

'Don't be late or she said she'll leave without you.'

I thanked her profusely and she said she was sorry she couldn't do more for me.

I rang Deirdre to find out how to get the shuttle and book a car to get me to the airport on time. Then I rang Naomi Wolf's number and left a message to say I was coming to Washington and could I interview her some time in the afternoon.

Finally, I left a message on Betty Friedan's answering machine: 'Hello, Betty, it's Susan Mitchell, the Australian who has been leaving messages for you all over the country. Thank you for allotting me the time to talk with you. This is just to confirm that I will meet you in the foyer of your Washington hotel at 8.30 am on Wednesday 31st May. See you then. Good bye.'

9

MARILYN FRENCH
PART II

Day Six, 6 pm: Her apartment, TriBeCa, New York City
Marilyn looked rested and much less frail when she opened the door to me this time. She said some days were better than others and today she was feeling fine. She offered me a drink, I said I'd get it but she insisted on walking slowly to the kitchen to do it. That will of hers, that spirit, was indomitable.

The photographs on top of the wooden cabinet showed me faces of similar determination. You just knew these were women not to be messed with; they were her mother and her grandmother.

Her study was a neat, immaculate room (Marilyn had once told me that even her spice racks were in alphabetical order) but very comfortable with bookshelves, a baby grand piano that she still plays and two couches. I settled back for the rest of her story. She knew exactly where we had left off.

'By the time *The Women's Room* was published I had been denied tenure at Holy Cross. I was really frightened, I was without a job. Fortunately Harvard was very kind and gave me a fellowship for a year, and by the time that was over *The Women's Room* had been published and I had a lot of money. If that had not happened I knew I would have had to scrounge by teaching introductory courses at various little schools that hired adjuncts; it would take five of those courses to support you.

'I don't know why it was so hard for me to get a tenured job. I got one at MIT and then the dean decided I was too old. I was over forty. I had a book with Harvard Press, I had very good teaching reviews, most of my colleagues liked me, but I couldn't get a job. So I did two years of promoting *The Women's Room*, one with the hardback and one with paperback.

'I went everywhere. The interviewers certainly understood what the book was about, but they didn't like the message that women were angry. They didn't like the message that women were unhappy with their lives and my women in that novel are angry and unhappy with their lives – as just about every woman I knew was. They didn't like that message, so they shot the messenger. Or they tried to. They did some damage, they injured her. It's not easy to go from city to city and to be called "bitch" and "cunt" and names like that by men. An Australian television interviewer actually called me a "cunt" just before we went on air. He was a man who had given up being gay to marry and have children and he said he was really a feminist. Then he proceeded to recite every foul thing any man had said about women going all the way back to Descartes. Just before the cameras went on him he smiled and said, "You cunt." I had a choice of sitting there for the interview or getting up and walking off.

'I was called everything. I was called terribly foul names on British radio. It was just a very bad experience. If you have five or six interviews a day, and two of them are hostile and nasty and three of them are vicious, then you can't come back home from that and not feel shot down and wounded. I don't think anybody could. I just burrowed into myself and tried to write the next novel and tried to keep real anger out of it, although I'm not sure that I did.

'Bleeding Heart is a much less angry novel than The Women's Room, but they did something to me, those two years of hostility. Now when I go out and people are very nice to me, in other words I'm accepted, I have a lot of trouble feeling comfortable. It takes me a while before I can trust an interviewer. I go into any TV station or radio station or even newspaper print interview very tense. I don't know what to expect and I don't think that's particularly good. I think you come across better if you're easy and relaxed and agreeable. But I am not able to do that because of what happened with The Women's Room. And that continued with Bleeding Heart, it didn't just vanish.

'I didn't do very many interviews for the Shakespeare book. Her Mother's Daughter was so many years later and by that time the reviewers had more or less accepted me. Then I wrote Beyond Power; but The War Against Women got people just as upset as they had been with The Women's Room. It only got five reviews and although I did go out and do a lot of interviews, all of which got published, the interviewers were not hostile on the whole, it was the reviewers who were.

'I never expected to write a best-seller; never in any of my dreams did I expect that. It was a total shock to me. I really didn't think I would ever be able to make a living. I thought I'd be published but I thought I would have to stay married to someone or get a job because I didn't think I would ever earn enough living out of my books to support myself. So I was very shocked when *The Women's Room* made that possible. It was nice.

'I don't feel anything about fame, to me it's just an illusion. It's not something I take seriously at all. What matters to me is the quality of my work. I wrote for twenty years, sending novels and stories out, and I got rejected for twenty years. For twenty years the world of publication told me I was no good. The last fifteen they've been telling me I'm good. I can't believe one any more than I believed the other. I could only trust myself, I could only believe in myself. My publisher said that if he'd gotten the manuscript of *The Women's Room* two years earlier he would not have published it, but things had happened in his private life that had really opened his eyes to the way the world treats women and because of that he was open to this novel.

'In *The Women's Room* I said in the narration: I know that you're going to be angry that all the men in this book are nothing but stick figures, which in truth I don't think is the case, but they are far less developed than the female characters and I don't understand male motivation in many cases and admit that I don't. I don't think men themselves understand their motivation. I had seen so many men destroy their marriages and destroy their families and I do not know what goes on in their minds, what they're thinking when they do this. I can watch them, I can observe, I can write down the details of what they're doing and the anguish I see in them but I could not give you a motivation for their behaviour. And so many reviewers said, "Oh, the men in this novel are nothing but stick figures," and I thought, "I really gave you your line to use."

'So I thought I'd write a book in which the man was not a stick figure, in which he comes as much alive as the female lead and in which his motivations are examined as closely as those of the female, and that's why I wrote *The Bleeding Heart*. Victor, I think, is a very sympathetic character and is gone into in great depth and that doesn't prevent him from, in some sense – I won't say exploiting because I don't think he really exploits – treating women as somehow less important than he is; acting as though his desires, his needs, should in some sense dominate the woman as well as himself.

'On all the television programmes women are still treated as if somehow or other their real purpose in life is to make men happy, to understand them, to support them. If they don't do that they're bitches. Certainly I filled the female role for many years, there's no question about it. I was married for seventeen years, I did everything, everything! I was the one who put in the new window sash, I paid the income taxes, I did the cooking and the cleaning and the raising of the children and the holding of heads during vomiting and all the rest of it I did. He didn't do anything that I can think of. He mowed the lawn. I earned the money too, I was working. I didn't earn as much as he did but he didn't earn such a lot.

'*The Bleeding Heart* was received horribly. By the time that book came out everyone was saying *The Women's Room* was a classic and how could the person who wrote this classic novel write this book? They forgot that *The Women's Room* received terrible reviews. It had infuriated reviewers; they hated it. But they hated *Bleeding Heart* as well. I think they thought I was condemning all heterosexual relations, which perhaps I was, but I don't think that was foremost in my mind. I was describing a particular heterosexual relationship and showing what happens in it, where it goes wrong, and creating a character as I said. I think very highly of Victor, I like him, but that doesn't keep him from behaving in ways that will drive women away. I would have left him for the same reason Dolores, the main character, does.

'At this stage I was still living in Massachusetts. I was doing an awful lot of travelling. I had my place in Florida, in fact I wrote *Bleeding Heart* down there, and then I decided to move to New York because I was having to come here such a lot. And my kids were here, and my family. So in 1979 I moved down here to an apartment on Central Park West and I've been in New York ever since. I think I was very depressed. I had failed. I had been denied tenure at Holy Cross and been out of a job. When that happened I lost my Holy Cross friends, whom I had really loved. They dropped me as soon as they heard I didn't have tenure. They said that it was too painful, that they'd had this experience over and over again and they didn't want to get any closer to me than they were because it was going to hurt them too much when I left. So they stopped being close to me right away. All except a half a dozen. Then when I got famous, or whatever you want to call it, well-known or had a success, I lost the others, who couldn't stand it that I'd gotten, as they said, beyond them. In New York I had a couple of friends but not a world, not a community, which I was used to having.

'I expected my success to be very important to my mother, to change things for her, because in some sense it was for her I did everything. And it didn't. She was getting old, she was sickly and she was getting really irritable and grouchy and wretched. She had emphysema, she had arthritis. She wasn't happy. I bought her a house. She told me she wanted the house and she wanted me to buy it for her but then when I did she said I was trying to kill her by making her move at her age. So success did not bring me happiness. I felt very alone, very unappreciated. It took me a couple of years to get over the trauma that success brings. I don't think anyone knew that, I don't think anyone had the slightest idea of how I was feeling. I concealed it all. Completely. They would have seen me as someone very independent, maybe a little bit edgy. Certainly a person who wouldn't take shit from anyone.

'When someone first gave me *Sexual Politics* I didn't want to read it. People were always telling me I was neurotic and angry and I didn't want to get any more so. When I did read it I realised it gave me a set of terms that was wonderful and of course it validated my experience in the sense of "somebody else sees this, it's not just me". Which is what woman after woman wrote to me about *The Women's Room*. What it really did for them was validate their experience. Someone else sees things this way, it isn't just me.

'I was fifty when I moved to New York and fifty-three when I had my first affair with a woman. It happened because she pursued me. She was someone I was attracted to but I had great reservations about getting involved with a woman because I didn't believe that I felt the same kind of desire for women that I did for men, which I think is true. But she was very seductive and she was very loving to me. I was with her for about five years and although I have very bad feelings about the way it ended and her behaviour, and I have a lot of very different ideas about her character now than I had then, I think that on the whole she was of benefit to me. She was a person who helped me. I was still very depressed and she tried to help me get out of it. The woman I was involved with was a flirt, a seductress, and the character in *Her Mother's Daughter* was not. But the affair with the woman gets Anastasia out of a depression.

'I still would never have lived with anybody. I told you, I can no longer live with anyone because I am too likely to be at their beck and call. It's just too easy to me for me to fall into a role of putting someone else first. I don't think I was that way by nature, I don't think I was like that as a young girl, but I think that all those years of motherhood trains you to be a different kind of person. When my children are just with me over the weekend – nowadays of course I don't do much, they do everything for me, the lifting and the cooking, and I help do some of it, or I should say it's at my direction – I'm always thinking about what they would like. Not just what they would like to eat but what they would like to do, what they're feeling, if they're upset, if they're having a quarrel, what can I do to make things better? When they're around, I'm not going to say I'm secondary, but I'm certainly not first, I'm one of a group and my concerns are for all of us. The only way I can think of myself is if I stay by myself. I don't think that's necessarily a bad thing. I think that when people live in groups they should think about each other.

'These days my children take terrific responsibility for me, since I've been sick. They didn't do it before. Not that I was totally at my friend's beck and call when I was involved with her. I stood up for myself more than I ever had in my marriage or with Joe. But that's probably because she was totally self-involved and did what she wanted to do and insisted that I do it too. I had a very good example of her selfishness in front of me. I was absolutely monogamous when I was with her. She wasn't. That's what broke us up. She's since broken up with any number of people. She's a psychotherapist.

'What I learned from that relationship is the double standard that I maintained. I took shit from her that I would never take from a man. I was tolerant of things in her behaviour I would never have tolerated in a man and when it was all over I realised I had been with my husband again. I swore I would never be with anyone like that again – a double-faced, tantrum-throwing, loving person; Dr Jekyll on the one hand and then Mr Hyde. I had been involved with exactly the same person: one of the most loving people I've ever met and one of the most vicious. I am clearly attracted to these people. You see my mother was all I had and she was very cruel in a lot of ways. She also gave me everything she had. So this was what I was used to. I don't have any confidence that if I were to get involved with someone again, man or woman, it wouldn't be someone just like my husband. It seems to be what I do.

'After being in therapy I got a little less depressed and then I met a man who apparently writes books about this now. He's a shrink and he talks about depression as an inevitable part of life, as a very real response to life. And that is what I think it is. I think it's why all the women I know over fifty, with maybe a few exceptions, are depressed. I think most men are too. It's a human response to what life does to us. It's depressing to look around the world and see what goes on and if you are not depressed there's something wrong with you. It's not a debilitating state, it's simply an attitude towards life. Depression has never debilitated me, there has never been a time when I couldn't work. There has never been a time I couldn't have a love affair. There has never been a time I didn't go to parties, except now, for other reasons. Depression is a difficulty in experiencing pleasure, a reluctance to experience pleasure. But I don't think I feel that any more, I think that's gone. I'm a sad person because I think life requires that we be sad. If you're not sad you're a liar.

'I wouldn't call Gloria Steinem depressed. I said there were some exceptions. Bella Abzug I don't think is depressed either, although she's very sad, especially since her husband died. My closest friends, my coven – Gloria, Esther, Carol – none of them is depressed but a lot of other people are. Gloria looks for the optimism. She looks for the woman who is doing wonderful things on an Indian reservation or in some little town in the South, a woman who's organising this or that. Gloria finds these people everywhere and they cheer her up and they give her heart and they give her hope, and that's how she maintains herself. Carol is just full of joy. It must be from her childhood. She must have been raised with joy like Grace Paley.

'I don't look around the world and see all that joy, I see pain and I also think that pain is the test of experiences. You need to find the pain in a person to know them. But that's not all I see out of this, I see a lot of pleasure, I take a lot of pleasure. Of course since I have been sick there are a lot of pleasures I used to have I can no longer have. Some things I know I'll never be able to do again. That makes me sad, but it's not a tragedy.

'Gloria [Steinem] was trying to get inside herself in *Revolution From Within*. I'm not trying to get inside, I've always been inside. The outside world has always been of secondary importance to me and it remains that way. I don't care what people think about me and I don't care what people say about me. I don't behave in a way to please others. Even with my closest friends I only care to some degree. The result is that people very much accept me the way I am. If you really don't care, people accept you. I've always been more or less like this, but less so, of course, when I was young. When I was a teenager I think I was rather paralysed; even though I probably didn't care as much as my sister did, or as much as some of the other kids in high school, I still cared very much and it was probably one of the most painful times of my life because of that. When you're a teenager you don't know what's expected of you or what you're doing wrong, why people like other people, why they don't, what makes somebody popular or not. I didn't have any idea of those things and that was painful. But as I grew older I cared less.

'The fact that I could go on writing for twenty years without having any encouragement gives you some idea of the amount that comes from the inside compared to the amount that comes from the outside. I am a great survivor.

'*Her Mother's Daughter* was written as a gift to my mother. She died before I finished it but she read the beginning and loved it. She said that I had given voice to her feelings in a way that she couldn't have.

'Bud French was probably the most tragic and difficult element of my life. I almost went under with him. Surviving that marriage was like surviving a concentration camp, and that's what made me strong. I survived it when I could very easily not have. I was very close to suicide for much of our marriage. But I couldn't leave my children with that, and I couldn't leave them with him. I loved them too much. I had to stay alive for them. That's not in *Her Mother's Daughter*, and that was the worst ordeal of my life. Bud is dead now. I really loved him, but he was a very sick man.

'*Her Mother's Daughter* is really about my mother and her effect on a putative daughter, Anastasia. The book is about the influence of mothers and daughters and how even if you hate your mother you carry her in you and you pass it on to your own daughter. But the portrait of my mother is accurate. It's true that the female characters in my novels have a lot of sex. I did too. There's a time in your life when you want to experience sex just for itself and anyone who's attractive is fun. I didn't find it alienating and I enjoyed it very much. It was freedom for me. The kind I never had when I was young. That book got good reviews.

'Success has not brought me any of the things that I thought it was going to bring. It didn't bring me everlasting love. The kind of success I had being a feminist and being a woman is very different from the kind of success I had read about the old writers having. I wasn't lionised by society, I wasn't invited to tons of parties. I was an unwanted person. I was a feminist, an angry woman. It didn't make me popular, but in time, with some effort, I built a community of friends. It's true it was entirely women. I'd always had a lot of male friends and I missed that. Men were simply too afraid of me and too wary.

'My mother was not made happier by my success, she was made jealous of me. She would say very mean things. It had apparently been important to her to feel better off financially than me and when she no longer was she became very resentful. She would say things like, "How can I buy a present for you? You have everything." And this hurt me. But you get used to those kinds of things after a while. I realised what was going on with my mother, I stopped expecting her to be happy for me, and indeed she was awful to everyone – it wasn't just me. I built a new life so I was no longer depressed.

'The desire for love and happiness ever after and sexual love has nothing to do with reasonableness or logic. That desire goes on whatever is happening. It's like a fantasy. At this point in my life I have this broken body. I lie in the bed every night and I can't imagine anybody even touching it but, as I say, there's no rationality in this area.

'My latest novel is about a woman in her sixties who makes a fool of herself wanting a man. This woman was me and the man in question did not return my feelings at all. I don't know to what degree he saw that. He ran after me but he just didn't want it to be more than a friendship. I assumed that anybody who ran after you that way wanted it to be more than a friendship but that was the wrong perception. I felt humiliated. I have never been left except that one time but I had experienced rejection from various people.

'I have a male friend I've known for about thirty years, we were lovers many years ago, and his bitter complaint is that women don't realise that the man is always the one who has to do the asking and therefore gets all the rejecting. He's never believed me when I've said that women get rejected too. Maybe they're not the ones who ask for a date but they pursue people in their own way, and maybe a little more subtly than men do, but they do it. And they get turned down the same as men but he doesn't believe that. I don't think there's any woman walking around on the earth who hasn't experienced that. There was a boy I really loved at the same time I knew Bud and he had asked me to marry him but in a very nasty way. What he wanted was for us to sleep together and I wouldn't sleep with him, even though I wanted to, because I was too terrified. He said, "All right, we'll get married then, if that's what you want." I said I wasn't going to marry someone under such circumstances. But I couldn't go further with him because I kept having this vision, as I told him once, that if I married him I would be down on my hands and knees scrubbing a bathroom floor. And of course when I married Bud that is exactly where I was, although I didn't think I was.

'The stories of those boys from my college days and what happened in their marriages is one horrible disaster after another. The one I was really in love with did eventually get married. He beat his wife, his daughter became a prostitute and his son ended up in jail. He was a very brilliant, talented man. He became a lawyer, he became an expert in antiques, but he destroyed his life and destroyed his family. So did just about everybody I knew in those days. Between alcohol and brutality, my mother's choice was not the worst choice. Marrying a man you thought you could control was the alternative to marrying a man who would control you. Men who controlled women beat them, were unfaithful to them and were drunks. There's one couple left from my early years who have stayed married to each other. They've been through hell but they have stayed together and it's good; to a large degree, he is a controllable, passive man.

'I don't think we had a lot of choice in an age when male supremacy was taken for granted. The only chance a woman had of having a voice, or anything in a marriage, was to marry a man she thought she could get control of. I married such a man. I could control him in public but never in private. I don't know if it's different now, I'm not young now. I don't see things being really substantially different. I see things being a little better; men are more likely to be involved with their children but they still beat up their wives, they still drink too much, but there's much less of it than there used to be in this country, which is a very good thing.

'Most of the people I loved have died from lung cancer or cirrhosis of the liver. The only person now left alive from my real youth is my sister. Everybody else is dead. My father is still alive but he's not a part of my life. He's just there. Mine was a generation lost to sexism and masochism that really grew strong after World War II. We'd have a party on Saturday night and we'd all be so hung over we'd get together on Sunday and start all over again. Weekend after weekend.

'The message of *Our Father* is not as positive as it may seem. All of the writing and the articles of the last ten years are about the fact we are a post-feminist age and feminism's over because it's gotten what it wanted and so we don't need it any more. That really upset me and I thought: everyone doesn't have to be a feminist for feminism to have an influence on society. I thought I would write a novel testing that out. The characters are women of different ages, different classes, different colours, different religions and they do reach a tentative understanding, but it's very fragile. They get together for this one Christmas; after this, who knows what will happen? For that one moment they can have harmony and say, "This is a bad thing, what this man did to us, and we have to stop it." In the face of the enemy they can come together and fight. But can they stay together? Can they really work together? I think it's very hard.

'I didn't do any promotion work for this book. I finished one draft of it before I was sick and three drafts from the hospital. I had to revise it after I got better. And then I got sick again, and that's when it came out, so I wasn't in much shape to do promotion. I feel very disconnected from that book because I was so absent during so much of its life history.

'When I was diagnosed with cancer, death was a definite future. They told me I had a year. I really got confused; I heard what they said and I read all these things about miracle cures. I thought: "I have one chance out of five of living." That wasn't true, I didn't. But I told myself I did, and I did.

'It changed me a lot because I'm no longer able to be as independent as I was, so I have to tolerate my own neediness now in a way I never did before. And that is really hard for me. There are things I can't do myself. I've learned to accept that. I don't live in the future any more and I always used to. I don't think I have a future, so I won't live it any more.

'I was fascinated to read in the *Times* some months ago that they did psychological tests of people who were happy. Now here's where I question this. How can you know that somebody is happy?

But, anyway, when people were happy the sections of the brain that deal with the future shut down. When you're happy you're living in the present, you're not living in the future as you usually do. It seems to work in reverse as well.

'I'm not going to say I'm a happy person, but now I live entirely for the present because I don't really believe I have a future, and probably I am happier than I was before. I don't expect very much from life, and I always expected everything and wanted everything and I wanted it all at once. That's not very realistic and it tends to make for unhappiness. I've come to expect a lot of affection on the part of certain people and just demand a certain degree of pleasure every day. I make it for myself even if it's only looking out of the window. I take pleasure in comfort, if I can just get myself comfortable. I can't always. I'm in pain a lot of the time.

'If someone read all of my work I think they would get a picture of women's lives in the west in the twentieth century, and there will come a time when that will not be generally known. The novels stand as sociological documents. I think I treat my women as full human beings. The things that upset them, the things that concern people, are not just men and children, which is what men assume about women all of the time. Male books are about human beings questioning life. Female books are traditionally about domestic violence. I think in my books the women question life in the same way that male figures do in their books, although I don't think there's a single reviewer who has ever picked that up. Even the great female novels of the past were involved with "who's she going to marry?" and usually end with her deciding who to marry. A Jane Austen novel presents you with a sociological picture of nineteenth-century England, the middle classes and the life of the women is pretty well circumscribed. I don't think that readers are yet used to the fact that women nowadays, or a lot of us, are dealing with other things, with questions of the meaning of life or asking what does a life do from here? I think I was one of the first people to do that.

'I hope I write with a great deal of care about prose and rhythms. I try not to get bogged down with the rhythms of high-flown prose but to create conversational, casual, personal rhythms.

I do aim to write beautiful prose. I have never had anyone say that I did, so I don't know if I've succeeded or if it's just not something people see. I guess I'm pleased with my body of work. I haven't re-read it and I never will. I'm sure that if I did I would find it wanting in all kinds of ways.

'Most of my greatest joys I've enjoyed alone, but it's the life I wanted. It just stopped a little too soon. But who knows, maybe there's more on the way.'

Marilyn had booked us a table at a nearby restaurant. Elegantly dressed as always, she took my arm for steadiness and we walked, arm in arm, the two blocks to dinner. At least in New York people did not come up to us and tell her she made them leave their husbands.

There was an easy physical presence about her that made me feel we had taken this walk every night for years. She possessed the dignity of someone who refuses to be bowed down or diminished by her illness. Over dinner, even though she did not eat very much, she enjoyed my pleasure in the food and we talked about her new novel *My Summer With George*. Nothing will ever stop her writing. To her it is like breathing.

It was a warm, pleasant night and as we strolled back to the apartment after dinner I told her how my book never would have been started without her initial support. She dismissed her part in it. Praise is still not something she accepts with ease. Criticism, it seems, is much more familiar territory.

I persisted. I thanked her for believing in me and the book. I thanked her for what she had given me. I knew it had not been easy to relive all the pain that she had experienced. It had taken great courage. And honesty.

'I'm a survivor,' she said.

'No, Marilyn, you're much more than that.'

10
BETTY FRIEDAN

Day Seven, 8.30 am: Washington, DC

Early morning call. Very early morning. Into the limo waiting outside the apartment for me. Out to JFK, onto the shuttle and into another car waiting at the other end in Washington. I don't talk much in the early morning.

'Traffic's a bit heavy today, ma'am.'

'Will we get there by 8.30 am?'

'I should think so, ma'am. I'll do my best.'

Surely she wouldn't leave without me if I was a few minutes late.

At exactly 8.29 am I ran into the foyer of the hotel and said to the woman at the desk, 'Would you ring Betty Friedan, please, and tell her Susan Mitchell is waiting for her in the foyer.'

I sat down and waited. A man rolled up the rug and mopped the floor around me. Ten minutes later she arrived, glanced over in my direction and walked straight up to the desk to complain to the woman about a letter she wanted re-delivered. The woman behind the desk started to say that it was not possible. Betty cut her short.

'I have rung the post office – they said you need to speak to the delivery manager. I will speak to the man who delivers the post. Right?'

She turned to me. 'Hurry up. I haven't got much time.'

I jumped up and collected my things. She looked at the rolled-up rug next to the plastic yellow sign that said 'Danger – Wet Floor', and said, 'Is that yours?'

'No,' I said, and wanted to add, 'I didn't come on a magic carpet.' She probably thought it was my bush swag.

I followed her to the kerb where she waved her arms frantically at every cab that went by, even though they all had people in them, all the while keeping up a torrent of monologue that went like this: 'I'm just so busy. I have so much work to do. Why don't you just read my books? I have no time to waste. Do you understand? No time to waste. Just read my books.'

'I have read your books, but . . .' I tried to reply.

'Just get all you want out of them. It's all in there. All I have time for is to let you ride in the cab with me. If that's not enough, then too bad. I am so busy. I have no time to waste.'

Finally she flagged down a cab with a woman in the back, got in the front seat with the driver and ordered me to get in the back. I did as I was told and, much to the surprise of the woman sitting next to me, took out my tape recorder, turned it on and held it up to the front seat where Betty continued to talk, half-turning towards me in between giving instructions to the driver.

'About three times a year we have a symposium in Los Angeles, Washington, New York or Chicago, or whatever, on separate aspects of women in the media like advertising or movies or coverage of the Persian Gulf war. We do studies about the number of times that women are mentioned or reported or photographed on the front page of the newspapers and the number of women by-lines. What we found out in the first studies was that while women are 52 per cent of the population, even from the sheet numerical count only 15 per cent of the space concerned women and in some of the best newspapers like the *Washington Post* and *New York Times* it was under 10 per cent. You understand what I'm talking about?'

'Yes,' I said.

'I have no time to waste. So, anyway, then we began studies of the editors and asked for comment. The editor of the *New York Times* said, "Well if we covered tea parties there would be women on the front page," and so we publicised that and the women who worked in the *New York Times* were so furious that they all wore tea bags to work the next day and made the management meet with them.

'So it began to improve and it's been steadily growing up to 25 per cent. But this year it's taken a fall again down to 19 per cent and I think it reflects the backlash against the women here. You understand the word "backlash"?' [Not so much a question as a bark.]

'Yes,' I said.

'You know we have a terrible political situation in America today with this Contract on America – you know, Gingrich and the attack on affirmative action and the economic frustration of men affected by down-sizing.'

BETTY FRIEDAN

'Yes,' I said.

'You know what "down-sizing" is?'

'Yes,' I said, thinking but not daring to say, 'I'm from Australia, not Afghanistan.'

'Right. All right. And so they manipulate the angry white males, to say nothing of the black males. They are manipulated into the backlash against women, backlash against racial minorities, against government, against welfare. There's a war on welfare mothers that's going on. The reason that I'm so frantic and so busy is that I came to Washington this year. I had spent ten years writing the *Fountain of Age*. It was not the only thing I did in those ten years. I was also teaching and lecturing. I was distinguished visiting professor at both University of South California in the Spring and occasionally at New York University in the Fall. So I was working on this book and then it came out and I did the book tour. It was a number one best-seller in Australia. Did you know that?'

'Yes,' I said.

'Anyway, I was here in Washington on my book tour and I had dinner with Marty Lipsits. You know Martin Lipsits?'

'No,' I said.

'Friend of mine, eminent political scientist, and Marty said: "Why don't you come here to the Smithsonian, at the Wilson Centre for scholars?" So I said, "Well that would be interesting," because I've always enjoyed coming to Washington for a day or two at a time on a journalistic mission or a political mission. I've thought it might be fun to live here if you were really involved and I was coming to the end of something. So I came in the Fall and they asked me what I was going to work on and I said policy implications of the *Fountain of Age* and my work on women.

'I'm not active in the politics side of the women's movement any more. It irritates me too much, it's not a good use of my time and I don't need that kind of power, but I am concerned with the vision, with the linking. While I was in California I ran a think-tank on the evolution of feminist thought, trying to bring policy makers together with academic theorists because women's studies have become so deconstructionist, abstract and removed from life and politically correct. The movement itself seemed to me to be stuck in rhetoric that was okay twenty years ago but not with the younger women today. I began to feel very uneasy that there was too much focus on sexual politics, rape, date rape, violence against women, sexual harassment, pornography, even abortion. The right to choose is essential, but we've won that battle in the US. There are skirmishes, the right wing keeps trying to bomb clinics but basically there is such a consensus on it in America that even the Republicans, even the Contract on America folks don't really try to take away your right to choose. It's important that women are being able to blow the whistle as they are now on rape; violence against women may well be increasing but it is a symptom, don't you see, it's a symptom of this economic thing, and the real threat to women's empowerment is economic. So then in recent years I applied the same thinking I had to women to the whole question of age and what older people need is not more nursing homes, because the research I put together for the *Fountain of Age* shows there's no serious deterioration for people ageing in the community, especially if they use their functions until they are well into their eighties. So here they are now, not only being forced out at sixty or sixty-five, but the down-sizing of jobs is mainly getting men over forty.

'In the last five years there has been a significant decrease in the income of college-educated white males, American white males, not high school dropouts. We know about the blue collar but this is college educated, that's from the down-sizing. I saw that even before we saw it in the 1994 election. I saw that as part of the backlash against women and the tactics of the last twenty years that we have used on sexual discrimination, and the separate movements of identity politics and women's movement, gay and lesbian women, are not going to be adequate to these problems and might even increase the polarisation of America. What we need is to transcend the polarisation. There's a dwindling number of jobs so do you say up the women, down the men? Are you going to say keep on the older people, don't hire the young? There's already a danger, there's already a backlash against the women, there's already intergenerational warfare and there's already an attempt by younger people to say, "Oh, well, why should older people get all the social security? There won't be any for us." Now you can't lie down in front of it, you can't. There's an attack on affirmative action from the Contract on America folks which means even further pitting the white male against the black, against the women, against the immigrant and so on. So I've organised a seminar at the Wilson Centre of policy makers, called "A New Paradigm: Beyond Polarisation", transcending polarisation and a new vision of community, if you will.

'I think there should be a campaign for a shorter work week for everybody. Although women don't make as much as men, the service jobs that women maybe do are increasing, whereas the blue collar jobs and the middle management jobs are being phased out. But those service jobs are being farmed out, contracted out, made temporary, whatever, with women having no protection of that kind of job, no benefits. So what we need is, first of all, benefits to cover part-time work, we need a campaign for a shorter work week and we need incentives for businesses as an alternative to downsizing to offer the flexible kind of job-sharing work schedules that would suit the needs of women and men in the parenting years.

'The two main problems women have today are jobs, getting them, keeping them, getting paid for them, and their work in home, their work in families. And there's a lot of stress on them because the structures haven't changed sufficiently. We should have a campaign for it, women and men, old and young, boosting the needs of women and men in the parenting years who are doing eighty-hour weeks. A new paradigm of thinking is involved, a new vision of community and a redefinition of the corporate bottom line and of personal success. So that's what I've been working on. I was supposed to write a memoir and I didn't.'

At this stage the woman in the back of the cab paid the driver and made her escape. I seized the time to ask a question as Betty transferred herself from the front to the back seat, next to me.

'All this work is important – symposiums, getting people together,' I said.

She snapped back: 'I told you what this was. This is not just getting people together.'

I asserted myself. 'No, let me finish. I'm asking a question now. What I'm wanting to know is, is it really your books that remain that permanent agent of change?'

'*The Feminine Mystique* is probably the most important thing I did. But *The Second Stage* is also important, and there's *The Other Half*, and my *Fountain of Age* was also important. I will make a book out of *A New Paradigm*. Then I am supposed to be writing a memoir which I've barely started. I wrote a new chapter in my life instead of the memoir, but I will begin working on that seriously this summer. Since I'm in Washington I got involved again because really dangerous stuff is happening. They have had me go up to see some Senators about the war on the welfare mothers, the attempt to scapegoat welfare mothers. I mean it's a minuscule part of the budget but they are making them the scapegoat. Do you understand the word "scapegoat"?'

'Yes, Betty, I do understand the word "scapegoat".'

'As soon as you say to me, "But it's the books that count," I get all guilty again. [Laughs.] But this new vision of community is something I feel strongly about. Did you know *The Feminine Mystique* has just been published in Russia? I thought they should have published *The Second Stage* as well. Russian women have been working and now they're being pushed back into the home again, just like women here were in the 1950s.'

While she had been sitting next to me in the cab talking at me, I took a close look at her. She was dressed in a long, patterned navy and white button-through dress in a granny print style. One of the buttons on her dress was undone but I thought if I told her she might order me out of the cab. She hadn't done her hair. Her shoes were beige with scuffed worn-down low heels. Her eyes were bulbous like an owl's and I had the impression she was not really seeing me except in a blur. There was no real eye contact. Her nose was long, her skin that of a seventy-year-old woman, her nails were chipped, uneven and needed cleaning. Her mouth, however, was young and when she laughed, briefly, I could see a young girl in that smile.

When we arrived at her destination, she did not ask me to join her. I simply followed her, like a faithful dog, into the conference venue.

The signs said 'Freedom Forum – Women, Men and Media Studies'. We went up in a lift and entered an anteroom where coffee, pastries and food had been laid out. Betty got herself a coffee as various people came up to talk to her. She gave each one about two minutes before she moved on to the next. One woman told her about the possibility of her hosting a new television programme.

Betty said, 'So, I should do a programme with you.'

She said to another, 'I'm going to China at the end of this week, you know. But first I'm going to see my daughter-in-law become a Rabbi.'

When people stared at me, standing two paces behind her, and she felt obliged to explain my presence, she said, flinging an arm in my direction, 'This is an Australian – what's your name again? – Susan Mitchell, that's right. She's writing a book on books that changed the world or something.'

The women smiled and looked interested but Betty Friedan was not there to talk about me. Everyone moved into the main conference room where about forty of the top women (and some men) involved in all aspects of the media – producers, presenters, newsreaders, press secretaries – sat in a square behind long tables covered with white tablecloths. Connie Chung wasn't present. Too bad. She'd have a story to tell. The press were told to sit directly behind on benches that ran along the wall. I sat down next to a journalist from the *Washington Post* who was researching an article on Betty.

'She's hard to pin down,' she said.

'Tell me about it,' I said.

'Who else is in your book?'

I related the names, keeping my voice low when I mentioned Gloria Steinem, as I'd been told Betty's animosity and jealousy are such that she may have refused to be in a book with Gloria.

The journalist said, 'I think Susan Faludi is too hard on Betty when she says she sold out. That's an unfair spin.'

Cameramen were positioning themselves behind strategically placed cameras.

'It's going live to air on C-Span,' said the journalist. I noticed Betty at the top table combing her hair and putting on her lipstick. And smiling.

At exactly 9.30 am the camera lights went on and a man from Freedom Forum welcomed everyone to the conference and said that 'Women, Men and Media' had been originally launched at a conference at the University of Southern California on the twenty-fifth anniversary of Betty Friedan's society-changing book *The Feminine Mystique*. One of the aims was to develop new strategies for women in the media to advance the cause by creating an umbrella organisation that would monitor how women were hired, promoted and covered by the press and then create round tables around the country to bring both women and men from within the media to discuss the information and to find solutions. The co-chair of this organisation, Nancy Woodhull, took the microphone and outlined the issues, before asking Betty to react to the latest study and give an overview.

When Betty spoke, without notes, she was animated, alive, articulate. She basically covered the same ground that she had summarised for me in our taxi ride together, except she added:

'Where are the voices of women? Are women just lying down mutely, passively and accepting this moving in on their rights and on their welfare? I happen to know, because I've been in Washington this year, that there were major press conferences held by the presidents of all the women's organisations, the council of presidents protesting the attack on affirmative action, protesting the attack on the welfare mother. I happened to be on the Capitol steps myself with other women leaders protesting this. In other years this would have been news – the women's response, the women's outrage. It was not covered. It really is symbolic annihilation. There were cameras and reporters there but it wasn't covered. We're here today to discuss this and maybe figure out what can be done about it, what it does mean, why it's happening, because I think this shows we are going back to *The Feminine Mystique*.

'The definition of news in recent years is more and more polarising. Polarising our society, polarising our nation. It's all win or lose, guns and violence, war, foreign or domestic. There is a glaring absence of a vision of community and this is both true politically and in the media. Last year, the *Washington Post*, which had been abysmally bad in its coverage of women, it was under 10 per cent when we first started, suddenly showed a big, big improvement.

'When we investigated we found out that a woman had been promoted to metropolitan editor and there was suddenly much more coverage of community, of positive actions about drugs, and stories that showed women more. We felt from the beginning that part of the symbolic annihilation of women wasn't a conspiracy but that there was a tremendous male blind spot in the definition of what is news and in the assigning of stories.

'When women are covered, do they have to just fit into that male model? Take the coverage of Hillary Clinton. Hillary cannot be ignored in terms of a real voice and real seriousness and concern with issues and she is being covered with some ambivalence. But I do not feel that there is anything wrong with coverage of Hillary taking into account, as it did, her trip to the Far East and other aspects of her complex existence as a woman that includes motherhood and marriage, even frivolous stuff like her clothes, her hairdos. This monolithic male model is not necessarily the model that women want to fit into. I offered a little unsolicited advice to the First Lady, well maybe it wasn't that unsolicited, but anyway, I said: "I like it that you had your picture taken in black velvet in *Vogue*. You know, I like it that you gave your recipe to that cookie contest. I mean, you're not just a brilliant career, you are all these things."

'There is a complexity of coverage there and I think it would be a good thing if the coverage of men would show that complexity. There is certainly plenty of attention paid to men's behaviour between the sheets. It would be nice if men's coverage included a complete coverage in terms of their family. Let's not always measure by the male model. The coverage of Hillary is an interesting evolution – at the moment she's climbing out of this backlash against her but she is not just a brilliant career woman.'

Most of the other women around the table spoke and Betty chipped in from time to time. When she spoke, people treated her with the reverence and attention they afford matriarchs. She does in fact describe herself as 'the mother of the women's movement'.

A former CEO of one of the big television networks finally concluded by thanking Betty for 'hanging in there' and saying that if women wanted to stop the backlash against affirmative action, and he did agree that there was one, then they had to make sure that all women knew that they would be affected, not just feminists and women of colour. They had to make it clear that Newt Gingrich's wife and sister and daughters would also be affected.

One of the black news journalists around the table agreed. She said, 'If you just say women will be affected, they will just think it's women of colour; you have to say white women and not be afraid of saying it.'

At 11.30 am, when the conference ended, I talked to a few of the speakers, always keeping Betty within eyesight. Eventually she was free and I went up to thank her for allowing me to be present. She said, 'You got enough didn't you?'

I asked plaintively what she was doing for the rest of the day. She said that after lunch with Marlene, a media commentator, where they would plan next year's meeting, she was going to the doctor, then she was meeting her assistant Hildie to do some business, then she was taking dinner to a sick friend.

'Well he's not sick. He's had a triple bypass. I won't be cooking anything though. I'll be picking something up.'

I tried for one more question: 'What has driven you in your work?'

She said, 'You know, my father used to say to me when I was five, "You have a passion for justice." Well, I guess I did. I never set out to start a women's revolution, that just happened. For me it was just part of something bigger. I am passionately interested in the community and perhaps since I've written the *Fountain of Age* I'm more conscious of the sense of the meaning of your life in terms of what will go on after your life. Not just your children and your grandchildren.

'I have marvellous children and incredible, wonderful, beautiful, bright, very individual grandchildren. My passion for helping to make a vision that keeps evolving is as great as it was about feminism. I continue that passion, but for me now the great need is a larger vision of community to transcend the polarisation of a women's movement that stays in its narrow gender focus. That would merely feed the polarisation and I never did see it as women against men, I did see it as the absolute need for women to move into their whole personhood and their full participation in society. Research shows in the US the addition of as many as two women to a state legislature changes the agenda in the direction of life. So I'm thinking, all right, we're adding the women and we will not be pushed back even though there's the backlash now, but what are we adding the women for? It's not just the matter of simple justice. The agenda has got to go more clearly in the direction of life. There is a need to transcend all these different separatist kind of movements to the vision of one community. It's not just women versus men but, somehow, women's voices added to men's must add that dimension.

'Someone said, "What are you going to write now after the *Fountain of Age*? The next life?" No. I will write a memoir but I keep adding new chapters to my life and this *New Paradigm* and *New Vision of Community* is my new chapter.'

'It's clear that your passion for justice is still there. It hasn't dimmed since you were five.'

She laughed. That seemed to please her.

'Talk to Marlene, you know Marlene, I introduced you.'

'Yes,' I said.

'Well I've known her since this organisation started – she and I started it – talk to her about me.'

'I don't think you quite understand what kind of book I'm writing.'

She waved to Marlene, who joined us.

'Where are we having lunch and our meeting?'

Marlene told her and she said, 'I'm going to the Ladies.'

I told Marlene that I had seen her on television on a press panel discussing Connie Chung's sacking, where she had said that it wasn't a gender issue.

'Not in her case,' said Marlene. 'Connie's never done a thing for women in her life.'

'So when she is sacked she screams, "It's because I'm a woman."'

Marlene snorted. 'Exactly.'

'Will she get another job?'

'She will. But lots of women don't. Her sort does.'

We began to discuss the dilemma of being part of an organisation that actively promotes women in the media and helps a woman to get a top job, only for her to ignore the women who worked to get her there and then actively distance herself from them. I could see Betty returning.

I walked towards her to shake her hand and she sailed right on past me. I turned around and called out to her back, 'Thank you, Betty.' Without turning around she called out, 'Have a good trip back to Australia,' and disappeared around the corner with Marlene.

I didn't have to meet Naomi Wolf until 3 o'clock so, a little stunned, I caught a cab to the Smithsonian, the history museum. As we passed the Cenotaph surrounded by all its flags flapping patriotically, I reminded myself I was in Washington, DC, the national capital of the United States of America. After this morning's conference and my own experience I realised that our cultures are not very different. Certainly not in the media. We didn't, however, have little seventy-four-year-old women like Betty Friedan writing feminist books, organising national conferences on Women, Men and Media and getting generous sponsorships for them, or writing letters to the President or, in our case, Prime Minister, addressing the need for a paradigm shift or giving advice to the First Lady on her media image. You did have to admire the energy of this woman.

11
NAOMI WOLF

Day Seven, 3 pm: Her office, Washington, DC

Naomi Wolf was given a tough time when she arrived pregnant in Australia on her last book tour with *Fire with Fire*. In 1990 they had adored her because in her best-selling book *The Beauty Myth* she was having a big chop at the powerful beauty industries. In 1993, however, it was a totally different reaction. So nasty to her were some of the more vocal Australian feminists, particularly in Melbourne and Sydney, that I was amazed she had agreed to ever be interviewed by an Australian again, unless forced to for book publicity. The print media had really given her the 'tall poppy' treatment; she was made to look like a bonsai by the time she had completed her tour of public meetings. Mainly they said that after attacking the big guns of advertising, fashion, cosmetics and pornography in her first best-seller *The Beauty Myth*, she had totally sold out to these same forces of capitalist exploitation in *Fire with Fire*. A journalist in the national newspaper *The Australian* accused her of writing lines that come from tampon ads and asking women to pelt their oppressors with cotton wool. They are words meant to sting.

Sitting on a bench soaking up the sun outside a café called Animal Crackers, opposite the zoo, where we'd arranged to meet, I stared hard at the photo of Naomi on the back of her book. I wondered if perhaps, like Gloria Steinem, they hated her simply because she was beautiful. At 3 pm precisely, I walked into the café and saw a person hunched over a newspaper.

'Hi,' I said. She looked just like the photo, only more normal, less glamorous. Good-looking in a sturdy, healthy way. I decided that the background music playing in the café was too loud for the tape recorder and she suggested we go to her office. It was in a big impersonal building a few doors away. A packet of Huggies disposable nappies dominated the table by the front door and the entrance to two light, airy rooms with computers. When we sat down opposite each other, the full light on her face – she wore no make-up – revealed strong, striking features. I had to stop her calling me Ms Mitchell. There was something of the polite, respectful, earnest PhD student there. Although no student in Australia had ever addressed me in that fashion. Not with our rampant egalitarianism. I could get to like it. When I sought to regale her with my experiences of the morning with Betty Friedan, she looked genuinely alarmed. But then we settled down for the interview.

Here she was, married to one of Clinton's speech writers, living a respectable, ordered family life in the country's capital, a heartbeat away from the White House. And she was a first-time mother. From the light that beamed in her eyes when I asked about Rosa, her baby daughter, she was totally over the moon about it all. It was a far cry from growing up in the Haight-Ashbury district in San Francisco in the mid–'60s. ('Are you going to San Francisco? Be sure to wear a flower in your hair.')

'What you've got to imagine is something that hasn't really existed before or since, which was this halcyon moment from about 1965 to 1972 when everything that could be transformed was happening in my neighbourhood. The gay liberation movement, the women's movement, the lesbian movement, gay pride day was just beginning. This was San Francisco in the '60s and '70s. I remember the hippies, I remember the free store where you could just go in and take something and walk out with it. I remember being in peace marches in my stroller. I remember, when I was a little older, the bath houses. I didn't go there but it was very normal for me to see guys in leather chaps, kissing in the street. I thought the whole world was like that. Growing up in the Haight-Ashbury area in San Francisco in the '60s and '70s, I was surrounded by lesbian separatists wherever I went. It was just my everyday milieu. There was Ms magazine on the table, there were Dykes on Bikes down the street. The most radical feminist lesbian literature was in our house because my mum was studying that community as an anthropologist. San Francisco was an extraordinary place and time in which liberation was just in the air and in which intolerance was the stupidest thing anyone could imagine.

'It was also very important to me that I went to one of the only good public high schools in the country. White kids were in the minority. The majority were Asian kids and black and Filipino and

Hispanic. So hierarchies based on race never made sense to me because I had been educated in one of the few real meritocracies. The school was free. White kids were a completely insignificant, politically powerless minority in the school. I think that's a great perspective to have as a white person in this culture.

'I'm the youngest of two children, I have an older brother who's an earth scientist. My dad was a teacher at San Francisco State College. My mum was a graduate student most of the time I was growing up and so some of my strongest memories are of her writing her thesis and us not disturbing her. But it was a very egalitarian family from the beginning. I don't know what happened to my dad because he is seventy-two now and he grew up until he was six in Transylvania, Romania. Not a very progressive background. It was orthodox Jewish. He was always committed to equality in our household and he was very much a primary caretaker along with my mother, and very nurturing. It's been a very big influence on me because I don't recognise some feminist stereotypes of masculinity in my father and brother. They're nurturing men. Culturally we were middle class, but we were always broke. My mother was twenty-three when I was born and she was at graduate school, so she had not done much yet professionally. My father was fifteen years older. There is a half-sister who did not live with us.

'I cannot tell you how great it was to be a teenager in San Francisco in the '70s. Gender was completely fluid. The high school was so focused on academic achievement that the most prestigious people tended to be Chinese girls who were just acing all their classes. There was never a sense that boys did better but also, in San Francisco, the ideal was a kind of poly-gendered reality. If you weren't bisexual in high school you had to pretend to be in order to be socially acceptable. It was a very different place and time than the rigid 1950s.

'I think everybody is bisexual but I got interested in boys pretty young and had a steady boyfriend throughout high school. We were all experimenting all the time with everything. It was a uniquely gentle place. It was extraordinary. Boys took boys to our high school prom. There was a prom queen who was a guy in another high school. The feminists who set the tone of second-wave feminism were rebelling against a rigidity of genders in their high school experience, which was profound. But when I was growing up it was full of this sense of abundance of sexual masquerading and camp and play. Great times.

'I would wish that kind of education on everyone. Especially my daughter, Rosa. I don't know if it's possible to provide it now. It was part of the times, it was before AIDS. I hope it will come back in her lifetime but we can't guarantee it. I was incredibly fortunate. I think my upbringing also determined the tenor of my vision of feminism. *Fire with Fire* is much more optimistic and inclusive than some feminisms. A lot of that came from my personal experience and the influence of the gay community in San Francisco. People were making alliances across lines of gender in the interest of liberation so I didn't grow up seeing men as the oppressors. I grew up seeing gay men particularly as fighting their own struggle for recognition and acceptance.

'I was also very influenced by my father taking me very, very seriously as a writer. My first poem was treated very seriously. I'd be talking with my dad about what I'd want to do, maybe I'd want to be a judge or something, then I'd say, "Oh, but I can't do that, I'm a woman and the world is closed to women." He'd say, "I don't ever want to hear you saying that. You can do whatever you want." He wasn't minimising the obstacles that women faced but I'm just repeating that I was very lucky to have been raised in a family democracy. So probably I have a more optimistic sense of genders being able to live in harmony.

'On the other hand, I was anorexic at thirteen. I wrote about this in *The Beauty Myth*. A kid in my Hebrew school poked me in the stomach and said, "Watch it, you're getting chubby." Even though I was living in this idyllic place in many ways, I was still reading *Seventeen* magazine. The dominant culture was still the dominant culture, so it was for the same boring reasons that everyone else gets anorexic.

'The social forces are very, very powerful. As amazing as my mum was and as much of a pioneer as she was, she was coming out of a generation of women that were stifled in their own youth. She was struggling with being a very beautiful woman and trying to be taken seriously and trying to take herself seriously as a scholar. I'm sure I sensed her insecurities.

'It's interesting that I talk about my father being such a clear marker for feminism and I have only started to tell you about my mother. That's partly because my dad had the luxury of being able to know that women were strong whereas my mother, coming out of the 1950s, had to struggle to find her own strength and that has happened in the course of her lifetime.

'My grandmother was a professor at state college in Stockton, California. She was always an activist, she started a mental health clinic in Stockton and a contraceptive clinic for migrant women. She's always been a real pioneer. She was the daughter of Russian immigrants, Russian anarchists.

'The one thing I hated was the fact that we were broke all the time. I think that the experience of it has scarred me. Of course, broke is relative; we were never on the street. I do, however, remember the first of the month being a time of tension. It made me resentful. It made me very very angry because I didn't know how I was going to get to college.

'My education was appalling until I got to high school. I knew I was bright and I knew that I was falling behind and my peers were able to go to private school and get a decent education. My parents were hippies. They don't like it when I say that, so let's say they were free spirits and they were profoundly anti-materialistic. In a way God has really blessed them because their attitude was: objects aren't important, financial security isn't important, God will take care of us. And God did take care of them beautifully. But my brother and I have become terrified about financial insecurity. My parents moved to New York and have a wonderful life and are really an illustration of karmic abundance. They gave away everything valuable all their lives, much to their children's dismay sometimes, and now it's all come back to them. I'll give an example. My dad was going to get his pension after years of service to the state of California and my mum had to move to New York to start her career after all that training. In a typically proto-feminist way, my dad was going to move with her. He had the choice of waiting a year and having a commuter marriage, as many people do, and getting his full pension, or else following her across the country and taking a financial loss. My dad's in love with my mother and he's this romantic guy, and so he just sold up everything at a garage sale. I'm still tearing out my hair thinking about that. Because they bought their stuff at garage sales, they were Victorian antiques that no-one wanted in the '60s. I would kill for them now. They sold it all and they showed up in New York.

'My dad is always having projects come his way. I admire them. My mother became a therapist years later in her fifties and now has a thriving practice and my dad writes his books and they're fine.

'It's much scarier for children than for adults to be financially insecure. They had exactly the lives they wanted, which were lives of freedom from being concerned in any way with material wellbeing. But the pressure was on me when I was fifteen to somehow get a scholarship to college. That's a lot of pressure because I wasn't going to get to college if I didn't get a scholarship and that's why *Fire with Fire* talks so much about financial security. So that was one of the hard things about my being a teenager.

'Certainly in the feminism I grew up in, power was a dirty word. Some feminists picketed me when I was in Sydney, Australia, in 1994. They had T-shirts made with my photograph on it in sniper sights, which I thought was a bit harsh. I think they thought that from a "radical" perspective this is very much a reformist book and that upset them. The back of the T-shirt said, "I'd rather have a revolution than a feminist boss." Well I'd rather have a feminist boss than a sexist boss. This peculiar version of feminism in which you are radical by not touching anything that could actually change the world is common in the first world right now. I think it's a perversion of the great radical tradition.

'I had to work very hard in the last two years of high school, and I got a scholarship to Yale through sheer terror. Yale doesn't do merit scholarships, so I had to get into Yale and then I had to get financial aid. I studied English Literature. In many ways it was very exciting. It was also a shock because I had never been around rich people, or so many white people; I had never been around an east-coast class hierarchy before. It was a shock. But it was also intellectually very stimulating.

'My high school had been very very competitive because I was competing with Vietnamese boat kids who were twice as terrified as me of not getting to college and twice as hard-working. So I was fascinated by power and by the assumption that these rich kids had that they were entitled. That sense of entitlement fascinated me because I realised that the one thing to distinguish the "haves" from the "have nots" at that age was not intelligence and not hard work and not even money so much as this attitude of entitlement to power, which is precisely what I try to get across in *Fire with Fire*.

'I don't know how they viewed me. It would depend on who you were asking. Actually I was very happy there. I came from such a tolerant environment that I didn't particularly care what people thought of me and that gave me a sort of carte blanche to do what I wanted to do. I had left a wonderful boyfriend behind. He was a very sweet guy and now he's a biological scientist at University of North Carolina, last I heard. It was a sad break but it was very much in the season of things. Every freshman was leaving people behind, but he had been a lovely introduction to maleness. He was the son of a single mother, which I think is part of the generational shift where a lot of pro-feminist men were raised by single mothers and they can be very compassionate toward women because of that. I think any primarily heterosexual woman is well inoculated against real jerks by having a nurturing father, but I'm still a woman in this culture and that allure of dangerous or cruel or judgemental or elusive animus figures is as strong for me as for anybody. I've managed to not have my life destroyed by such men, but we all know about leather jackets and motorcycles.

'The most important thing I got from Yale was a close-up look at how power really operates and, paradoxically, at the language of meritocracy. Before Reagan was elected and before new barriers were set up, when I first went to Yale, it was on the tail end of an optimistic surge where women and African-Americans and Mexican-Americans could get into Yale through dint of sheer hard work. There was a sense of the beauty of democracy, and of a cultural tradition that could be open to all. Whereas when I won a Rhodes scholarship and went to Oxford, I encountered Yale's evil twin. It was classist, racist, anti-Semitic, nasty, elitist. It was a foul manifestation of education as a treasure which only the priest class are entitled to touch. For the first time in my life I encountered the kind of sexism that withers women by simply laughing at them. This cynical, sneering British sexism was what caused me to read radical, leftist, feminist academic theorists.

'I was planning on being a writer because that's what I saw everyone around me doing. I would have been content to make any sort of living as long as it was steady. Dad writes fiction and was a pioneer in the literary criticism of horror movies and books like *Frankenstein*. From him I very much got a sense that you don't have to be Shakespeare and you certainly don't have to be Jackie Collins. A writer is a craftsperson who sits at the computer all day long and just works.

'So *The Beauty Myth* started out as my thesis and I've still got a shelf of books waiting to be turned into my finished thesis. I was getting so annoyed at the sexism of Oxford and was simultaneously reading people like Adrienne Rich who were saying – to paint her position broadstrokes – that objective enquiry was phallocentric. That led me to believe that for me to pursue scholarship in the Oxford mould would be betraying my sex. So I was increasingly writing these impassioned polemical attacks on the representation of images of women in nineteenth-century fiction. My adviser, though a perfectly sympathetic guy, kept saying, "This won't do, they'll never pass this." I was thinking, "You pig, how dare you say that? I'm going to go off and write my subjective impressionist woman's voice view of this subject."

'I produced an unreadable and unpersuasive totally subjective version of *The Beauty Myth*. I then got a contract to write a book along these lines but my editor, Jim Landis at Morrow, said, "Go back and write this again." I eventually snapped out of it. I was trying to do something which there aren't a lot of models for, which I think is very valuable. I was trying to combine rigour and objectivity and good journalism and good research with evocative language, lyricism, subjectivity. "Masculine" and "Feminine" together.

'I now think that aspect of Adrienne Rich's work is wrong and the world view of the '70s and '80s feminism is what younger women are right to start questioning. It is not true that critical enquiry has to be phallocentric. I shouldn't put this all onto Adrienne Rich. She's a great poet and a marvellous essayist, but the unfortunate by-product of me reading her books at a time when I was surrounded by the most heinous form of sexism is that she persuaded me that the kind of poetry I was writing was phallocentric. The fact that I haven't written any poetry since is unfortunate because I was a damn good poet. And I had been writing it for a very long time. It's kind of hard to go back to. I will eventually I suppose, but it's sad.

'My uncle is a writer about psychology and he told an agent in New York about my book and the agent let him give me his number. It was a wonderful way out because I had absolutely no idea how I was going to make a living after graduate school. For two years when I was writing *The Beauty Myth* I commuted between Oxford, Edinburgh and New York. I became involved with a Scottish guy and went up to Scotland to write and to live with him. It was quite a wonderful place to write because it was fairly far outside of the culture I was critiqueing, so it let me stand on the periphery and say the kinds of things that it's harder to say when you're surrounded by those values. He is now an attorney in London. We split up. I can't say that my success had nothing to do with it. I worked very hard on that book. I'm happy to own it. It's a good book for a twenty-six-year-old to have written.

'I embarked on a huge promotional tour, which was very scary. I was breaking up with my boyfriend, or rather he was breaking up with me, and the book was very controversial in Britain. All my life I'd been writing things about which people would say, "Wonderful, here's an A for you." People in my life had generally liked me and had been quite warm to me. Suddenly people were attacking the book from all sides and attacking me from all sides. But I had to keep going. It was easier that their attacks were so stupid. Attacking me because I'm young is not smart. It wasn't as wounding as it could have been if someone had actually tried to debunk my thesis. But you can't debunk the thesis because it's true. I do remember thinking, "Everyone hates this book so much I'll never be able to publish again, my career is over."

'I got a reasonable advance, but a book takes years to write. *The Beauty Myth* made it possible for me to live off my writing, which is a great blessing. I've gotten better about trying to accept that I deserve to be paid what the market will bear for my work. I have not gotten as good as I would like to be about handling money, understanding it and using it wisely.

'Now that I've got a daughter and I'm helping to send a relative through college I feel much, much more confident about thinking of myself as a breadwinner who's entitled to do the best I can for my family.'

Right on cue, the door bell went. It was the baby-sitter delivering Rosa to her mother. From the moment that baby was in her arms I could see it was a love affair. Still polite and respectful, she asked if I minded if she breast-fed her while we were talking. Rosa was a good baby. After she had finished Naomi put her over her shoulder and she belched on cue. (The baby, that is.) Naomi cooed, 'Good for you. Oh good spitsky.'

When the baby was over her shoulder she could concentrate on what I was saying. But when she placed the baby in her lap and it lay there gazing up at her, she was lost. It was like looking at a modern version of a Madonna and child painting.

She resumed the interview.

'So I did the promotion in the middle of a heartbreaking end to a four-year relationship. I came back to this country feeling completely shocked at my experience in Britain. I talked to my grandmother. At eighty-two, she was able to put things in perspective and say things like, "Big advances have always been heralded by sniping and attacks." What also made it easier were the letters that started coming in. That's always been my publishing experience, that controversy will be raging in the newspapers or among the cultural elite and in the meantime I'm getting all these letters from women saying this is absolutely right. In the end that is the real thing, that's the only thing that counts.

NAOMI WOLF

'So I was back here preparing for US publication and I met the man who would become my husband. There was quite a long period of figuring out that the other relationship was doomed. Our deal is that I keep my husband out of my professional life and he keeps me out of his – let's just say he's a great guy. So I was starting to see him, the book came out in the US and caused another huge fight, a very scary fight. I was up against the big guns. The beauty industry is big money here, so is cosmetic surgery. There is every reason to believe that the magazines were put off by these people. They really pulled out all the stops against me initially. Even though at the time it was incredibly painful, one thing that I was learning to do was fight back. I found that I rather enjoyed it. I'd always argued against stupidity and injustice and sexism. The attacks got personal at Oxford and the UK but in America it had a different tenor. By the time it came out here it was a best-seller. I went to Holland and Italy to promote the book.

'The years from 1991 to 1994 were spent learning how to have the kind of job I have now, which involves travelling constantly, lecturing, meeting thousands of women, going to all sorts of communities. That's an amazing part of what I do for which I'm very grateful. Then I was writing *Fire with Fire*.

'It's not a job many people can teach you about and I'm not very organised by temperament but I am very, very hard-working and very disciplined when it comes to my writing and my speaking. When I go out on the road I try to give each commitment 150 per cent because it's important to people. I've been to many communities where my talk to a group of young girls was their first exposure to feminism. It's damned important to make it a good and empowering experience.

'I do believe in God. I don't know what else can explain this universe. And having my daughter is unbelievable, incredible. It's a total revelation. Now I'm writing a book about female desire and I've kept a journal about my pregnancy too.'

The phone stopped her flow of words. She smiled.

'This might be my husband. Do you mind if I take it? Come on, baby. I think it's Daddy calling us.'

From the tone of her voice and her genuine delight I gathered it was her husband on the other end of the line. When she returned to her chair, however, and positioned Rosa over her shoulder, she picked up where she left off, without missing a beat.

'I started a group in New York when I was theorising or working up ideas for *Fire with Fire* and the resource was committed to doing what I advocated in the book. It got so many women so many jobs, so many contacts, so many rises in pay. It was incredibly successful. It's foundering right now because a few of the women do all the work. The next step, for every woman to give back to it, seems to come much harder.

'Not taking responsibility for power, not taking responsibility for fostering and producing relationships that build and generate power is our fault. It's interesting that my male peers who came of age at exactly the same time are right now on the hill, in the White House or down the street trading power around. I was trying to invent a structure for women to do that.

'I am wary of the sentimentality of "sisterhood". I'm Jewish and I have a deep sentimental attachment to giving back to my Jewish community. But I'm very aware that sentimental attachment can very easily turn into tribalism, elitism – witness the occupation of the West Bank. It can turn into a world view in which Jews are better than other people, in which I owe more to my own people than I do to the black kid down the street who can't get into college. I think we have to radically question all kinds of tribalism. I think that we will really evolve and move into a vision of humanity in which there is no such thing as one peer group that's more cherished and that you have allegiance to humanity as a whole.

'The men who I respect don't owe more allegiance to their sentimentalised view of brotherhood than they do to humanity. The white people who I admire face the fact that they are born into an implicit identification with white people and they choose to extend their sense of belonging to non-white people as well. The men I admire go beyond their sense of affiliation with other men and they make a choice to stress their bonds with women as well. The only reason for women to organise to get more women into positions of power is precisely because women get less of it simply because they are women. The minute that women do not get less because they are women, we should pack the tribal identity in.

'I believe I am no more a sister to my sisters than I am a sister to my brothers. I should affiliate with welfare mothers who are not represented in a democracy – not because we're both mothers in some mystical plane, although that's very nice, it's a wonderful emotional bond – but because it isn't fair that they are not represented in democracy. Some feminists have attacked my engagement with capitalism, but many radicals have used the stock market to help poor people. The bus strikes that Martin Luther King led in the Deep South in the '50s and '60s, particularly in the '60s, were using capitalism, the power of the consumer, to advance the cause of justice. I'm talking about using our women's clout to achieve justice, not justice for individuals but justice for the oppressed.

'If you read my book carefully you see that everything's premised on giving back. Let me give you a model. I earned money from my writing, and my relative, whose dad died when she was little and whose mum is struggling as a single parent, wasn't going to get an education, so I was able to help educate her. I think that's a wonderful use of resources from woman to woman to open up opportunities which enable her to make choices that she didn't have before.

'A more global model is Emily's List. It has been attacked in both Australia and in the UK on class terms, which I think is absolutely idiotic. It's women contributing money to empower not just women politicians but to empower politicians who can then represent the poorest and most disempowered women in our communities. What other form of advancement do we have except for leaving it all to the state, which I do not think is the safest way to empower women because another administration can get swept in which does not have women's best interests at heart.

'What I want to question is that psychological reflex which I think goes deep into what turns girls into women in this culture. It goes like this. It is very dangerous and threatening for some women to get something because if they don't give back they will have something and I will have nothing. Whereas before we all had nothing. I'd like to point out that women are uniquely susceptible to that thinking. As sad as I am that the group in New York isn't thriving, a lot of women have better jobs because of it and I'm glad of that. In the African-American community not every initially impovershed black person who has gone on to the middle class goes back to the ghetto and gives back. Does that mean that it's bad that they're not living in poverty? Hell no!

'My baby's white and she's going to have a lot of options in this culture. Down the street in South East Washington, which is one of the most depressed areas of America, an African-American mother may be on public assistance, may be not supported by the father, certainly without daycare. It is sentimental for me to suggest that she and I share a deep bond that is political on the basis of our shared motherhood. It is right for me to act on her behalf because it's the right thing to do but not because there's some cosmic bond between us that's any deeper than the cosmic bond between me and the homeless guy down the street who doesn't have a baby. I feel a very deep sense of allegiance to women simply because they're women and therefore get left out of things. That's where a lot of my loyalties lie but I do think it's dangerous to sentimentalise any allegiance because that turns into chauvinism sooner or later. Then you get into this messed-up feminist organising principle of whose reality is the defining reality of how we feel this bond of sisterhood. Is it that we are all victims? Okay, well that unifies us in a way but that's dangerous and sentimental because I'm not as victimised as the woman down in South East Washington. Is it that we're all able to give birth? What about the ones of us who aren't interested in giving birth or who are not able to give birth? It gets immediately into very rocky territory philosophically.

'*Fire with Fire* is saying that the millennia in which women are subordinated are over if you choose to make them be over in political terms. The hardest thing will be conceptually for us to start thinking of women as the ones who run things and letting go of the self-image that being a woman means being the reactor to events beyond our control.

NAOMI WOLF

'I don't just write books, I do a lot of activism, but I don't think I'll ever run for office. For now I'd like to finish these two books and I still dream about getting my doctorate. I mean that literally. I want to raise my daughter. Oh God, look at her. She's better than any video game. That gaze. For a long time I felt that she didn't really know who I was except a pair of breasts. But just last night she was giving me this look and it lasted for a long time. I said, "David, what's wrong? Why is she looking like that?" He said, "Naomi, she's in love." It didn't occur to me. I hope that we'll have another baby. I want to start a catalogue or a clearing house of wonderful books and toys for girls so that girls her age and younger will have terrific empowering books and toys for growing up which we didn't.

'I want to keep speaking, which I enjoy very much. I think this book about female desire is going to be a whole new, very interesting conversation. I'm not looking forward to the controversy on that one but I have to accept that this is the way my life appears to go.

'All my books are saying that women are much more powerful than we've ever realised, so let's look at how that is. I think that women are far more sexually powerful than the current framework in which we discuss desire allows. Most women intuit this, they remember it at some deep level, but feel that somehow they're monsters because they feel this great life force to be excessive compared to how nice girls are supposed to behave. I think that's worth looking at. In Australia they have seen too much of a schism between the individual and the collective in my work. Ninety per cent of the recommendations that I made at the end of the last book are about collective action. I think that women certainly need to gain power individually and collectively. I don't see a contradiction. Emily's List is the biggest lobbying group in the country now, that's a hugely big deal. Emily's List decides who gets elected in many ways and that's with only six million dollars. Imagine what they could do with sixty million. Literally a national coup is within our grasp. So we all have to say, "It's up to me, it's up to us." The backlash is continuing but we're turning so many corners so fast and we've got to start noticing it. The United States just decided that it will allow refugees from sexual violence to claim immigrant status. That's a big deal. The violence against women Act got passed. This is where I'm going to break forth and scream. It is a little frustrating to write books that are met with howls of outrage and disbelief only to have it become the conventional boring wisdom two years later. Two years ago I told the feminist community that it had to stop thinking in partisan terms because feminist issues were going to become bipartisan, that it would lose its constituency, because the Right was going to start talking about women's issues. Some of them howled me out of the room and now we're seeing that one of the reasons the Republicans got elected in the United States was because they started to talk about women's issues. Feminist organisations can no longer rely on a constituency based on seeing Republicans or Conservatives as the sexist party. We'd better figure that one out because we're going to win or lose the next election on the basis of that.

'Feminists of my own community were appalled at me for talking about women who might not be pro-choice but who care about women's issues. And yet that voting bloc is determining the next election because we've seen, as I predicted, that there are plenty of women in this country who are not pro-choice but who don't want to get raped, who don't want to get beaten up, who want rapists to be locked up for a long time, who want equal pay, who want equal status and they're not necessarily a bunch of Stepford wives. That's my warning against seeing feminism as a partisan issue rather than a human rights issue.

'The other thing that needs to be done is to make the fight sexy and fun. All my heroines and heroes did that. I'm just reading Emma Goldman's letters to her boyfriend. She's the one who said, "If I can't dance it's not my revolution." Martin Luther King was always saying, "Walk in love." He did. There is a Vietnamese peace activist who says, "We are not our suffering."

'Revolutions and revolutionaries can be joyful. Gloria Steinem was really important to me when I was growing up because I was looking for a role model of a woman who was brave and strong and fearless and joyful. I think Gloria walks in love. She's generous, she's open-hearted.

'As a young girl growing up you want to feel that once you get to equality there'll be happiness there. You see some visible feminists who seem very bitter. The sad question to ask is, "If your equality is so great, why are you so bogged down?" There have been plenty of times when I have been bitterly unhappy and thought, "The battle is not worth it, it's just not worth it, I'm going home now." But ultimately the struggle for justice is a joyful thing to spend your life doing. It's life-affirming.

'I read Phyllis Chesler's work and I respect it. Kate Millett's analysis is first-rate. I thought *Revolution from Within* got a bad rap. I actually think Gloria Steinem very much achieved in that book what she said she valued, which was a pedagogy of the inclusive. She actually addresses some very complex and sophisticated ideas in very clear and simple language, which critics tend to scoff at because they're insecure; and her insistence on a kind of spiritual truth, that comes from within, scared people in the chattering classes who very much base their self-esteem on being cynical, being critical, being ironic, being distant and being not spiritual. Her emphasis on childhood, which I think a lot of people carry deep wounds from, made that book almost a test case of how truths that hit too close to home are often dealt with more harshly than plain bad writing is. I don't think it was a stupid departure for her. I think that properly read it was a very political book. It's true that before you can have a wall coming down in the East, each person who brings about the fall of the wall has to have some inner shift that makes it possible for them to think that it's time for the wall to come down. I think that history will be much kinder to that book than her contemporaries have been.

'I think Alice Walker is a lovely writer and a lovely essayist. She's also a role model. The position of the public intellectual, which was so well established in the nineteenth century in England particularly, has really been on the decline. Now in this country it's primarily African-American men and women who still practise a kind of public instructive prose. Her essays are valuable because she does weave together the lyrical, the narrative and the didactic.

'You ask me: "Why is there no British or Australian equivalent of these American women?" All I can suggest is that British misogyny expressed by the male cultural elite is more scathing than it is in just about any other country I've been to. It is much easier for me to make my case in Britain, get on a plane and go home, than to have to live with the British press and get my sense of identity from that community. There's a kind of sexism in the press, both highbrow and lowbrow, in Britain that you just can't get away with in any other English-speaking country. I think that's what shrivels the confidence of some British women. It's terrifying. I've met some amazing young British feminists but it's much less threatening for a culture to import its feminism than to let a home-grown commentator take the stage. Many of these English-speaking countries import their feminists and then send them home. You suggest that in Australia it may be the tall poppy syndrome, cutting down your successful people, especially successful women.

'In terms of the press creating a younger feminist versus older feminist dynamic, it's always tempting to look at divisive tactics in the press as being anti-feminist or gendered, as they so often are. But in this case I think there's an inbuilt drama to a younger generation rebelling against or resisting or revising the truisms of an older generation. That's been true with the battle of the classics versus the moderns and it's been true of the last generation. I don't think it's innately gendered for the media to play that up although, of course, there's always an element of divide and conquer in the coverage of feminist issues. When a young man or a young male movement is overturning or challenging an older male establishment, drama is acted out. It's Oedipal and it's about celebrating the continuity of male power and, ultimately, it's about the updating and revising of male power. Whereas when there are differences of opinion, as there are right now between younger and older feminists, the press tends to say, "Look how weak they are, look how they can't even agree," rather than, "Look at what a vibrant movement it is that renews itself in every generation."

'I don't think there's a lot of disagreement about what inequality looks like. I think any feminist worth his or her salt wants women to have 52 per cent of access, power, money, not to be raped, not to be beaten, not to be discriminated against in the workplace. So let's nod to these continuities. I do think that there is quite a significant shift in thinking going on right now, though, which goes basically like this, which is a summary of some of the argument I made in *Fire with Fire*. The thrust, at least in the United States in the '70s, of much of feminism for that brief, shining moment when it was a popular and populist movement, was egalitarian, it was reformist, it was aimed at access to power and equality. During the evil '80s, as Susan Faludi has so eloquently pointed out, there was a countermeasure against women and in that time some of the aspects of '70s into '80s feminism, that are now being challenged, came to predominate. What predominated in the '80s, when straightforward egalitarianism seemed more and more out of favour, was reflexive stress on looking at the exclusion of women and a reflexive suspicion of looking at how women have been able or can try to or do have access to power that they're not using or can use more effectively. Alongside this there was a critique of sexuality that was often centred on the work of Catherine McKinnon and Andrea Dworkin but which was very influential and which tended to universalise what was dark and oppressive and scary about heterosexual relations. It made suspect in some ways a pleasure-loving assertion of heterosexuality. That's what we women of my age and younger inherited as the feminism establishment, which can produce a pretty grim and sometimes paralysing world view.

'The bonus of that kind of world view is that you know your enemy. You have a clear enemy, it's unified. There is a dogma. You know who your friends are and who your allies are. It's very, very seductive in that way. And let's face it, there are conspiracies against women. I mean, I think that *The Beauty Myth* was very much written in that tradition and it doesn't mean it's inaccurate. Women are systematically brutalised, tortured, raped. All of that is true but now this is what we have to do. Women do have a preponderance of political power. In Western democracy women are moving up from 59 per cent to 73 per cent of the dollar. Younger women's earnings are equal to younger men's earnings now. There is a lot of power we're not using and I think that what's starting to happen to younger women is a critique of the kind of universalising of patriarchies that are entirely hostile to women and a passionate interest in looking at how we can use the power we have. The fact is that history has moved on from twenty years ago when Ms magazine was saying that the judicial system is completely anti-woman, and the best thing we can do is to boycott the wedding of an alleged rapist. That may have made sense twenty years ago when that observation could well have been largely true. But to do that now when feminist jurisprudence is at the forefront, when there are women judges and women attorneys transforming the judicial system, is a kind of despairing. It's almost a historically inaccurate position to take. That is the shift I see and that I hope is happening.'

As Naomi was going down in the lift with me, I asked what being famous was like.

'There's this assumption that lives change radically when you enter the public eye. You get a lot of mail and attention from the press and have a busy schedule and a public persona. But it shouldn't affect your everyday life if you have commonsense. We mostly hang out with parents of little kids. We're going to a baseball game tonight with our friends and five or six babies and toddlers. It's a life that I think most people who value being a family in a community with their neighbours would identify with. Yes, it has been very interesting to be able to meet some of the people who make the headlines, but that's not real life. Real life is going to Fresh Fields supermarket to do our shopping, real life is the mornings that I spend with the baby, reading the paper and getting her dressed for the day. I look after her in the morning, she has a baby-sitter in the afternoons when I work on my book. In the evenings my husband takes over and I rest. That's my life.'

As we stood on the pavement waiting to flag down a cab she told me she was hoping to go to Brazil in the summer to talk about her books. Would her husband and Rosa go with her?

'He won't but I haven't decided about the baby yet.'

She jiggled the baby up and down. Rosa smiled.

NAOMI WOLF

'You've been to Australia though, haven't you, baby.'

'Very good *in utero* influence too,' I said, like a true patriot.

Those on the far right of politics have a lot to learn from Naomi Wolf. If you want girls to turn out to be good and contented wives and mothers, happy to live in a nuclear family, you must ensure that they have a feminist mother and father, a hippie upbringing, total sexual freedom and a high-quality education in a multi-racial, coeducational state high school. It's simple really.

12

INTERLUDE III

10 pm: 'My' apartment, West 69th Street, New York City

Having caught a cab to the Washington airport, boarded the next shuttle to JFK, got another cab to my apartment, had a shower, poured a glass of wine, switched on the television and stretched my tired body out on the bed, the phone rang.

'What fresh hell is this?' I said aloud.

'Hello.'

It was Nancy Grossman. The Cadillac Queen. 'Quickly. Put your telly onto C-Span, you're on.'

'What do you mean?'

'It's some conference and you're sitting there in the background, making faces. It's so funny.'

And sure enough, on the C-Span channel in a replay of this morning's forum, every time one of three women on my side of the room spoke, and they spoke a lot, there I was in the wide shot sitting behind them reacting to what was being said; smiling, frowning, yawning, scratching my nose, taking my coat on and off (still having trouble with my personal thermostat), appearing to sleep. I have Betty Friedan to thank for my being immortalised on film at the Women, Men and Media Forum, Washington, on 31 May 1995, performing a satirical version of Marcel Marceau and a Greek chorus. It was not exactly how I imagined my fifteen minutes of fame.

13
ALICE WALKER

Day Eight, 3.30 pm: The Lowell Hotel, East 63rd Street, New York City

I had woken up with a blinding headache that made me feel bung-eyed. I was trying to run through my notes on Alice Walker but the words kept jumping on the page. The appointment for my interview was 2 pm in Brooklyn. It was 85 degrees Fahrenheit, which is hot in New York City, and I stayed in bed under the overhead fan, feeling like a dowager with the vapours in a Somerset Maugham story. The reality was I would soon have to get up and go to the bank to get some more cash on my credit card. Not something women characters in Maugham's stories ever had to do.

The phone rang. It was Joan, Alice Walker's assistant in San Francisco, informing me that Alice had moved from her daughter's house in Brooklyn to The Lowell Hotel on East 63rd Street. Could I meet her there? 'Certainly,' I said, grateful that I wouldn't have to endure a long, hot taxi ride to Brooklyn in the chaos of Friday afternoon traffic. Half an hour later the phone rang again. Could the appointment be changed to 3 pm? 'Fine,' I said. 'How about 3.30?' 'No,' she said, '3 pm is fine.' I hung up and lay down on the bed. At least it gave me more time to try and rid myself of the headache. I took another painkiller. The phone rang again. Joan said, '3.30 is best.' 'Great,' I said and collapsed back on the pillow.

Later when I walked up Columbus Avenue to the bank it was still very hot. I stood in a queue, zombie-like, overdosed on headache tablets. After what seemed an eternity my turn came, and the woman behind the counter refused to give me any money without seeing my passport. I searched frantically in my bag. My passport was back in the apartment. I had no time to go back and get it, come back to the bank, get the money and get to my appointment. I pleaded with her. She said, 'Would you like to speak to the manager?' I said, 'I'd be delighted.'

After five minutes of going over my story with the bank manager, he said he was sorry but I'd have to show my passport. They were the rules.

'But I need the money to pay for the cab to get me to the interview with Alice Walker. You know, *The Color Purple?*' He was not impressed.

'I have a terrible headache. I simply can't go rushing out in the heat. I'm pleading with you.'

He was unmoved. I was teetering on the edge of hysteria and pain when the bloke from the wine bar where I had bought my South Australian wine said, 'Hi there. What's the problem?' I explained. He said to the bank manager, 'I can vouch for her. She's Australian and she just lives up the street.'

The bank manager smiled and gave me my cash. It is a truth, universally acknowledged, that good wine can save your life.

The foyer of The Lowell Hotel was cool and quiet and dark. If only I could have laid myself down on the floor and pressed my poor forehead and my flushed cheeks to its marble chill. Just for a few silent minutes. Surely they wouldn't mind.

Instead I said, 'I'm here to see Alice Walker,' and duly caught the lift to suite 14A. Alice opened the door wearing a long batik dress and no shoes. She looked tired. We were going to be a great pair.

'So you'd had enough of staying at your daughter's place.'

'Oh,' she said, 'you know, the only comfortable place to sit at my daughter's is on the bed. And I've just been re-visiting all my siblings and that's meant sleeping in so many lumpy, uncomfortable beds. I'm so tired.'

I promised it wouldn't be a long interview and said if my eyes looked peculiar it wasn't because I was on hard drugs.

'For me being a writer wasn't a conscious decision. When I was at Sarah Lawrence as a student in the late '60s, I suddenly realised that I had a complete book that I had written. I was traumatised having got pregnant to someone that I had actually broken up with, and this was before abortion was legal, so I had to find an abortionist. I had no idea where to go and so, in that period of real conflict and transformation, as it turned out from someone who didn't know what to do or if she could do it, to someone who did it anyway and lived to tell the tale, I realised that I had written this book. It was my first book of poems and I gave it to my teacher, Muriel Rukheyser, who was a really fine poet herself. She died some years ago but what I realised even before that was, when I was really feeling conflicted and alone and scared and needed to know what to do, I would write something. It didn't necessarily tell me what to do, but it was an activity and activity is really an antidote to all kinds of scary things like inertia and feelings of despair. So my first book of poems, *Once*, was published after I graduated and the first section was all haiku because I had discovered Zen and Esau and Basho and Japanese haiku poetry and loved it.

'I wasn't aiming at absolute precision. There is a whole little formula where it has to be so many words. It's a good way to teach it, it's a good discipline. Mine didn't quite do that but they were still haiku, and they were really very good for me because somehow I was able to write about my feelings, about nature, with that sense of immediacy where, instead of explaining, you're absolutely showing things like a snapshot. And that's how I thought of it. A lot of them I wrote while I was in Africa and then I came back to finish my last year at college. That's how I started. The editor that Muriel sent the work to took this book before I graduated and then published it afterwards.

'Gloria Steinem is beginning to write poems. In fact I read one of her poems when she was in San Francisco last time and it was a great thrill for me because she's always been reading my poems when she speaks, and she uses them in her work, and I have wanted to do the same. So finally in her last book there's a poem and I read it while I was introducing her. We admire each other. She has wonderful balanced skills of public ways that I don't even aspire to because I'm not as fond of the public as she is, but I admire her grace and she's an incredible fund raiser for women.

'I liked *Revolution from Within* very much. I like Kate Millett's work a lot. I think she's a wild, wonderful, crazy woman who is very insightful. I remember reading *Sexual Politics* long ago and saying, "Yes, this is true." I love her novels. I loved *Sita*, I thought it was wonderful. I think she's very brave in the way she wrestles with her own frailty, her own craziness, almost literally. I think people like her, however difficult they may be for other people, and I understand that sometimes she can be that way, lets in a lot of light through the cracks. And how necessary was that analysis of Mailer and Miller.

'*The Women's Room* didn't grab me really. It's been years since I read it but it didn't go bang, bang. It didn't connect with my life. I read Susan Faludi's book, I thought it was so good, I wrote a blurb for it. Naomi's book I decided I could only hear on tape. I bought *The Beauty Myth*. I haven't got to *Fire with Fire* because I have decided that at this point there are books that I am not going to read. I'll listen to them, maybe, but I'm just not going to read them because I don't have time and there are other things I want to read.

'Right now I'm reading a lot of Buddhist thought. I just bought a very interesting book yesterday by a psychotherapist who was trying to bridge the gap between Buddhism and psychotherapy. I'm also reading a book called *Loving Kindness*. It's about natural Buddhist practice. I've read a lot of Jung. I like him a lot.

'We always lived in the country and I was just there last week and was able to see once again how really beautiful it is there – the hills, big old oak tress and pine trees. It's right in the middle of Georgia. This is the Deep South. Very hot in the summer, wonderful peach trees everywhere. My sister and I went to a roadside stand and we got peaches, not from my little area but just a bit below it, where it's just a little hotter – peaches, melons, peanuts, pecans. There's a section near us where we grow a certain kind of onion, bidahlia onions, very good onions. So there's a sense in my growing up, a sense of having wonderful, really good-tasting food. It was just completely taken for granted that everyone would have a huge garden so that you would always have excellent stuff to eat. I realise now that it was all organic. It was all healthy.

'Recently I was talking to my brothers and we were all saying how wonderful it was that our parents were together because I see how few people seem to have had that experience of two parents always in the house. When my older siblings were growing up my parents were healthy and very much in love and the house, I think, was a very happy one. When I grew up, because I was the last of eight children, by then my parents were sickly, especially my father, and they had seen a number of their dreams really destroyed. So they were very different people.

ALICE WALKER

'My mother was happy, because her nature was a happy one and she could pull herself out of anything just by her will. My father was not, I would say, a very happy man by then. He had bronchitis, he had diabetes, he had heart trouble, a long list of illnesses, and he was married to my mother who was very strong-willed, and very anti-sexist. He was a sexist person because every man in that area was sexist, and so were many of the women, and of course he was always up against racism because the white people were very racist.

'My father and my mother were both farmers and dairy people. They milked dozens of cows every day. My brothers helped with this. I did some farming, I picked some cotton, not very much, because by then the whole economy was changing and people like my parents weren't able to make much of a living, making crops and share cropping, so they were often forced to leave and go to the north. We never went but most of our relatives went to the north, or they went somewhere else looking for work.

'I started school at four because my mother would have had to take me to the fields with her and she couldn't really work carrying me and looking after me. So she asked her friend who taught first grade to let me come in and be in her class. In fact I have just spent a wonderful morning with this woman. She's eighty-one years old now, and we were talking about what it was like, and she said that I was fine, that I kept up with the other children and I seemed very cheerful. I think it was because she herself was such a sweet woman, and she still is, she's just weary. And this woman is so amazing, because all these years whenever I go to see her she always wants to talk about my life. She says, "I remember when you were born, and I went there two days after and I brought you some clothes, and your mother was doing this and your grandmother – my grandmother was a midwife – was doing blah blah." This time I was determined to find out who she was before I knew her. So I asked her about her mother and tears came to her eyes, and she said, "Well my mother died when I was twenty-one years old, she died during the change of life, she had a haemorrhage," and then she looked at me and at eighty-one, she's barely creeping around, and she said, "You know, I've been sixty years without a mother." And she obviously feels it just as much now as then. I was so glad I asked her about her life. I'm going to go back and talk to her some more because I realised I had been so good with this woman who had such an impact on my life. So I was going to school every day with my older brothers and sisters. I loved it. We were all bright, everybody in my family is very bright.

'When I wasn't in school we were always running around playing, making up our own games. There was one game that we made that was like a foot see-saw, you put a board across a rock and one person would get on one end and one on the other and one would jump down on that end and toss the other way up and jump down and toss that one up. It was great fun, I loved it. And there were creeks and we would go wading and play in the water. I was specially treated being the youngest. I was called Baby Alice and I think I was hugged and kissed until I just had enough, until I couldn't take it any more. And they dragged me around everywhere, carrying me on their shoulders and they would chuck me under the chin and tell me how cute I was.

'But I think I really missed my mother. I never really understood that I had to go off to school because she had to go to work, and I think I just made the best of it. That was a pattern that continued through all my adolescence and teenage years. Because she always had to go off to work and I always had to do something else because she was working. And I was a child who greatly loved her and I still love her even though she died two years ago. So I think that was hard. Because of the economy, my siblings were working almost as slaves, so they left too. I have this sense of people always leaving, always from my child's view. For no reason they suddenly just disappeared. They had to go but this meant that every single relationship that I ever had with my siblings was interrupted by leaving.

'I've gone back to see who they really are, and to reaffirm that there was this period when we were really a family. I think it's something that is hard for my family to really understand. We often say that we have such dissension in our family and we don't know why. I think it's partly because of this. It has an economic political foundation which, because many of my siblings haven't studied and haven't learnt to think that way, they have just tended to think was because of our different personalities. But in each case I think there's the pain of having tense sibling relationships and loving each other and just not understanding why suddenly that person's disappeared. None of them had the education I had. Only one sister went away to university. My other sister did not go to college, she is a cosmetologist. One brother went to college, stayed for a couple of years and dropped out, and that was it.

'I was fortunate that I had grandparents who were interesting old people. They were mysterious because they had lives that I didn't know anything about, I only heard whispers. I was very curious because I knew them as sweet, old, patient people. It just amazed me that they had lovers and fights and that my grandfather carried a gun. Actually, my father's mother was murdered when my father was eleven. She was a very young woman. I think the impact that story had on me was that she had been murdered by someone who had wanted her to sleep with him. She'd said no and he had killed her. The mystery to me was that she was always blamed for her own murder. And that really is, I think, the foundation of my womanism.

'I sometimes use womanism instead of feminism. I don't always because it's the same thing except that it's black.

'But I just couldn't let that go. How could your own murder be your fault? Really. How could it? There she was saying all that she could say as a married woman with children, she was saying, "No, I can't go with you, I have five children." And this man shoots her anyway. And she died after a couple of days of great agony. I recently took her name as my middle name. Her name was Kate. Her ancestor was Irish on the white side. Anyway, so that's the beginning of me wondering why it's so different if you are a woman. If she had been a man, we would have heard a very different story.

'It didn't make me angry because she was just a picture on the wall. There were these old photographs that looked like paintings. She was a peach, the inside of a peach, this face; just hanging there. So of course this is a wonderful mystery to a child. "Who is this woman, why is she here?" "Oh, that's your grandmother Kate, she was killed by this man." I think my father really believed all the stories about his mother. His father was so traumatised by the murder that he then tried to figure out what she'd done to entice this thing. He passed this on to my father, who was much more sexist because of that than he would have been. In the role of protector he was always trying to protect his girls so this wouldn't happen to them. So that was a very defining event in all our lives.

'I had so much anger at my father. I once tried to knife him because he used to beat my sister, very much in the style of "trying to keep her pure, trying to keep her virtuous" and "trying to make sure she wasn't like his mother". And that meant in his mind that she couldn't go on dates, that she had to be kept right under his thumb. So she was constantly rebelling by sneaking around and so he would physically abuse her. I hated it. I just couldn't stand it. I was really little, about seven or eight, and I went and got the knife when they were fighting, when he was beating her up, and my mother was trying to get them separated and I was going to plunge it into his heart. But I only came up to his belt. I often think of that because I think that was also a defining moment in a very complex way. Suppose I had managed to kill him, what would that have done to my life? And at the same time it pointed to my need and my deep desire to assist and defend women against injustice. It once again affirmed what I loved so much about my mother, that she was a strong woman and that he could not physically best her. This was one of the greatest gifts that she gave all of her daughters, that unlike many women who could be battered, who could be cowed, who could be beaten, she could not be. Not by him anyway. By the system, but not by him.

'I think that it is very difficult for black children to blame their mothers because usually that's the only person they have. However, when they do reach a point where they can encounter in themselves the ability to blame, they often go overboard. Until a certain point she is blameless and then you began to see that maybe she wasn't and then you just dump everything on her. But generally speaking, I do think that in our culture the mother has been so clearly heroic. I mean it hasn't been any mystery what she's been up against. So it's been very difficult for children to blame her even when she is blamable. I am a mother and my daughter is blaming me regularly. But she has been brought up in a different culture. Well it is very painful, but what can you do? All I can say is I did my best. Her blaming hurts though. It does. A lot.

'In one of my stories, I quote this colonial white woman who had just made this very unconscionable generalisation about black people's lives, and it was really horrible because obviously she lived off their labour, their land. Her people had taken their land, eaten their food and worn their clothing, and then she says, "But black people have the secret of joy so, whatever we do to them, they will survive it." But you don't. Really, some people survive, but many people don't. I mean, look at Africa. So what the character Tashi learns in this book is true, that there is a certain degree of joy in resisting tyranny. That is wonderful. I mean, it's the same joy that the people in the French Revolution felt in the beginning before they tipped over into tyranny and craziness themselves. So I think there are kinds of joy in that resistance movement.

'I see myself as much more than a survivor. Much more. Because in my life there is a lot of joy and, again, I think that when you just survive there's a good feeling about that, but the best feeling of all is to really feel at home on the planet, connected to it in a way that is all yours. I do feel that. I have always felt that way.

'My background is that of a country person who woke up in the morning and ran outside and for miles there was nothing but just wonder, just trees giving fruit, and then leaving that and coming to somewhere like this, like New York, where it's very different but still full of wonder. You cannot deny that we live in an incredible, magic place. The world is almost too amazing to be believed and it's that feeling of wonder and happiness that I enjoy and want to share. That makes me more than a survivor, rather a celebrant and someone who is really happy to be in on this part of creation. Some people may call that a sentimental view, but I don't care. It makes absolutely no difference to me what anyone says and that's pretty much always been the case. It's not just my sense of myself but my sense of the enormity of what we're in that is so strong.

How could it possibly matter? I mean, it matters on the level of people not hiring you for a job, people not letting you into a restaurant to eat, people not letting you use a library, all of which I have experienced. But on the level of just how tiny people are in the scheme of things and how little anyone really matters, including me, it's ridiculous really to be concerned. Then, on the other hand, I have been called everything, so to be called sentimental is nothing.

'Even though my daughter is at the stage of blaming me, there's growth in that too. I went with her recently to the therapist with her father. She's twenty-five and as I was sitting there I was thinking, I love the therapist because she agrees with me at this point. She always says, "When you've done your best, what you do now is you shrug." So I think that even though this is painful, your child has to be reminded that the reason you went away from home was because she could no longer tolerate public school, where she was being threatened with beatings every day, so you had to go off and take two or three jobs you didn't want in order to put her in private school. This is all stuff they forget, they don't even know this really until you remind them. So you sit there and you listen to this long gripe about how you weren't there, and where were you, until finally you do say – and I do feel that to have brought her into this world where she can now eat the plums and the peaches and the pecans and the watermelon, and dance and be loved, that's no small thing. And that's what my mother did for me. And what her mother did for her. And whatever our failings, the gift outweighs that. And I think that some time in the future my daughter will really believe and comprehend that.

'I must say I do wonder how people continue to have children. I think there should be at least a moratorium on reproduction. I see no reason why people should continue to have children in the face of the disaster that has befallen us as a planet. I think that a moratorium worldwide would really help people to think again about what they are doing. I'm not even saying they'll never have them, but just have a moratorium. It says a lot about our honesty and integrity, it's just very selfish. What about the child? And what about having more than one? There's no reason to have more than one. And especially in the west where every one you have has to have a refrigerator and maybe two, and a car, maybe two. The forests will go, because they'll all have to have big old houses and wood and I just don't see the point. I understand that people want to experience the wonder of having a child but it seems very short-sighted.

'I had my first sexual experience when I was sixteen. I was indifferent. I don't remember it being especially momentous. Sex has not been a driving force in my life. For me, it's always about love. When I've tried not to combine love and sex, I've really felt very empty. I think it's because I always feel the need for a feeling of worship in lovemaking, the feeling of something being really sacred and close to you. Close to the blooming of a tree. I mean, it has to be something really as wondrous as everything else, it can't be less wondrous and, when it is, it just leaves me feeling very bored. I'd rather be doing something else like walking through forests of redwood trees, reading a good book or walking by the ocean and seeing something that really is arresting.

'I dated the same guy throughout my high school years and into college, and then I went out with another one and then I was married for ten years and then I was in a marriage-like relationship for thirteen. I always have very long relationships that are lots of work but are really deep. In fact, I was reminded of that when I went to the therapist with my daughter and her father, because our history is that in the '60s we married, and we were the first inter-racial married couple to live in Mississippi in this century. And it was a great strain. And you know just how much energy it took to do that and to have a child, and he was fighting all the racist laws as a lawyer and I was writing books and our love was very deep and really sustained us wonderfully for seven years. And then we just broke down. I had not lost respect for him or for his work and he had always supported mine, but there comes a time when you have been stared at too much and people have just presented too many obstacles. There are only so many laws that you can change before you start to feel like somebody else will have to take this on, it's too tiring. And it's very curious, though, because I think he was very aware that it was the best time of his life, because he was doing what was right. He's probably the bravest person I've ever known, and he was very attractive.

'Maybe our daughter wants us to understand that her life has been just as hard too, though different. We thought we had made her life so much easier than ours, so what could she possibly have to complain about? She said, "A lot." We had joint custody because that was the right thing to do. The old way, which was to have a child go with the mother, was just ridiculous. You have two parents, you don't have one. But, as it turned out, what this did for her was that it made her feel very split, like she was the only one who understood both places, because she was the only one. He went on to marry a Jewish woman who was very traditionalist, has never had a child, and then there was me – I was still outspoken and always was and she just couldn't conceive of my being able to take care of me and of us.

'So I sat there in the therapist's office and kept thinking, "Well, what more could we have done?" Should we have had her stay with me all the time, which she eventually did most of the time, or should she have just stayed with me for a couple of years, or should she have been with her father? That wouldn't have worked because he's really not there. The best thing, of course, is to have the mother and father both there. Anyway, she's twenty-five, I get back to that, she's twenty-five, she's graduated from Yale. There was an article in *Time* magazine in which she was named one of the fifty most important writers coming along in America. And that's what I was really working on by going back to see each of my siblings, because I know there is love underneath the strife. And I wanted to recollect it.

'Actually, the way this started was that my favourite brother has leukemia and he wasn't expected to live longer than six weeks. This was several months ago and I met with him and that brought up all of the ways in which I loved them, not just him, although he is special. I think they couldn't help but be a little envious of me, mainly in terms of privilege, what I can buy and where I can go, but at the same time I have been extremely supportive of them and their children. So again I don't know what more I could do and whatever negative feelings they have, they will just have to deal with.

'At university I studied literature, philosophy, history. My first job was in the welfare department as a social worker. Like many of my generation in the '60s, we thought that we could help people like that, but you could never really help them enough. And that was just so frustrating. So I would do that in the day and then I would come home. I lived in a flat with another woman and I would get my old typewriter out on its stand and write stories of life. Boy, was that exhausting. So I guess I felt like I would always have a "job" job and I would write at night, and I actually did that for a while. It was just necessary. I felt that there were so many things that I needed to understand and I needed to work on them in a way that would permit me to go deep rather than skim, and the problem with having a "job" job was that you're so beat at the end of the day that it's hard to go deep. You've spent the whole day trying to get furniture for a mob of nine and they have just come from Alabama and she's a mess and the children are sick and you just don't have it at the end of the day. I did it as long as I could. I never held on to many of those "job" jobs very long. Six months at the most.

'I went to Mississippi and I started to register voters. This was in the full swing of the civil rights movement and I taught and I wrote history texts for the teachers and the children but, even then, even though I loved that, the bureaucracy got to me. And finally I couldn't do it. I hate meetings of all kinds. I just find them tedious and boring and I get sleepy the minute I sit there. Anyway, then I taught at the university, at two black colleges. That was good, I liked that. I had really incredible students, all movement oriented, and they were very responsive, and so I did that and I wrote my first novel and I had my first baby all by the time I was twenty-five.

'It turned out to be just fine and then I wrote an article for the *New York Times* magazine, just talking about how basically boring it was to be in Mississippi. I had gone there in the first place because I always felt really insulted that you could live in a country and there were some parts of it that you were afraid to be, so anyway, that was my thing. I was going to Mississippi where others were too scared to live. I had done that and so now I was free to go. So Gloria read this and, somehow, I don't know whether she called or wrote or whatever, and she just said, "If you do leave you have got to come and be a contributing editor on Ms magazine." I thought, "Okay," and I came. We bought a ruin, a limestone, four-storey, eight fireplaces, sweetly elegant old nightmare ruin that we restored. It took all the money from my husband's law practice. We did it and I thought it was just the most beautiful house I had ever seen. But it gave me a deep sense of freedom to leave it because I had really created this incredible dwelling. I remember the fireplace in my study had great, beautiful deep green tiles and there was all this beautiful woodwork. But it was so nice to know that you could choose your life, make a new start. So I stayed with Ms magazine for I think four years or so. I would only go in once a week and I bought a little house. I earned a modest living. Then we sold the first house and I had my share to help me live on and then I got a salary from Ms. And I have spoken and lectured in every state from Iowa to Idaho.

'I had a little kid and was by myself so I hit the trail and that's what it was. Then I decided that even though we had this darling little house – which was a sliver of a house, it was very narrow, about 12 feet, but really sweet – this is madness. Now Gloria makes New York feel like a village. When I'm here I hang out with her, cruising, dancing, eating in the restaurants, going to plays, having a wonderful time but, otherwise, give me my own little place, let me sit on my swing and look out into a million trees and that's me. So I packed up my few suitcases and I left my house to some friends who rented it from me and I left my daughter with her father and I went to California, where I had a lover. It was not easy, circumstances were terrible, but in the end we are still very good friends. I just talked about this with my former husband. I told him that he just completely withdrew from me and finally, after fifteen years, I asked him why, and he said he didn't really know. Anyway, this lover has grown in leaps and bounds over the years until he was a wonderful person. I have had women lovers as well. Because I have fallen in love with whoever I fall in love with.

'It's all about your spirit. My spirit has always been about collusion, curiosity, and loving the spirit of whoever. I love being this way. So then I moved into a tiny apartment and lived there very happily because it was a co-operative working-class place. I wrote *The Color Purple* and I won the Pulitzer. So I sent Rebecca out to find a house for us, and she did. Winning the Pulitzer was not something beyond my wildest dreams. I really don't keep up with prizes, very much. Winning it changed my life but the problem with that is that now "Pulitzer Prize winner" is almost a part of my name and it seems to imply that my work has value only because of this prize, and that's total bullshit. Who are these Pulitzer people? Are they people that I really care about that much? I don't know. In other words, you can only be honoured by people that you honour. It's taken years to think about the ways in which winning a prize of this sort has meaning. And it has meaning mainly because it means something to other people in terms of recognising something that without the label they perhaps wouldn't see.

'Most of the women writers have one book for which they are known. I think it's better that people have something to grab onto, and then maybe they can move onto other things. That is true of me too. I think of the books that I've loved by authors, there is usually one that goes to my heart, and after that one I say, "Gee, this is an interesting mind, this is a great heart, let me see what else she has done," and then I go on. The result of winning the Pulitzer was a mixed bag, actually. More books are sold, therefore more income. This was very good because my mother had become an invalid and needed care, so that I felt that I could do that. And in the beginning all the letters from readers were interesting, but over time it was really more than I could deal with. For a while I would just put everything in a room and shut the door on it, but now I have this great assistant, Joan, she's wonderful, she saves my life daily, what an angel. She's just the sweetest woman in the world. But before I got her I had inducted a good friend of mine to try and help me and it was a total disaster.

So I decided that I would not have anyone. I would just throw the stuff in a room and shut the door. I did that and one day Gloria, bless her heart, said, "No, you can't do that, you have to have someone to help you," and I said, "Oh, after this disaster with my friend I can't think about it." She said, "Well you should think about it." She thought about it and she called her friend Sidney and Sidney said, "I've thought of the perfect person," and it was Joan, who was changing her life, and that was many years ago. Now it's terrific. But I think I will one day get back to just closing the door, because there is a certain joy in that too. Not the bills, because then people come and harass you, but all the other stuff that people keep asking you to do, write me this, say that, go here, go there, make up this, like you are a company.

'I don't know if you know who Margaret Walker is, but she's this wonderful, seventy-year-old writer down in Mississippi, and I think maybe from her I learned this possibility of just ignoring people, because that's what she does. She just literally ignores them and thinks no more about it. As she will tell you, "I never answer letters, I never know whether you've sent it or not because I don't bother to open them." And I think that is just so good of her. When you look at her life, she raised four children, taught all her life in colleges and had a long marriage to some man, and then she wrote an amazing book called *Jubilee* about her grandmother who was a slave, and it took her twenty years to write that book. In fact when I met Langston Hughes, he told me once he went to visit Margaret and she wanted to show him the book, and the manuscript and the sheets of paper were everywhere. She had to go and collect them all together – they were everywhere because of all the children and all her duties.

'I sometimes say that by now I have met everybody I want to meet anyway. The high point for me in the last couple of years was meeting Fidel Castro. Now that's somebody I wanted to meet. Because I love the Cubans and I love the Cuban revolution. I've just been gung-ho for them since the '60s. I was a great fan of Fidel's and Che Guevara and Celia Sanchez and all of them. I met him because I was actually doing something for the children of Cuba. I was delivering medicines and we delivered such a big bundle that everybody in Cuba was just really happy and that's how we met. I liked him a lot. He's extremely human – very smart and very warm and philosophical, and I really appreciate that in leaders, that they are real people. I've never seen anyone go through so many unplanned emotional states in one meeting as he did, just unselfconsciously – angry, sad, tearing of hair, practically – and then laughing, and then just being very friendly.

'Fame is good for opening doors, which is good for fund raising. I used to do an awful lot of that and that was clearly because of *The Color Purple* and the movie and all of that. It had its problems, but overall I liked it. And my sister founded the Color Purple Foundation in Eatonton, and so we have adopted classes and we have provided pencils and paper and whatever else they needed. Our first little class graduated from grammar school. Eatonton is where I was born, it's in the middle of the state of Georgia.

'The bravest people I've met? Well I think Fidel is very brave. I think Gloria [Steinem] is very brave. I think Winnie Mandela's very brave. Oh, she's always had bad press and they are really determined to get rid of her. Now that's probably the only person that I can think of who I would really like to meet now. I've met Nelson. I would like to meet Winnie, but not just to meet her – I would like to know what her side of the story is because some of these articles are so weird and they are fussing at her. She was complaining because Nelson's government was rolling out the red carpet for Queen Elizabeth, wining and dining her and her entourage while millions of black South Africans are going hungry. Well I can understand that, I mean, why should anyone wine and dine the Queen? I don't get it. I mean, not in South Africa, but actually, as far as I'm concerned, not anywhere else either because you're really wining and dining the very symbol of the colonial presence that has done you in.

'What are the things I've done that I'm really proud of? I stood by my mother until her death. I have put my daughter through the best educational systems in the west, although I have many reservations about its goodness. I have been a very good friend to my friends and I have been very supportive of organisations and groups that help children and women and men. In terms of my work, I have taken on everything that had my name on it, everything that I felt that I could do and that I could do really well. I feel quite good about my life. I used to just run all over the place and do every speech and every rally, but I don't do that much any more. After working on the issue of female genital mutilation for almost five years I was pretty tired. There are ways in which that particular subject is so draining, and just thinking about how no matter what you do, how many children you save from this, there are thousands of women who were having this experience and what this means for them.

'It was after finishing the novel and then making the film that I knew I needed a sabbatical, and that's what I took. I just had a year of doing very few public things. Instead I got a dog, Marley, a Labrador puppy, and I spent a lot of time in the country. Out of that time in sabbatical came another book which was published in the winter; it was my accounting of what it felt like to have my novel made into a film in Hollywood.

'I'm prolific, but totally without trying to be. I don't really sit down for three hours or four hours every day. I do it when I feel it. Although that's not always true. I remember when I started *The Temple of My Familiar*, I had just thought, "Oh, I really should start on this," but I didn't really know what to start on and how to do it, and then one day I just made the decision that I would just sit up in bed, grab my pad and start working, and then every day I did that. I do everything in bed. So I started out forcing myself to do it, but it ended up being my longest novel. The world that you create just keeps getting more and more interesting.

'I would not describe myself as ambitious. Ambition is more artificial. I would describe myself as blooming. I mean the self that I feel in myself is one that blooms rather than climbs. You have to set some goals, you have to say, "Well, I'm going to work on this book for a year, two years at the most, because of contracts and deadlines." So you have to have order, but in terms of just being ambitious, I mean, why would I be ambitious? Because competitively I don't feel that.

'The saddest times in my life, oh, I don't want to go there. Too recent. I'm at that point, I keep trying to remember who wrote it, you know, where the whole point of life is to get to where you began and know it for the first time. T.S. Eliot. That's exactly where I am. And I felt that so strongly on this pilgrimage through my childhood, staying places with my siblings, that I see them for who they are and know them in a way that I don't think I could have known them when I was younger. Even reconnecting with my former husband, I could see him in a different way and really acknowledge what we were up against. It was too much for any two people. For me what has been really interesting in this period is that I have had to really look at the ways in which I caused my own problems. I mean, it's not that I didn't know I caused them earlier, but I was not willing to work on them as much as I am now. This isn't new but there's a way in which it feels new. I am really committed to harmlessness and I can see how I have really hurt other people. Sometimes it's inevitable, but I mean to the extent that you can help it, I think you really have to work on it.

'I've always had what I now recognise as a physical chemical imbalance so I've been plagued by very deep depressions, and out of these depressions I have really been very hard on people, especially people close to me. My lovers, my daughter too, and when I would withdraw she wouldn't really know what was going on. I decided that the time had come, in a recent relationship where this had cracked it up, to really try to get to the root of it. Not everybody has chemical imbalances, but there are other things in life that are possibly fixable, but you don't really let yourself be taken to that point of saying and doing the work, because for whatever reason, you think, "Well, you don't love me etcetera." But now I really feel very committed to doing what I can to be sure that my presence in the lives of the people who I love is not a wounding one. Ever.

'You develop habits. They are the way you deal with things and they are familiar. The only problem is that they really screw up other people, because other people don't always understand. When I was with my former husband, I was telling him about the same issue and he typically came to my defence and said, "But I understood, I knew there were times when you couldn't really help it," and I said, "Yeah, I know you did and that was really great, but what about me?" Because at some point it really isn't about people accommodating you, it's about you trying to take control of what you can control in your behaviour and not inflicting it on people. The way I dealt with it, often, was just to disappear, and it worked pretty well. But then maybe with menopause we have all kinds of other things happening and so we don't have the energy to disappear.

'I fought oestrogen tooth and nail. Tooth and nail. I said, "This is a natural process." But I've only taken it for a month and I think I do feel better. It's a very interesting time though. The story I was telling you about my first-grade teacher's mother, there are ways in which we need to be reminded that this change is a difficult one, and is life-threatening sometimes, in various ways. I mean, her mother literally died. I haven't died yet, but I have these amazingly complex emotional feelings through which other people have had to try and walk, and they have been blown apart. I just really don't want to do that.'

After the second side of the tape clicked off I knew she'd had enough and needed a nap. So did I. She opened the door to the side balcony that came off the living room and we stepped outside. Standing there side by side we had the whole sweep of the city before us. But Alice was looking elsewhere.

'Look at those peonies about to bloom,' she exclaimed. 'And those beautiful roses on the trellis next door.' It was true. In the middle of New York, suspended on the fourteenth floor, small plots of spring flowers were blooming. The air was clear. Beneath us millions of people were going about their business and their lives in a few square miles of city. Before I left I showed her the tablets I was experimenting with for menopause and she wrote the name down. We laughed at the fact that we who pretended to be such worldly feminists were really just hostages to our hormones. And our ignorance.

Okay, Germaine, so you were right about the change. And it is time to talk about it and share our experiences.

It was noticeably cooler when I stepped into the street. My headache had almost lifted and I realised I'd had nothing to eat all day. I walked across the road into Madison Avenue where a little French restaurant caught my eye; a bowl of broccoli soup, an avocado, string bean and grapefruit salad with mustard vinaigrette, a glass of red wine, a bottle of Evian and a cappuccino later I was a new woman. Well, almost.

14
KATE MILLETT

Day Nine, 11 am: Her farm, Poughkeepsie, New York State

There had been some worrying calls back and forth between me and Kate Millett, who has a loft in the Bowery and a farm in Poughkeepsie, two hours drive north of Manhattan. We settled on an interview at the farm and Jane Galvin-Lewis offered to drive me.

At 9 am Jane was sitting out the front of my hotel in her Jeep with a little porkpie hat on her head. I had not seen her at all in the last week as she had been performing in a play in Atlanta, but she had rung me often to check on my progress. Like a lot of people who live in New York City, for whom the choice of which route to take anywhere could become at least a thirty-minute discussion, she wanted to talk to me about the best way to get to Poughkeepsie. I, however, had a list of directions from Kate and refused to negotiate alternatives. Jane agreed to follow them, reluctantly.

Our two-hour drive was, as she kept saying, 'a dream run', which meant that we could talk about things other than the traffic. Jane is not someone who meditates while being forced to queue in long lines on freeways. In fact she takes it as a personal failure that she has somehow ended up in the wrong lane, as if it will somehow shape her life's direction. Perhaps she is right, perhaps life is like choosing a freeway. If you make the wrong choice it's sometimes hard to get off. Or you see signs saying, 'Stop. Go back. You are going the wrong way.' Sometimes it seems you never even get out of the backroads, let alone onto the freeway. The point is, I tell her, that even if you do make the wrong choice and are forced to go out of your way, in the end you can get onto the right road.

'But think of all the time you've wasted,' she said, honking her horn at some poor driver who had only looked as if he was going to cut into her lane.

I must admit to some apprehension about this interview, because several people had warned me that Kate was not an easy person to deal with, that she was subject to dramatic mood swings, sometimes in the middle of a conversation. I was not to be surprised if she suddenly, having been absolutely charming, turned on me and ordered me out of her house and off her property. Jane, too, had heard these stories over the years and hoped that our two-hour drive would not be in vain or end in disaster.

'I'll come in with you and make sure everything is fine, then I'll leave you to get on with it,' she said. 'I've got some reading I want to do. I'll come back and pick you up.'

'Fine,' I said, secretly wishing that she would at least be on hand if things became difficult. No-one would mess with Jane.

As the Jeep pulled into the drive a well-built woman with long hair the colour of stainless steel and thick glasses came out to greet us. It was Kate. When I introduced Jane she said warmly, 'Don't I know you? From *Ms* magazine. Aren't you a friend of Gloria?'

She took us both inside her own barn which was one huge room with a bed at one end and a living area, kitchen and work area at the other. It was neat, comfortably furnished, with a wonderful feeling of space. She invited us to look around while she took a phone call. Jane called out to me to look at a sunken bathtub she had discovered in a verandah, where you could bathe underneath the stars. The art hanging on the walls, a lot of it Kate's own work, was not angry but sensual, full of soft curves and pendulous shapes.

Kate returned to collect me for the interview and invited Jane to visit the other buildings which house the artists and writers.

'I know they'd love to meet you,' she said.

I was pleased Jane decided to stay. It was a comfort in case the mood changed and we had to beat a hasty retreat.

Kate and I settled down by a wooden table under the canopy of a huge leafy tree overlooking a picture-book pond complete with ducks. It was very *Wind in the Willows*. She said modestly that they had created the pond, simply found a spring and made it bigger.

This trial-and-error experiment that she had been developing for the past eighteen years was finally starting to pay off, but that had not been her only aim. Her vision of an arts colony for women where artists and writers could apply to spend the summer working on the farm and their art had proved to be an outstanding success. The women who were there now spent the mornings as farmers, the afternoons as artists and the evenings eating, drinking and having lively discussions on art and politics. Kate divided her time between the country and the city, between her art and her writing, having hopefully the best of all worlds. The farm, which grows and sells Christmas trees – a near recession-proof industry – was an inspired vision and one that, despite bouts of mental illness and severe depression, she had managed to sustain.

'It is a piece of heaven,' I said, looking around me.

She nodded and settled back with a cigarette while a tall blonde woman placed a jug of iced water on the table in front of us.

'I thought you might need this,' she said.

'Thank you,' said Kate, pouring me a glass with slightly unsteady hands. It was all very civilised.

I noticed while we were having a preliminary chat that she thought very carefully before speaking. There were long pauses between sentences as well as paragraphs. Her voice was deep and nicotine husky. Lulled by the calm ripples of the pond, the seamless blue of the sky, the rolling green of hills, I changed gears to a slower pace and relaxed a little. The only thing that disturbed the peace and tranquillity of this pastoral scene was the frog who had the loudest honk I had ever heard. Either that or someone had just goosed a hippopotamus. Kate laughed when I said this. A hearty and generous laugh; a laugh that I could tell she'd had all her life.

'A lot of the child is still there in me. Even now. Especially my sense of equity and outrage, which I've always felt from about the age of five. I remember remarking to my mother that everybody who was a bigshot was male – George Washington, the Pope, the President. She said, "It's a man's world," and I said, "That isn't fair," and she said, "You're right." So I think I was waiting all my life for the feminist movement to re-occur, and it did when I was in my late twenties. I knew about its history because Susan B. Anthony was still on the postage stamp.

'I was born in 1934 and Mother was in the generation who were the first ones to vote so I was always thinking, "Where did it go? How did it disappear?" I don't think she knew where it disappeared either. Then Betty Friedan told us in *The Feminine*

Mystique. She explained how it had been engineered away by advertising in the women's magazines after the war and by pop psychology.

'From the time I was a child the world seemed to be tilted. It wasn't on an equal basis at all and then there were all the indignities about chores, what boys did and girls did. History was an obsession of mine. So a sense of injustice was inside me all along and then as I went into the workforce and looked at the opportunities in education I was really hurt by the disparity.

'My mother went back into the workforce after my parents separated. I was thirteen, she was about forty-five. My father was an engineer and a delightful, fascinating guy. He was a great deal of fun but his life didn't work out for him very well. He finally had his own company and it didn't succeed and just at this point my mother hit upon his long liaison with the woman who became his second wife. At that point everything burst apart for my family. Mother asked him to leave and then, with a lot of struggle and trial and tribulation, she established herself as a very successful underwriter of life insurance and she had a very good career. So she was a good role model.

'My father was so unhappy in his last years with us, it was liberating for him to be gone but I did love him a great deal and missed him. My mother depended upon me because I was the one daughter of the right age to be useful. I had a younger sister and an older sister, but my older sister was away at college. So I got all sorts of jobs and earned money and helped Mother. I had a good and close relationship with her. She was a wonderful mother. She died about two years ago and it's been a very great loss.

'As my parents' marriage fell apart I retreated into my room and books. Their divorce probably had a lot to do with my being scholarly. And the example of my elder sister too. She was studying international relations. Also, Mother had been an English major and I think I absorbed her college education by listening to her at the kitchen table on the nights that Daddy didn't come home. She would tell me what this professor said and what the other one did and what the stories were in the plays. She read aloud to me from the time I was a very small child – a lot of poetry and Irish writing, so I had quite a notion of books and a love of language. It was a very precious gift. I also had an aunt who sent me to Oxford, which really changed my life. You couldn't get a Rhodes scholarship in those days if you were a woman.

'Even though the English do not generally like Americans, I must say I was very happy at Oxford. It was an ideal world and at the time I had very little awareness of politics or class consciousness. I was swimming in a world of books and had a very nice tutor. I did rather better than they expected I would because, after all, I was only an American. I got a first-class degree in English. I felt like a little Irish running home with the prize.

'It was my aunt who wanted to send me to Oxford, but secretly I was having an affair with another student, a woman in my last year of college, and when the family discovered that they decided they'd forbid me to see her further. Or they said I couldn't go to Oxford. My aunt was appalled at my having an affair with a woman. But I got a summer job at night in a factory and earned my friend's passage and so we went anyway. My lover took some tutorials and was writing a novel. Later, when they found out what I had done, all hell broke loose. I was disowned by that side of the family, which was the side that was paying the fees.

'I have a book coming out this Fall called *AD*, which is about the aunt who sent me off to Oxford, who is a woman I adored. In fact she was the great infatuation of my youth. So it was an awfully complicated situation and the lover I went to Oxford with turned out to be a great disappointment. It was all very complicated. The love of one's family, the love for another young person, the whole thing of trying to figure out one's identity and make one's way. They broke with me but I went on still really loving my aunt and feeling very sorry that I could never be close to her again.

'I was astonished and delighted to get a first from Oxford. I came back to the United States and got a job teaching English in the South, separating from the lover during the process. I fell in love with the fine arts and decided I would be an artist. So I went up to New York to do that; you simply had to go to New York. I lived there for two years and then went to Japan for two more, and when I came back I had all the trouble getting a job and earning a living that women were experiencing in those years. This was around 1960 to '61.

'I'd been a practising artist in New York and in Japan, and when I came back to the United States from Japan I needed to earn a living in order to be an artist. So I taught English again. Then it became apparent that I had to get a PhD, so I set about doing that and *Sexual Politics* came out as my thesis. But it was very much affected by the fact that all the student strikes had been going on – Cambodia, Vietnam – and I had been fired from Barnard College at Columbia University for my political beliefs and for supporting the student strike. So because I was fired I could make a much braver thesis than I might otherwise have done. So that's how *Sexual Politics* came about.

'Simone de Beauvoir and Betty Friedan were both influences. Especially from this distance, one's aware of how much one owes them. From the point of view of other feminist influences and support, those books were very important. I imagined that I was only concerned with the books I was analysing but, in retrospect, I realise how much I owe to the other pioneer books.

'Coming back from having studied in England and in Europe I was aware of the prosaic nature of American academic writing and I wanted to give my PhD some sense of irony. Humour gives it a kind of balance. I really enjoyed *The Female Eunuch* for that reason when I read it for the first time. *Sexual Politics* did become a best-seller overnight and it was, after all, just a PhD thesis, which usually nobody would bother to publish. Having been let go by the university I was, of course, penniless and in peril. The advance was a very tiny sum but the fact that I got it published was plenty. For it to make all that noise was astonishing. When I wrote it I knew I was having an awful lot of fun. The first chapter especially was just outrageous fun to do. To use that energy that we were all getting up together in the feminist community and then to apply that to the academy and literature and culture as a whole was great.

'Being on the front cover of *Time* magazine was a mistake. I didn't want to be on the cover. We were, as you know, against the star system and so it was against my expressed wishes. It was done with a painting because I hadn't wanted to pose for a photograph.

KATE MILLETT

So you go from being a struggling artist on the Bowery and living that life, to TV and the whole media circus. It was very, very confusing. For a couple of weeks it was fun, then it became a nightmare.

'On the other hand, one was able to speak for the movement and for feminism, which was a great opportunity. The truth of the media is that first you're exploited and manipulated until you become this big balloon, which later they then puncture. And puncturing me was supposed to puncture feminism. They called me bisexual even though I had told them I was a lesbian. We handled it very well in that we gave a press conference, all of us. Gloria sat next to me and held my hand and we endorsed gay liberation. So it was a great step forward politically.

'My life changed in the sense that, having written a best-seller, you get to be able to write more books. I was living with Fumio Yoshimura and he was going to be deported so we legalised our love affair and got properly married. It was a genuine love affair. He was a delightful, wonderful person.

'The feminist movement had brought us into loving each other as women again, which was something I'd done before and which was involved with the changes everybody was making in their minds and their lives. The imbalance in the system that I had noticed at five was reinforced. Patriarchy was and is everywhere – in the government and the economic system and the educational system. But we were making a little progress at that stage. I'm sure we felt that the revolution was just around the corner. On the other hand, we had begun with just a handful of women in New York and our successes astonished us. Our first breakthrough was integrating the want ads in the *New York Times*, which then changed the nature of employment in all the other newspapers throughout the country.

'Why did *Sexual Politics* take off in the way it did? Timing. There we were beginning a movement and we needed a book. *Sexual Politics* came out at the right moment and was, I guess, sufficiently persuasive. De Beauvoir's *The Second Sex* changed my life in that way, absolutely. I was at Oxford when I read it and going to Paris on all the vacations. I thought here finally was confirmation of all I had felt and known since I was five. I also move between autobiography and fiction and nonfiction like de Beauvoir.

'When I called the book *Sexual Politics*, so many places couldn't understand that as a term. Did that mean who Jack Kennedy slept with or what? They found it hard to see sex as a political category, to nominate it as a political category, like class or race. For others it clarified things a great deal. I mean nineteenth-century people had talked of patriarchy too, but then it all got lost and forgotten. And in fact to link sex and politics together was so astonishing for some places that they wouldn't use that title. The French called it *Les Politiques de Males*, the politics of males. The Germans called it – this is awful when they change your titles you know – *Sex and Domination* and they all said, "Oh, but *Sexual Politics* wouldn't make sense in German and French." In America the publisher, Doubleday, decided on a first cover which was a picture of two arms arm-wrestling – one brawny male and one fragile female – and I said, "No, under no circumstances can you issue my book behind that cover." So we ended up with a plain white cover.

'If I look back on the young woman who wrote *Sexual Politics*, there's a lot of her still in me now. The rebellion is still there and the insistence on logic and clarity. I felt very keenly that I was making a reasonable argument. And my sense of irony is still very strong. These traits are recognisable in all my other books too. *Sexual Politics* was the theory and *Flying* was the praxis of the life we were living at that moment. Everything was changing so swiftly and was so exciting. After *Sexual Politics* came *The Prostitution Papers*, then *Flying*. My next book, *Sita*, came out of the end of a love affair. There have been a few of those, very important in my life.

'They said nasty things about *Sexual Politics* right from the beginning. They poured vitriol on the fact that I was rocking the boat. I feel that almost all my books offend in one way or another. I didn't set out to offend, just to write the truth. In the 1970s I was writing *Sita* and *The Basement* and doing a good deal of art shows. There was an awful lot of my life going on at once. I had mentally crashed by this time. It was all concern about how much I could get done. I have a great need to accomplish and achieve; it seems to power things, it seems to be the energy source. I am disciplined when I work. When I'm in a book I do it every day. If I'm composing it's about four hours, if I'm revising maybe six or seven. But my books take a long time to write, usually about four years.

'At the end of the 1970s I was having a lot of exhibitions. I had mental breakdowns in 1973 and in 1980, but I still tried to work in those bad periods. In the 1980s I wrote *The Basement*, which is a story that made a huge impression on me many years before, in 1965. It's about a girl confined to a basement by the people who are taking care of her and eventually, through endless refinements of cruelty, they killed her with the accusation that she was unchaste. It happened in Indianapolis and it seemed to me a great metaphor for the way our necks are snapped in adolescence under the accusation of sexuality, a sexuality we often don't participate in and hardly understand, but it's our crime and establishing that guilt in us makes us easier to control. That seemed to me a parable, overstated but, because exaggerated, a clearer version of something that's done on a very small, subtle scale to the generality of women. Just at an age when they might become powerful, effective or free, they're accused of sexuality and suborned. Things have changed today but our neck is still there and this process has a big role in the psychic submission of women, which has a lot of social and cultural effects.

'The reaction to that book was a great disappointment to me because I'd worked on it so long. I was holding onto this terrible discovery for about fourteen years. It's been reissued now and it's hanging in there. It has a lot of readers who remember it very well.

'I put off writing *Going to Iran* about that time and wrote the book about my aunt, which is only now being published. Prior to this it struck them as too literary. There's a kind of resistance to accepting me as a literary as well as polemical writer; in the United States, not in France.

'I bought this farm in 1970. It was a place to work away from New York and it was very inexpensive. And I love it. And I guess the 1980s for me were making the farm and creating a colony of writers and artists.

'Where am I with feminism now? This is the feminism. I'm practising it. There's a whole network of women artists here from a number of countries. They apply to come here. They work in the morning on the farm and do their own work in the afternoon. We had to support the place so this seemed to be one way to do it, and in order to keep it going we have to keep our trees going. Now it's virtually self-supporting. It took a long time. It takes ten years just to grow a tree. So we've been gradually building it and making it nicer and nicer, and I get a great deal of fun out of it. It gives all these young artists and writers an opportunity to spend their time with each other and their time on their work. In the art world, you see, there wasn't anything for women, so I wanted to make a different situation for young artists and writers coming along. We've been doing it about eighteen years now.

'My book *Going to Iran* is pretty much self-explanatory. It was wonderful to have that opportunity to participate in history, in a revolution that almost happened and then, alas, one that became a reaction. It was eye-opening for me to see naked political power, the patriarchal force at first-hand, and the hatred and hostility. It didn't make me more cynical, rather more chastened. Cynical means you have given up, and I haven't. I think it also led to my book *The Politics of Cruelty*, which focuses on the whole issue of political force and brutality. In Iran my life was certainly in danger. I was terrified. We were arrested and deported. The longer I stayed there the more I wanted to be deported because we really could easily have been imprisoned and executed. It was a time of many executions and I was really lucky to get out. That telephone call I just took was someone who'd been at the colony once and was calling to say that she'd just read *The Politics of Cruelty* and how the book had meant a great deal to her. That's very gratifying.

'Then there was *The Loony Bin Trip*. Very hard to get published. Psychiatry is terribly powerful in the United States. This book was anti-psychiatric so publishers just couldn't risk it, the culture police in fact were working on them. Even writing it was a revolutionary act, but to get it published was certainly very difficult. It took about five years. And the response has been fantastic. It's still making the rounds in paperback, not only to people who finally have a book that speaks for them but also to lots and lots of women in psychology, and professionals and therapists.

'I don't believe in mental illness, as diagnosed and described. I believe that people are in crises, that they have troubles in life, that they get to places where they can't cope. That's what happened to me. I learned a lot about powerlessness. I did do a good deal of time in therapy and I think therapy probably helps deal with a loss of confidence, self-doubt, things like that. The main problem for me is the standards I set myself. I'm very proud that I had a chance to write these books, but I'm tough on myself because there are so many things I should get done. I've got more books to write and I'm having a retrospective of all my sculpture in a couple of weeks from now so there's still a lot to do. I just had a sculpture show in New York last season.

'The aunt I loved has died. It's hard to know whether she would be proud of me. All that bourgeois respectability was so much a part of her, whereas my mother coped with my life brilliantly – and it was a lot to cope with.

'I've never had any children. I don't think I regret that. My mother and I had very different opinions of things but we had a lot of political agreement too. Somehow it all came right in the end. I think Mother did a whole lot of growing to encompass what I was on about. My sisters went along with me to a point. It was very important to me to maintain contact with them. I wanted to bring them with me to whatever place I was headed, rather than separate from them.

'The Politics of Cruelty is based on the idea of injustice and an extension of patriarchy as well but now we're looking at it in international and political terms. It's essentially the same old oppression, the same old systematic power and domination and cruelty. In this book I was trying to bring feminism into world politics. It's kind of a feminist analysis of a phenomenon that we don't pay enough attention to. The brutalisation of government is a force in our time and it might not be seen the same way if we didn't take a feminist approach to it. Rather than as an aberration, I saw it as an extension of patriarchy. Floundering and in trouble, it becomes more and more violent and reverts to torture. That's what I was trying to do in *The Loony Bin Trip* and *The Politics of Cruelty*, and probably in *The Basement* as well.

'The analyst, the theoretical pioneer, is still strong in me. The crusader in the streets is not part of me so much now. I don't think the women's movement will disappear again. I'd be interested to know how Robin [Morgan] and Gloria [Steinem] were responding to America now. The right wing is making quite a stab at dismantling a lot of what we achieved. But through their own affinities and relationships with their own daughters, a lot of men can become very sensible when they realise they are affecting the fate of their daughters and they can put that relationship ahead of their automatic military commitment to male power.

'There's always a hassle in me between art and writing although I try to accommodate both of them. It's like the conflict between the farm and my own work. If I answered every request or contribution I wouldn't get the book done. The urge to love and have sex and passion is not as strong as it used to be – leaves me more time to work. I get intellectual stimulation mostly from reading. I read almost everything, very widely. I read a lot of fiction, trying to see how to do it better. Yet how to do it always comes out of what's happening. But I guess narrative device or craft gets tucked away somewhere. I never watch television, or very rarely. I talk with friends. Sometimes I'm lonely. You know you get very wrapped up in a book and it is a solitary thing to write one. So I miss companionship and intimates.

'I don't find intimacy difficult. My relationship with Fumio lasted about ten years. But I am still friends with him and with all the other lovers I've ever had so that these relationships are now decades long. That's very important to me. Certainly I believe it's possible to have a relationship last twenty or thirty years. All kinds of people do it. Maybe it's a bit harder for an artist. I'm not sure what kind of relationship I would envisage now but it might be less all-encompassing. I wouldn't become so engrossed. But I don't know that you can ever outline what you think about love. It surprises me, you know. You never really know when it is going to occur. I'm very convinced of the importance of deep friendships; long, on-going friendships.

'What's it like to be me these days? It feels overextended some days. I'm always trying to get things finished. I'm more aware of time now, or that it's closer to when the final paper has to be turned in and there is a kind of pressure to finish. By now there's a sense of an oeuvre of work rather than just a book as an inspiration. I'm concerned now with the design because the fabric is longer. The concern is to make it all fit together and make sense.

'The Politics of Cruelty was very important to me that way. I spent a lot of years on it, about seven, and I saw it as a public work on behalf of people who couldn't speak for themselves.

'If it were all to end tomorrow I would like to be remembered for trying to create compassion and for breaking down jails and cages and confinements of all sorts. It's important to me to have put time into working against oppression. I don't think there was a time when I never would have been concerned with political prisoners suffering under torture. Imagination is what is important. You have to be able to imagine what it's like to be the girl in the basement or somebody looking at an electrode, so that there's the will to stop it.

'Of course I care what other people think of me but you can't let it affect you that much. It's like dealing with critics. If I get a wounding review, well I just try to live with it. Joyce Carol Oates reviewed The Basement. If I were to re-read the review it probably wouldn't be as wounding as it was at the time. She seemed to find the book too dark, and we all know hers are too, so that was a strange reaction.

'I've read some of the younger feminists' work. The one that I respect the most is Faludi because I think she really did her homework and proves her case very well in Backlash. It's important to marshal the evidence. De Beauvoir was my major influence. I was lucky to know her for sixteen years and to see her every year, virtually, for that time. I met her in 1971 and I went back every year to Paris to see her, so she was an important mentor. Oh, she was wonderful, a marvellous mind and very kind. People don't normally think that of her because she was very scrappy too, and certainly opinionated. She had very decisive ways but I always thought she was tremendously kind, and compassionate to all kinds of causes. She became the conscience of France and a lot of the western world.

'When *Sexual Politics* first came out I was the caricature feminist, but I worked very hard against that. I really did want to persuade people to a reasonable argument.

'You don't get change without consensus. I don't think you can force people. You can legislate but before you can get legislation you have to do a great deal of persuading. I see myself as a human rights worker. I think there has to be a process of education to change hearts and minds. Ultimately of course you're confronting people with the power of your resistance to whatever they believe, and when I say persuading and consensus I don't mean the powers that be, you don't persuade them. But if you persuade enough people, that's an avenue where you might make some progress. And I think the history of American civil rights is probably always in our minds as a reminder that we did, at a point in history, arrive at a better consensus. Of course puritanism is a strong stream and a wicked part of the American soul, and is much on the rise again too. It's that combination of hostility to pleasure and sensuality at the same time as this obsession with money and greed and that Darwinian survival thing. It's as if the country were being run on behalf of business interests. That's terrifying, it's very far away from the archetypal American dream and our better side of democracy and constitutionality.

'I once told a British journalist that my sister and former lover had me incarcerated in the bin. And it was funny because when we told him we were all sitting together, all friends again. He was astonished. It was all true and they had been operating under the current notions of American psychiatry, which they fortunately finally let go of too. I forgave them for it. I think they even finally forgave me for being different, so that's probably how you make progress; by that process of understanding, of seeing conventional ideas as funny, something to be suspicious of. I was on lithium for a while. That mental difficulty has been hard for me to deal with, as it is for everyone. Whatever difficulties people have in their lives, it's pretty evident, right on the surface.

'Probably everyone has contemplated suicide. I did, and a number of times very seriously. But the work goes on and there is always something else to finish, that does sustain me. There's so much injustice of more and different kinds. So many of the causes that came to me I wouldn't have guessed or predicted.

'I've been writing about my mother and dealing with the oppression of age. The treatment of the old is terrifying – the disrespect and manipulation and imprisonment and drugging. My mother was confined for a very short period in a nursing home and just plain hated it, and I rescued her from it, took her back to her apartment whereupon we had a lot of rehabilitation to do and hard work, but it worked out. She was able to live there until her death. And it was the life she wanted. Whereas I tried very hard to save her sister from one of these places and couldn't, and they were holding her virtually prisoner. She was there against her will and they were drugging her. It was deplorable. This is a perfectly innocent person, perfectly sane and rational. But between the family, the system, collusion between the doctor and the whole set-up of the institution, I couldn't win. No-one was listening to her.

'It's breathtaking how much people don't listen to the old. Especially when in other cultures they are revered, esteemed and really listened to. And of course it could happen to us too. I don't want to be 103. It's not something I would devoutly wish for. I fear that helplessness. Seeing the situation that Mother and my Aunt Margaret got into I think we're all wise to fear it. The way the aged are treated really has to change. That treatment can't go on. The important thing is to make elaborate plans and build a support system for yourself and have enough money to last. I guess I'll just go on writing and running the farm. And hoping for the best.'

Between more jugs of iced water, telephone calls and some interminable pauses, Kate had nevertheless conveyed the essence of her work and her life. Using fewer words than many of the other women I had spoken to, she thought carefully about the ones she chose. She was essentially an intellectual, thrust into the public glare of an 'in your face' movement. She endured it because she believed in the good it could achieve. Unlike some of the others, there were no well-rehearsed lines, no stream of carefully selected words. She was hesitant, there was frequent lighting of cigarettes, and she was interested in engaging in a shared conversation rather than a standard question-and-answer interview. Her responses to direct questions were short and measured; like stones thrown into a pond, it was important to watch the ripples. I sensed that she was sick of people prodding and prying into her mental breakdowns and did not ask her to re-visit them.

Details, times, places were not of concern to her, the distillation of the experience was what counted.

We'd had a companionable time sitting by the pond but somewhere behind us we could hear thunder. Never one to ignore a symbol I said, 'Time to go,' and we moved over to the next set of buildings where Jane was sitting holding court on a chair surrounded by what looked like a circle of blonde Amazons. She was beaming.

'I have had a wonderful time,' she said. 'In fact I might even come back for a weekend and do the cooking.'

As we were leaving one of the young women asked to take our photo with Kate. The three of us stood, arm in arm, smiling for the camera. It was a far cry from the forbidding scenario that some had predicted. Kate Millett could not have been more charming.

As we hit the road again, Jane said, 'Well, the Goddess is sure smiling on you today, girl.'

'And you too, from the look on those admiring faces.'

She snorted.

The storm that was threatening never happened. The traffic was light and free-flowing so we stopped at a town called Freedom Plains for a turkey sandwich and a beer. Sitting outside, our elbows on the table, Jane said, 'Sure has been a dream run.'

'Well today has, anyway,' I said, thinking, 'Nine down, one to go.' And she was in Stockholm.

15
SUSAN FALUDI

Day Ten, 3.15 pm: Arlanda Airport, Stockholm, Sweden

I waved a frantic goodbye to Jane and watched her top hat bouncing through the crowd. I had managed to get a cheap ticket from New York to London to Stockholm and back to London, where I would board a Qantas flight home and immediately resume my university teaching duties. The timing was tight. Very tight.

My plane was thirty minutes late getting into London. I rushed headlong down vast corridors, running full-speed, nearly knocking down endless numbers of tiny Japanese people who stood steadfastly motionless on the moving walk-way. I finally arrived at my seat sweating, red-faced and distressed. The plane sat on the tarmac for another thirty minutes. Finally they announced that they had lost a passenger. I wondered for a moment if it could be me and I had missed a check-in point.

By the time the plane landed in Stockholm all I could see out of my window was rain. It was, according to the captain, 11 degrees. Not that it really mattered, as I was not leaving the airport. I pushed my way through passport control, customs and was the first person to burst out through the exit doors. A crowd of expectant faces stared at me. I searched them for the face on the cover of *Backlash*, which I had in my hand. I looked for a Faludi or a Mitchell among the signs that were held up. I suspected that she was not the type to stand there like a travel agent or a limo driver. I was right. And I was getting desperate. I walked among the crowd scanning the faces of strangers. I approached someone who looked vaguely like the photo. 'Excuse me, are you Susan Faludi by any chance?' The woman looked at me like I was mad or soliciting. Or both. This was hopeless. Why hadn't I made better arrangements? I never dreamed there would be so many people there. I found the information counter, explained my predicament to the woman behind the desk and asked politely if she could perhaps make a public announcement. She stared hard at me. I pleaded with my eyes.

'How do you spell it?'

The call boomed out over the public address system, in a Swedish accent. I stood by the counter. A small young woman with long, dark hair approached from the other side of the crowd. I looked hard. Yes. It was her.

I apologised for the lateness of the flight, even though it was hardly my fault. I asked the woman at the information counter if there was anywhere quiet we could go.

'No,' she said, blank faced. 'There's upstairs, but it's noisier than this.'

We chose a table by the exit doors as far away from the fast-food outlet as possible. She said her boyfriend was coming to pick her up at four o'clock. I looked at my watch. It was 3.15. I hastily cleared the table of McDonald's debris while she went to get a Coke. She was small, petite even, and stared at me with expressionless eyes. Her smile, when it appeared, was warm but her manner shy. From the careful, measured way in which she answered my questions, I could tell her mind was of the steel-trap variety, the kind that writes the book that wins a Pulitzer Prize.

'In *Backlash* I was firstly trying to make sense of a gut feeling I'd had. I was getting some strange signals from the culture. I was born in 1959 so I came of age at the very time when the women's movement was taking off and I saw the very dramatic difference it made in my mother's life and the lives of all the women in the neighbourhood where I was growing up. My mother was married, she was a housewife, which for some women would be fine. But she was a woman born too early and she was clearly meant to be a working woman, a writer, and she moved herself into this role that wasn't right for her. She was married for seventeen years and lived in the suburbs and wore house dresses and dusted furniture, and was completely miserable. There were a lot of women like her in my suburb and community. It was all very much like *The Feminine Mystique* and *The Women's Room*. In fact I remember my mother reading *The Women's Room* and then passing it on to me one summer. And it was that same summer that my parents' marriage fell apart, which was ultimately a great thing for her. It allowed her more freedom and enabled her to go back to work and to become a whole person again.

'My father was an immigrant from Hungary but, as immigrants often do, he had the most extreme view of the American dream and wanted a wife in the suburbs in a house with a white picket fence. I remember over dinner when I was in adolescence, my mother asking if it would be all right with him for her to go to work. She wanted to work at the local newspaper and he said, "No." And that was the end of it. That was the entire discussion. When her marriage ended she worked for a newspaper for a little bit and then she spent most of the time working for in-house trade publications. But she went right back to work when they divorced. I have a younger brother, so she had to for economic survival. In a way I am living out the dream that was my mother's.

'My mother and I had a very close relationship and still do. She was always a feminist, she just married very late. She didn't really want to marry and she wasn't someone who feminism just suddenly hit like a Mack truck when she was forty-nine. It was more a question of suppressing those impulses. She had lived in New York in Greenwich Village and was a bit of a Bohemian, a leftist, an activist. Then she pushed all that down and moved to the suburbs and baked cookies. She really felt that this was expected of her. My parents knew each other for six weeks before they married; my mother was twenty-seven and felt that she was the only person she knew who wasn't married. It was again all those pressures to conform.

'It's funny because when I look at the progress of my writing *Backlash*, it all began with a similar pressure from a *Newsweek* story about the so-called man shortage. And from the men in my own life calling me up and saying, "See I told you, you should have gone out with me three years ago." Just thinking about this now – it wasn't the same crushing blow as my mother's but I can see it, not consciously – it was really the development of the same thunder clouds that appeared on my mother's horizon so many years earlier. The most depressing thing to me through all of this was that I saw how much my mother struggled, how much all the women of her age struggled. She felt she had no choices, that she was unemployable, and I think she also absorbed that whole 1950s mentality of "you're nothing if you're not married with a dishwasher". How much that has changed, to the point that we can sit here now and say, "God, why would I want to do that?" But it seemed then as if there was no alternative.

'Yes, she's very pleased that I am a writer and she refers to *Backlash* as her grandchild, very proudly. I think one of my blessings from my mother is that she does not, unlike a lot of mothers, sit around and say, "When are you going to get married?" "When are you going to have children?" It's more, "When are you going to write another book?" And that's very freeing. I don't have that voice in the back of my mind.

'I was aware at such an early age of my mother's unhappiness. She, and to his credit, my father encouraged my academic aspirations. That's where I excelled. I was not a great athlete, I was not a cheerleader, so this was my arena of achievement. I think I had idle fantasies about driving a station wagon full of children but I think I recovered from those very quickly. By the time I was a thinking person I wanted to be a writer. Or my other thoughts were more along the lines of being an activist lawyer or a social worker and doing something that involved social and political change. I never thought of not continuing my education. I won academic prizes in public high school, which wasn't too hard. Then I went to Harvard.

'When *Backlash* came out, in that first year there were a number of things coming together: the Anita Hill hearings, Naomi Wolf's book, the film *Thelma and Louise*. And behind all this, the realisation from women that if they didn't get rid of George Bush they would lose the right to abortions. I think all that came together in the Fall of 1991 so that whole period through 1992 and through the presidential campaign was a very heady feminist period when it felt that something could really change, that there was this window of opportunity after twelve years of the Reagan dark shadow. And then it fell apart so quickly when the Congress became dominated by Republicans.

'Sometimes I think the book actually achieved more here in Sweden than it did in America. Right after it came out here they had this conservative government that came into power in 1991. For the first time since the 1930s the social democrats didn't have the power. There were these cutbacks to women's social programmes and talk about re-evaluating abortion rights and apparently when my book came out here it became part of this huge debate about, "We've got to get rid of the Conservatives."

'The Support Stockings is a feminist secret organisation made up of a lot of women in the media. They organised and were hugely effective, and because of their three-year campaign they were able in 1994 to get the social democrats to commit to ensuring that every other candidate on the party list would be a woman. And the Prime Minister committed to having a Cabinet that was 50 per cent female. They had an election in 1994 and the social democrats won. Now they have 50 per cent women in the Cabinet. From afar I thought, "Well this is wonderful, I'll come here and it'll cheer me up." But actually it's a numbers game and there's an extreme segregation here. The women are all in the public sector and the men are in the private sector. So there are actually more women in executive positions in US corporations than there are here. The power has shifted from the public sector and parliament to the private sector, which is where all the men are. Because of joining the European Union the Swedish parliament really has a lot less power and so the men have deserted the field to women. So the fact that there are so many women in parliament means that women are presiding over a government that's in a cut-back mode. Women are doing all the dirty work in parliament. They're the ones who have to cut out welfare benefits and maternity insurance because of the mess that the men left the economy in.

'I hope that *Backlash* endures as a useful tool to women so that when they read the next story about "women are all going back to the home" and when the story has no statistics they're able to see that this is a political message, not a scientific one. I get letters from women who say they made changes in their lives after reading the book. And the other thing that's been very gratifying is that I get letter after letter which says, "I thought the same way in the '80s and now the '90s, but for so long I thought I was the only one who thought it, and I thought I was crazy." Which was kind of how I felt. To know that other women out there feel the same way and that you're not crazy and you're not imagining it is great. I do ascribe a lot of the power of the backlash to the media. I could argue that part of that is because it's my profession but I also think that the media is now the real source of power.

'In coming here I've had a lot of discussions about this with feminists, and part of their argument about why they think women have been able to get the power so easily in parliament is because the power has shifted into these huge media corporations. So it doesn't really matter if you can pass a law in parliament any more, what matters is if you own the public airwaves and if you are able to influence public opinion, if you're able to reach people through advertising or pop culture. That's where all the money is and that's where all the power is. What's frightening about that is the people in power don't acknowledge that they're in power and don't really have a well thought-out political agenda. I mean, they're mostly driven by greed.

'In the media in Los Angeles there is one man who owns all three television stations. In America it used to be, "Oh, there's this man who is buying up," but now it's a whole conservative political bloc that has very astutely realised that the media is the way to power, and controllable power. Now you've got the national empowerment parliament and television run by a Christian coalition. Newt Gingrich is up to his ears in cable and TV monopolies. There's some talk among some feminists in California about buying a radio station, but it's too lame and it's too late and it's too little. We don't have that kind of money. Then there's the whole Internet thing, which a group of women with a lot of money should be buying into. We should be thinking about the future now. We're on the ground floor and we don't even realise it. Everything is changing so quickly.

'I don't buy the argument that we should form alliances with right-wing women. I mean, I don't have anything in common with them. I think that's a huge mistake, and as for conservative women who are against abortion, I don't even want to breathe the same air as them. I don't believe in a sort of essentialist idea that because we're women we have some special bond. To me the feminist movement is about not defining yourself simply by your ovaries. To me the basic lifeline of feminism is that people should be freed up to act in order to pursue their true callings in life. And to be able to act on the widest stage possible. But the other part of feminist belief is that you work towards not just getting that for yourself but opening up those paths for other women. That's where I think right-wing women get off the boat when they cut back social programmes. They cut back everything that would help other women enjoy that same freedom.

'I guess what I'm saying ultimately is that form of capitalist feminism is a contradiction. In my ideal mind I find it hard to imagine someone holding true to feminist principles and not being in favour of political and social change, because to me they're so connected. Somebody who is a right-winger is not in favour of change that makes life better for those less advantaged.

'At the end of the '90s I don't think women are going to go back. There's been a threshold that we've crossed. The '50s were an aberration after the war anyway, but we're not returning to a traditional division of labour because of the current economy and two-income families. But what frightens me is that people don't think or don't want to think politically. Certainly in the US, in the void created by all this focus on personality, cheap morality and celebrity feminists, progress is stymied. What is most discouraging to me is that a lot of people in the US seem to be aware that the right-wing is taking a hatchet to any kind of social supports. They know they are doing their best to turn the clock back, but I don't see any kind of political reaction to it.

'There's an immense feeling of defeat about using the political system to make change or coming up with any kind of resistance. We have the paradigm as recently as the 1960s for making political change for organising, for demonstrating, but there's a widespread feeling that that doesn't really lead to anything, it doesn't work any more. But nobody knows what to do instead. So you have a situation in the United States where the roof is falling down on everyone's head and we just hold little meetings and say, "Oh, it's really bad."

'There have been various efforts organised but nothing seems to take off, nothing seems to have caught fire. It almost did in 1992.

It was like we had this flame going and we were fanning it wildly and then it just snuffed out. I think there's a lot of anger but it's just not expressed as political organising, it's expressed as burning down buildings or bombing Oklahoma City federal buildings.

'There are a lot of these pseudo-feminists like Katy Roife, Rene Denfield and Christine Hoffsomers who are attacking feminism. Camille Paglia is just odd, she's just as mad as a hatter. But with some of these other women, it's a kind of rage that's turned in on itself. When I got here, people asked me about Christine Hoffsomers, but nobody's actually read her book called *Who Stole Feminism?* She's probably about five to ten years older than I am, but a lot of these women are quite young. Again it's that dynamic of power shifting to the media. These are women who are extremely concerned with getting themselves on television. It's pure opportunism. You read their books and you can tell they don't even care about the writing in the book. That's not where all their passion went, it went into getting a media coach and getting on the Donahue show and becoming a "celebrity". That is the goal. It's like young boys who go out and rape girls so that they can make a scandal and get on TV. It's the whole natural born killers mentality in a much nicer form.

'People may say to me, "Well it's fine for you, you have published an international best-seller." But the thing is, do you start out with that as your only goal? Mine started out as an article. There is no research or scholarship in these other books, which is extremely depressing. That's why if you look at these books that are coming out now that are attacking feminism, there are no facts in them. There is no effort to go out and interview anyone and there's no conviction behind them. There's no sense of political outrage. It's, "Oh this will sell, this is a hot proposal. I'll have a power lunch with the publisher." There's no vision behind them. They are completely based on negativity. It's, "Let's go after those older feminists, those feminists who made a name for themselves, and trash them." And that's the entire point – they don't have a new point to make, they don't have another fresh analysis. There's no message. They're not offering an alternative vision other than to pat themselves on the back for having managed somehow to get

SUSAN FALUDI

through the first thirty years of their life without any palpable discrimination. I'm actually surprised there isn't more of it.

'The hopeful, realistic, scenario is that things will get so bad in the US that Gingrich et al. will go too far and that will finally push people into action. We'll see something similar to the widespread agitation and activism of the Great Depression. The hopeless scenario is where the media controls everything and it gets worse to no avail. I do believe that too much has changed to go back and that in spite of all the layers of apathy and dejection and indifference, underneath all that, a lot of women – even if they don't really define it politically – do have this sense that they're part of this change. So even as it's being attacked, it's being celebrated.

'I hear this more and more and you can see it more in talking to the men. Men feel that women are on this great adventure, that women have a direction, that women, and I think this is true, have completely overhauled their notion of what it means to be female, what their role and identity is in society. And even in the darkest hour that's not only a great comfort but it gives one a great sense of mission and a meaning in life. In this country, even for all of the disappointment that nine months after this female government was elected there hasn't been much change, there's still a sense of, "We have a cause and we're pushing forward and we're digging our way out of something." Whereas men have no sense of what it means to be a man any more. That's why my latest book is on masculinity.

'My first job was at the *New York Times* but I was just a copy girl so it was actually a rather dreadful job. Thankfully I left. Then I worked on the *Miami Herald* as a cub reporter and then I went to Atlanta for the *Atlanta Constitution* and I switched over to the *Sunday Magazine* and found my stride there in the magazine. Then I moved to California when that magazine folded and got another job on the Sunday magazine in the San Jose newspaper. I did that for a while and then wrote the book and then came back and worked at the *Wall Street Journal* for a couple of years. Then I quit to freelance and write my current book on masculinity.

'The year I worked on *Backlash* I was very isolated and felt like I was going against the cultural tide and that I was seeing something that no-one else saw. I was the kid looking at the emperor with no clothes and everybody else thought the emperor had wonderful finery. So that was a very tough time, but in another sense it was deeply enriching.

'If we're talking personally, my childhood years were difficult. But a lot of people's parents break up, I don't want to make a big deal out of it. I haven't had any grand cataclysmic events happen in my life. Not yet. Ideas excite me. My passion is reporting and writing. It's my work. I don't do needlepoint. I don't go scuba diving. And I don't have hobbies. My life is pretty much built around my work. I certainly don't have enough money to be a full-time writer but I also like to be engaged in the world on a more daily basis. I'm at my most impassioned when I'm in the middle of a journalism project that I care about.

'Currently I'm writing about this whole supposed transformation in Swedish politics and I'm looking at the Swedish male dilemma as well. Men feel that women's gain is their loss and I don't think that's at all true. It's more that men look around to explain their losses and fasten on women.

'My boyfriend is here to be with me and he's a writer also. Oddly, I think *Backlash* had a very good effect on my personal life. It had the opposite effect to what you'd predict. I was on my own at the time I was writing the book, and since then it's sorted out all the loathsome men whom I wouldn't want to deal with anyway because they immediately attack me. Anyone who wants to avoid a feminist at least knows right away that my position is pretty clear publicly. Then I met Ross, my Sambo, as they call it here, which is a very weird term. Do you know it? Sambo is Swedish for someone you live with. He's been pretty insulted. He keeps seeing himself referred to as Susan's Sambo. Anyway I met him a year after the book came out.

'One of the mistakes people make is to expect feminism to produce happiness. There's a great line in *The Second Sex* where Simone de Beauvoir says the point of liberty is not to be in a state of rest, and that's what happiness is. Happiness is having that sort of static contentment, and that was never the goal of feminism. It was meant to free people up to take action, to agitate. Liberty does produce anxiety. When women claim to feel cheated or betrayed by the feminist cause because they say, "I have a job and a man and I'm not happy," well that's not feminism's responsibility or even objective. Feminism isn't a grocery store where you go to buy things. Those women have a very consumerist idea of what it means to press for feminist goals. It doesn't mean that you get to have it all. That's a very capitalist notion of what feminism is about. It's not supposed to give you a makeover or add years to your life. It's supposed to give you a richer political and internal life, which you can choose to live either happily or unhappily. The greatest feminists are not happy cheerleaders.

'I've been thinking a lot about Mary Wollstonecraft recently because she came here 200 years ago and wrote a book called *A Short Residence in Sweden, Norway and Denmark*. She was sent here actually by a ne'er do well, he wasn't her husband but he did impregnate her and then he took up with a much younger actress and jilted her. I'm certainly trying not to re-enact this scenario. But anyway, he sent her off to Sweden to fix up his business affairs which had gone awry. He was a ship's captain. She was in deep despair and came here with a broken heart, but she not only sorted out his business affairs, she compiled the letter she had written to him and turned it into a book, removing his name, removing any kind of evidence that she was writing to this creep, and it actually became a best-selling book at the time. Her passion and her ability to see everything in political terms and to believe in the importance of political change even after the French Revolution, I found very inspiring.

'Charlotte Perkins-Gilman is also a heroine of mine. She is somebody who thought of everything that the '70s feminists thought of, many years earlier, and never got the credit she deserved. There are also all these unsung women who, on a much less grand scale than someone like Mary Wollstonecraft, were determined to stick to their political beliefs and to not be dissuaded by the climate of the time.

'I consider the act of writing to be activist. I will go to meetings but I think you need to play to your strengths. It doesn't do the world much good for me to be spending all my time carrying placards when my skills are reporting and writing. There are all kinds of players who need to come to the table in order for a movement to take place, and we need writers, marchers, phone callers, people to make rousing speeches. I do a lot of speaking in colleges and I've rationalised the time spent by going to colleges where the feminist message might not be well heard. But I'm not Gloria Steinem, unfortunately. She's an incredible presence.

'If anything, as time has gone by, I've been more involved in, I don't know if theory is the right word, but trying to sort through what's going on beneath the surface rather than just saying, "Well this is what's happening." What I'm trying to do in this most recent book is not to write about what is happening, not just to document it like, "Here is the evidence," but to try to understand the underlying motives and forces that are compelling people to act in this way.

'The masculinity book is due in a couple of years. So the near future is just working on it. I'm only here in Stockholm until the end of July. I work at home as a freelancer. I do feature articles but I mostly focus on these masculinity questions. I'm doing pieces for magazine articles. I make a living. More or less. Money is always a prod to finishing your work. It's like an incentive to stop procrastinating. I think I'll stick with it as a profession. I don't think I'm going to run off and join the circus.

'Babies? I'm not planning to but I'm not planning not to either.

'Feminism, no matter how much it's attacked by the politicians and by the media, has made a formative transformation, worldwide, of women's perception of what their meaning in life is and I don't think that's going to go away. Women may go undercover for a while, they may be frightened, but they are never going back to the 1950s, or earlier, to the Victorian era. They will move forward again, eventually.'

After thirty minutes she kept looking over my shoulder for her boyfriend, Ross. Eventually she saw him and waved. When he came up to the table she smiled in a way I hadn't seen before. He was tall, older than her by about ten years I'd guess, with a quiet charm. He offered to get us a Coke. We declined and he went off to get himself one.

'He's cute,' I said to her.

'Part of his attraction is that he's unaware of it,' she replied.

When he returned he sat down at the table quietly and unassumingly so as not to disturb. I ploughed on but could sense the minutes ticking away. Surely she would give me more time. At four o'clock exactly she said, 'I'm sorry. We have to go.'

I asked for a little more time, she said it wasn't possible. I asked Ross whether he was working. He said, 'Not like Susan. Just on my own projects.' She said that the newspaper she was attached to was working her pretty hard. She wrote her articles in English and they translated them into Swedish. Ross said, 'Maybe it's just as well we can't read them. Some of the translations might be strange.' She apologised for the fact that she couldn't see me in Los Angeles. I apologised for the lateness of the plane. We shook hands. They walked off through the exit doors.

I stared at their backs. I must be honest and admit that there was a part of me that was thinking, 'Wouldn't you have thought she would have delayed her appointment and given me a bit more time. Even thirty more minutes would have made a difference. After all, I have flown halfway around the world to see her. This generation has no regard for other people's needs, they are so totally self-absorbed.'

Was this the generational clash that had been so sensationalised in the media? Was I feeling the pique of an older generation not having been treated with more respect? Or was this in fact what our second wave of feminism had taught Faludi and her generation of thirty-something women? Hadn't we said, 'Be self-directed, make yourself the subject in your own life, don't worry about what other people think, don't be a service centre for the needs of others, don't feel "obliged" to do things you don't want to do'? Was she, in fact, a product of all the books these older feminists had written? Was this their legacy? And should I be saying, 'Good for her'? Or was she all intellect and no empathy?

With time to spare before my flight back to London, thanks to a Qantas Club Card, I took myself off to the British Airways Club Lounge for a gin and tonic, to think about it.

Silence, however, was not golden, or mine. A crush of men, all sizes, shapes, ages and races, were grouped around a very loud television set, watching a Rugby Union match between France and Britain. They cheered and groaned and sighed. In unison. No cultural or generational clashes there. Sport was truly the cement that welded their men's house culture together. You could smell the bonding.

So was this to be how my journey, my exploration, my adventure was to end? Stuck in a Club Lounge, 90 per cent of whose privileged inhabitants were men, forced to be on the margin, a reluctant witness to a male ritual I could never join; at least not without a sex change. The next person who uses the term 'post-feminist' should choke on it. I had another gin and tonic.

So who cares about their sport? Let them have it. After all, we have our books, dangerous books, to read. And to write.

16

GERMAINE GREER

10 May 1995: facsimile from London
In the interest of your reading Dr Greer's own words and to avoid any possible misinterpretation, I include this fax. It is a great sadness to me that she did not make an exception for this book, worthy though she deemed it.

Dear Susan Mitchell,

Dr Greer decided some years ago to cease giving print interviews. She was fed up with being processed by celebrity interviewers for their own aggrandisement. The only way to proceed was to refuse all requests to be so processed, with no exceptions.

This is the only way she can be sure to avoid misrepresentation and it has worked so well that she is in no mind to change the rule. Yours is doubtless a worthier enterprise than most, but Dr Greer still prefers that people read her, rather than about her.

Yours faithfully,
Carol Horne
Assistant to Dr G. Greer

POSTSCRIPT

The women in this book are the scribes, the catalysts and pioneers of a social revolution which generated the most dramatic and long-lasting changes to our lives that we have witnessed in the latter part of this century. It is not women or even men who haven't changed, but the outdated political structures which move too slowly to embrace these changes.

To read the stories of their lives as they have told them to me is to chart the course of the second wave of feminism. As indeed, the personal is political. And vice versa. It is their personal stories of struggle and hope and despair and pain and joy that link us all. On one level they are extraordinary women; some of the best and the brightest of their generations. And yet as their stories have unfolded it is the ordinary, everyday, flesh and blood parts of their lives with which we identify. For we all, as women, I'm sure, have found meeting points, recognition points, in some or all of their stories which make us feel less alone.

This book was for me a personal journey. Later, much later, now that I have listened to the taped interviews over and over again and reshaped and reworked them into dramatic monologues that tell each woman's individual story, now that I am on another continent and my hot flushes appear to have been dealt with, I must confess that I am still high on the aftereffects of meeting these women and shaping their words. I hope that the book will give every reader this same sense of their own potential, of their own power to make a difference in the world.

But what of these women? What do they have in common, now that we have seen them together, side by side, in one book? What are the patterns that emerge, the themes that should be pursued and, dare I say it, the lessons to be learned for the future of feminism as we prepare to enter the next century?

I have named them the icons, saints and divas of feminism because each of them has one or all of these attributes. The reason that we have become obsessed with icons, particularly female versions, is that we have never really had any with whom we can identify or model our lives on. Hardly a day passes when we don't see the term used, often, I should add, incorrectly ascribed. An icon is someone who transcends their time and place, and these women – as makers and writers of social history and narratives of our times – will certainly live on in the lives of those who changed their lives because of them. Their body of work will outlive them.

We have chosen to canonise some of them as modern-day saints, to elevate them above the crowd, because we need to have women in that role and many of them have been attacked simply because they have been placed on that pedestal. With the attack comes the martyrdom and the adoration.

As divas they have stood centre stage, singing their literary arias to the world, full-throated and with passion. Some, it is true, display the characteristics of the prima donna – it comes with the role. Some have lived the life of the great artist devoured but not destroyed by tragedy. But what draws us to them is the work that has emerged from their lives; it is this that transforms and transcends them. Bold, daring, challenging, it captured our minds and our hearts.

We have learned from these women to find ways of making something worthwhile out of the most difficult and desperate parts of our lives and ourselves. We have witnessed them battling menopause, bad temper, age, even death. We have witnessed them enjoying flirtation, sexual ambivalence, breastfeeding and growing Christmas trees.

It is what I have shown lies behind the gloss of celebrity that both disturbs and attracts us. It is their very ordinariness, their basic responses to everyday relationships, that gives us all the strength to survive.

For example the complexity of the mother–daughter relationship and the importance of their mothers in all their lives is pivotal. Many of them have written for and because of their mothers.

Robin Morgan's dedication to *Sisterhood is Powerful* reads: 'For Faith, my mother. With love. Finally.'

And no wonder, given the fact that she never received a cent for all her work as a child actor.

Phyllis Chesler writes in the front of *Women and Madness* not of love but of the basics: 'I thank Lillian, my mother, for giving birth to me, and for taking care of me long before I could write such a book.'

Marilyn French wrote the novel *Her Mother's Daughter* solely to give her mother the voice she never had. It appeared to be the one thing she gave that pleased her mother.

Erica Jong concludes her midlife memoir *Fear of Fifty* with the lines: 'I am not my mother, and the next half of my life stands before me.'

In the first collection of her writing, *Outrageous Acts and Everyday Rebellions*, Gloria Steinem wrote 'Ruth's Song', for her mother, because she could not sing it for herself.

The breakdown of her mother's marriage provided Kate Millett with a role model of an independent mother who made her own living and it was her mother's stories around the kitchen table that gave her a love of literature.

Susan Faludi dedicated *Backlash* to her mother 'who as a young woman fought to preserve her independence in the face of her own era's "feminine mystique" backlash'. She admitted that she was living the life her mother always longed for but never had.

In many instances these women have absorbed the anger of their mothers and determined that their lives will be different, only to feel guilty when they are and sometimes punished because they remind their mothers of the lives they lost.

Their fathers have been either absent or supportive but never punitive or abusive influences. Sexual freedom, experimentation and sensuality have been major pursuits, particularly for the older writers for whom repression was part of their upbringing. They all exude a sense of adventure, a sense that your life should be something you create for yourself. Unlike their mothers, they pursued or discovered or forged pathways of escape from what was expected of them. They were all passionate in their pursuit of truth, freedom and justice. Time has never dimmed the bright flame that burns within them. To have witnessed these stories is to have been energised, to read them all together is to be exhilarated by life's possibilities.

Every day, however, it seems someone is either predicting the end of feminism or giving it a future fractured by factions and fights. These are simply the signposts of backlash.

There will always be the trashers, those who set up false notions of what feminism is and then write a book knocking it down. Or those who seek to make their names by trashing feminist leaders. And the media is only too willing to give time and pages to the smashers and the trashers.

These are very different from the fights between genuine feminists. Anyone who has ever pictured the women's movement as an all-female version of 'The Brady Bunch' or 'The Pollyanna Push' has clearly never had anything to do with it. The only difference between the genuine fights of the 1970s and those of the 1990s is that they are now undertaken in the public arena. In the early days of any radical movement there are enough people trying to destroy it without having fights in the public gaze. It is a healthy sign that now clashes of opinion or ideology or analysis are conducted in the open and become part of the mainstream of public debate. To admit to differences, moreover to be able to celebrate them, is a sign of maturity.

Feminism is meant to be subversive: its aim is to confront, shock, disturb. It is also meant to be fun, a joyful struggle. Those who seek to reduce it to a sanitised, salt-free, sex-free, low-cholesterol humourless movement seek to destroy its essentially anarchic spirit.

Mind you, the sisters grim have always been in evidence. Puritanism and wowserism are simply strains or strands of what is often a totally contradictory movement. The future of feminism will rest on its embracing these differences and contradictions, not denying them. It has sufficiently penetrated the mainstream for there to be strange alliances formed for individual issues. There will continue to be strange bedfellows as women of the Left and Right meet, if only for one issue, like rape or pornography.

There is no one feminist canon or ideology. There never has been and there never will be. To insist that all feminists should like each other and agree on everything is to insist on the very conformity that it opposes on principle. As soon as one feminist decides what is ideologically sound or correct there will continue to be another one who will attempt to disprove it. This is all grist to the mill of ongoing struggle and dialogue and a commitment to diversity.

Those who seek to whip up a generational fight between younger and older feminists are not treating the movement as a fluid, changing organism. While it is true that younger women, having reaped the benefits so hard won by an older generation of feminists, often do not wish to call themselves by that name, no-one should expect them to feel compelled to do so. The real point is that they live their lives by the feminist principles of self-determination, independence, equality and support for other women. Many of them act as if they have absorbed its tenets almost with their cornflakes. They assume freedom to be an inalienable right, not something that can be taken away. But no-one should expect them to be grateful or beholden. If they don't know the history of the gains and freedoms they take for granted, it is the fault of their education systems. You cannot be grateful for a history that has been withheld from you. Most of them are strong, tough and expect institutions to treat them with respect. Stand aside, they say, we are sexy, streetwise and savvy.

The young women now standing centre stage – legs astride, singing and writing rock'n'roll – exude exactly the kind of strength and sexuality that Greer was endorsing in *The Female Eunuch*. When I heard the report of Greer and Suzanne Moore, I was reminded of Kathy Bates's character in the film *Fried Green Tomatoes* who says to a couple of young women who stole her parking spot in the supermarket carpark, as she rams her big car into their smaller car: 'I'm older and I've got more insurance.'

Feminism is about liberty, and justice; not happiness. To blame it for failing to produce nirvana is to entirely misrepresent it. The word itself is a concept rather than a definitive, nailed-down checklist. As Rebecca West wrote in 1913, 'I myself have never been able to find out precisely what feminism is: I only know that people call me a feminist whenever I express sentiments that differentiate me from a doormat.'

No one group or movement or political side owns feminism. Not the Left or the middle classes or the academic theorists or the old or the young, not the radicals or the conservatives. It is more than the sum of its parts. It needs both the power of the collective and the power of the individual.

But one fact remains constant, rock-like: the dominant culture, which is patriarchal, will not share power without a fight; its aim is to bury its opposition; and in the past it has succeeded. But feminism will never give up; backlashes will come and go, change will ebb and flow, but feminism will never again disappear entirely. The social revolution that we have witnessed since World War II has now penetrated too far into the mainstream, but there will always be those who seek to slow down or stem the tide of change.

It is important that we celebrate the women writers in this book. Despite all the slings and arrows of criticism and envy they have withstood, they are all continuing to write. Their passion for writing and for feminism has not been dimmed.

This does not mean that their theory has always matched their practice, or that feminists have done and continue to do things that are not always ideologically sound or politically correct. Nobody's perfect, nor should we expect them to be.

These women have been very brave to have told us the true stories of their lives. It takes genuine courage to take off the public mask and make yourself this vulnerable. As wives and mothers and lovers and trailblazers they have never allowed anything to stop them writing or believing in the power of the word. They do not pretend to be anything other than what they are. If you don't like them, tough.

And where are we going now? By looking at where we have been, perhaps even knowing that place for the first time, it is possible to chart where we are going. There will be more diversity, a wider range of 'feminist' behaviour, a less judgemental sisterhood, a more diffuse women's movement. It will not march together except for major challenges and old times' sake, but it will vote in increasing numbers for women candidates and it will sing and dance and rock'n'roll. It will also continue to write books that are tough and true reflections of women's lives. Books that sing on the eyeballs of their readers and that catapult women into the twenty-first century full of a sense of their own power and their own potential.

These women wrote books that, even though they were based on scholarly research and academic analysis predicated on an intellectual framework, entered the mainstream because they were accessible to a wide range of readers. The failure of academic feminism is that it has become increasingly narrow and elitist in its use of post-structuralist jargon. The term 'best-seller' has never been a term of praise in academia, in fact it has been a death knell. It is heartening that younger writers like Naomi Wolf and Susan Faludi are continuing the mainstream tradition of the writers of the second wave.

It is in the electronic media that we see the most dramatic legacy. Mainstream commercial television, damaging though it has been in depicting the more extreme streams of feminism as if they were the only ones, has also given us female characters like Murphy Brown – a bright, intelligent, uppity woman with a sharp sense of humour and an independent existence as a single mother, by choice. Roseanne Barr – as a gutsy, working-class mother of three and wife of Dan – negotiates feminist issues on a daily basis in her series, and also in her life. Oprah Winfrey has been a trailblazer and a role model for feminists and women of colour. Her programmes, based on airing opinions and sharing of experiences, are a direct offshoot of the original feminist consciousness-raising sessions. She now speaks to twenty million people every day. Younger women such as Ricki Lake have continued this tradition for a younger audience. Donahue is the voice of a strong, sympathetic male intent on co-operation with women and their concerns.

The world of the video clip has brought Madonna into everyone's home as a symbol of a woman not threatened by but embracing sex and money and power. A self-determining woman. The generation that came of age with the knowledge of feminist principles may be wary of using the big 'F' word or of identifying themselves with some of the media's most common kill-joy projections of it, but they are using rock music as a vehicle for making powerful statements about gender. The big 'P' power word does not scare them.

In all these women, now household names, we witness the same thrusting energy, the same self-asserting anger, the same sassy humour, the same sexual aggression, the same commitment to bold, challenging, provocative disruption that we saw in Germaine Greer, Erica Jong, Phyllis Chesler, Robin Morgan and all the other women in the '70s spotlight. What was so shocking in their time is now almost taken for granted. This is often the fate of the social reformer.

Even the British royal family is not immune. Lady Diana Spencer, at one time the future Queen of Britain, gave an interview on television that rocked the western world, not to mention her royal relatives. Having suffered from the low self-esteem, self-punishing diseases of anorexia and bulimia, she decided to take control of her own life, and in the tradition of *The Feminine Mystique*, 'named' her problems. In the tradition of *The Female Eunuch* she rebelled against her oppressors. In the tradition of *Fear of Flying* she refused to be discarded as a sexual partner and instead took lovers on her own terms. In the tradition of *The Women's Room*, she chose to challenge and eventually remove herself from a marriage in which she was being destroyed. In the tradition of *Women and Madness*, she refused to be labelled 'mad' and 'neurotic', she refused to succumb to mind-numbing drugs and being locked away in clinics (or the Tower). And in the tradition of *Sisterhood is Powerful*, she sought female counsel and help from a feminist therapist, and so on. In short, she took responsibility for and control of her own life.

Big 'F' feminism is no longer one fast-flowing river surging its way through various countries; continents and countries, it has now spawned many other smaller rivers and streams and tributaries that run, artery-like, from one to the other.

These writers, together with thousands of others, have provided the working documents for changing the consciousness and the laws of western society. Ironically, Australia has, because of its political systems, managed to pass more feminist legislation than America or Britain, and yet it is from America that most of these writers have emerged and survived. Perhaps it is because American culture is the most powerful, perhaps because it is the most nurturing of its successful people, that the women in this book, unlike their counterparts in Britain and Australia, have continued to produce a solid body of feminist work. The fact that half of these writers are also Jewish may be a result of the role models they had earlier in this century – of strong Jewish women, like Emma Goldman, associated with radicalism, reform, intellect and idealism. Or it may be that the experience of the Jew as the outsider is very similar to that of the woman as outsider.

These writers and their books have taught us all to ask as women, 'How far can I go? How much can I achieve?' and to stretch the boundaries of possibility, to leap the barrier, to push out the envelope, to crack through the glass ceiling, to go where other women have feared to tread. In short, they have taught us to be bold, not to be afraid. To be brave enough to be yourself or the self you secretly want to become. As Robin Morgan's poem said, 'There is nothing you cannot be.' If this book gives the reader nothing else but that belief, it will have all been worthwhile.

Too many stones have been thrown by women against other women in the name of feminism. We have to stop being so hard on each other. We need to remind ourselves who has the real power. Of course there will always be times when tempers flare, when friendships are broken, when argument rages, when passions run high. This is proof that feminism is alive and well. Feminism is about change and change involves conflict, confrontation, discord. If you want harmony, then join a choir. But as this wave of the women's movement matures and grows in the confidence that it will not disappear again, feminists will be less insecure and less inclined to blame each other.

Younger writers like Wolf have accepted that differences will occur and that women do not have to agree about everything in order to join in an alliance with each other to promote female power, that they do not have to cast out their sexuality or their love of men or women to be good sisters. She has accepted the fact that some women will grab the gains of feminist struggle and not give anything back. There have always been the users and the collaborators but that is no reason to give up on sisterhood. It is not enough just to succeed; in so doing, you must make the path easier for other women.

Unfortunately, one of the by-products of 'consciousness raising' is an obsession with self. It seems to have been forgotten that 'speaking the devil' is only meant to be the first stage. So often what we witness is the obsession with self-advancement that so characterised the 1980s. Selfhood became confused with selfishness. With the gaining of individual freedom should come a sense of responsibility to help others. The point is not merely to understand your oppression in the world but also that of others and in so doing to act to change it. What often passes in the name of feminist action is nothing but verbal masturbation; women getting off on describing their own oppression and becoming professional victims. Context is a word too often ignored.

The women who make their reputations by trashing feminism or its main proponents will come and go and, in a sense, are proof that it is alive and potent. There's no point in trashing something that's dead or moribund. As long as they are named for what they are, their gains will be small. But it is important to deal with them, not simply to ignore them. Every generation has to learn the lessons of the past or else repeat them.

And of course it is true that even in western culture there is much that needs to be changed. Women and young girls are still being physically, psychologically and sexually abused. Not nearly enough of them sit in our legislatures, our boardrooms or the front of the plane. Anyone who uses the term post-feminist is simply wrong. Abuses against women in other cultures make these concerns appear trivial.

But like the disappearance and reappearance of the bra in a new guise, feminism is with us to stay. There are those who argue that as both a symbol of oppression and a mark of our sexual freedom, most recently in Madonna's breastplate, the bra is feminism's most hotly contested sign.

The battle for women's freedom and equality has not yet been won but, despite the backlashes, it never goes back to where it was. In the '80s, like the '50s, they tried to make women return to their homes and blamed them for youth unemployment. This did not work because the two-income family had become part of the economic fabric. As capitalism depends on an ever-increasing growth of markets, it will embrace the independent woman's dollar in the same way it has embraced the 'gay' dollar.

Feminism has been buried before and it could be buried again; there are certainly strong forces which would like to achieve that. We must know its history, we must know the real stories of its struggle. We must know that the history of feminism is our history and pass it on to every generation.

Its survival lies in its being a broad movement, in its embracing diversity, in its teaching and celebration of its own history, in its telling and recording its own stories, in its tolerance of dissent and contradictions in its own ranks, in its insistence on sisterhood and in its recognition and pride in its icons, saints and divas.

It is, as it has always been, a work in progress.

SELECTED WORKS

Note: wherever possible, the bibliographical details of first editions have been cited.

Phyllis Chesler
About Men, Simon & Schuster, New York, 1978
Feminism and Psychology: Retrospection of 'Women and Madness', Sage Publications, London, 1994
Feminist Foremothers in Women's Studies, Psychology, and Mental Health, edited by Phyllis Chesler with E.D. Rothblum and E. Cole, Haworth Press, New York, 1995
Marriage and Psychotherapy, Know Inc., Pittsburgh, Pa., between 1970 and 1974
Mothers on Trial: The Battle for Children and Custody, McGraw Hill, 1986
Patriarchy: Notes of an Expert Witness, Common Courage Press, Monroe, Me., 1994
Sacred Bond: The Legacy of Baby M, Times Books / Random House, New York, 1988
Women and Madness, Doubleday, Garden City, New York, 1972
Women, Money and Power (written with Emily Jane Goodman), Morrow, New York, 1976
With Child: A Diary of Motherhood, Lippincott & Crowell, New York, 1979

Susan Faludi
Backlash: The Undeclared War against American Women, Crown, New York, 1991

Marilyn French
Beyond Power: On Women, Men and Morals, Summit Books, New York, 1985
The Bleeding Heart: A Novel, Sphere, London, 1980
The Book as World: James Joyce's 'Ulysses', Paragon House, New York, 1993
From Eve till Dawn: A Woman's History of the World, Meulenhof, Amsterdam, 1995
Her Mother's Daughter: A Novel, Summit Books, New York, 1988

My Summer with George, Knopf, New York, 1996

Our Father: A Novel, Little, Brown & Co., Boston, 1994

Shakespeare's Division of Experience, Summit Books, New York, 1981

The War Against Women, Ballantine Books, New York, 1992

The Women's Room, Summit Books, New York, 1977; with Afterword by Susan Faludi, Ballantine Books, New York, 1988

Betty Friedan

The Feminine Mystique, W.W. Norton & Co., New York, 1963

The Fountain of Age, Simon & Schuster, New York, 1993

'It Changed My Life': Writings on the Women's Movement, Random House, New York, 1976

The Second Stage, Summit Books, New York, 1981

Erica Jong

Any Woman's Blues, Harper & Row, New York, 1990

At the Edge of the Body, Holt, Rinehart & Winston, New York, 1979

Becoming Light: Poems New and Selected, HarperCollins, New York, 1991

The Devil at Large: Erica Jong on Henry Miller, Turtle Bay Books, New York, 1993

Fanny: Being the True History of the Adventures of Fanny Hackabout-Jones: A Novel, New American Library, New York, 1980

Fear of Fifty: A Midlife Memoir, HarperCollins, New York, 1994

Fear of Flying: A Novel, Holt, Rinehart & Winston, New York, 1971

Four Visions of America, Capra Press, Santa Barbara, Ca., 1977

Fruits and Vegetables: Poems, Secker & Warburg, London, 1973

Half-lives, Holt, Rinehart & Winston, New York, 1973

How to Save Your Own Life: A Novel, Holt, Rinehart & Winston, New York, 1977

Loveroot, Holt, Rinehart & Winston, New York, 1975

Megan's Book of Divorce: A Kid's Book for Adults, New American Library, New York, 1984

Megan's Two Houses: A Story of Adjustment, Dove Kids, West Hollywood, Ca., 1996

Ordinary Miracles: New Poems, New American Library, New York, 1983

Parachutes and Kisses, Signet, New York, 1981

Serenissima: A Novel of Venice, Houghton Mifflin, Boston, 1987

Witches, H.A. Abrams, New York, 1981

Kate Millett

AD: A Memoir, W.W. Norton & Co., New York, 1995

The Basement: Meditations on a Human Sacrifice, Simon & Schuster, 1991

Flying, Hart-Davis, MacGibbon, London, 1975

Going to Iran, Coward, McCann & Geoghegan, New York, 1982

Intimate Relations: The Natural History of Desire, Yale University Press, New Haven, 1995

The Invention of Heterosexuality, Dutton, New York, 1995

The Loony Bin Trip, Simon & Schuster, New York, 1990

The Politics of Cruelty: An Essay on the Literature of Political Imprisonment, W.W. Norton & Co., New York, 1994

Sexual Politics, Garden City, New York, Doubleday, 1970

Sita, Virago, London, 1977

Writing Selves: Contemporary Feminist Autography, University of Minnesota Press, Minneapolis, 1995

Robin Morgan

The Anatomy of Freedom: Feminism, Physics, and Global Politics, Anchor Press, New York, 1982

The Demon Lover: On the Sexuality of Terrorism, W.W. Norton & Co., New York, 1989

Depth Perception: New Poems and a Masque, Anchor Press/Doubleday, Garden City, New York, 1982

Dry Your Smile: A Novel, Doubleday, Garden City, New York, Doubleday, 1987

Going Too Far: The Personal Chronicle of a Feminist, Random House, New York, 1977

Lady of the Beasts: Poems, Random House, New York, 1976

The Mer-Child: A Legend for Children and Other Adults, Feminist Press, New York, 1991

Monster: Poems, Vintage Books, New York, 1972

The New Women: A Motive Anthology on Women's Liberation
(edited by J. Cooke, C. Bunch-Weeks and R. Morgan), Fawcett
Publications, Greenwich, Conn., 1971

Sisterhood is Global: The International Women's Movement Anthology
(edited by Robin Morgan), Doubleday/Anchor, New York,
1984

*Sisterhood is Powerful: An Anthology of Writings from the Women's
Liberation Movement*, Random House, New York, 1970

Upstairs in the Garden: Selected and New Poems, 1968–1988, W.W.
Norton & Co., New York, 1990

The Word of a Woman: Feminist Dispatches, W.W. Norton & Co.,
New York, 1992

Gloria Steinem

Moving Beyond Words, Simon & Schuster, New York, 1974

Herstory: Women who Changed the World, edited by R. Ashby and
D. Gore Ohrn, with an introduction by Gloria Steinem,
Viking, New York, 1995

Outrageous Acts and Everyday Rebellions, Holt, Rinehart &
Winston, New York, 1983

Marilyn: Norma Jean, New America Library, New York, 1987

Revolution from Within: A Book of Self-esteem, Little, Brown & Co.,
Boston, 1992

Alice Walker

Belief in the Love of the World: A Writer's Activism, Random House,
New York, 1992

The Color Purple: A Novel, G.K. Hall, Boston, Mass., 1983

Finding the Green Stone, Harcourt Brace Jovanovich, San Diego,
1991

Good Night, Willie Lee, I'll See You in the Morning: Poems, Harcourt
Brace Jovanovich, San Diego, 1984

Her Blue Body Everything We Know: Earthling Poems, 1965–1990,
Harcourt Brace Jovanovich, San Diego, 1991

Horses Make a Landscape Look More Beautiful: Poems, Harcourt
Brace Jovanovich, New York, 1981

In Love and Trouble: Stories of Black Women, Harcourt Brace Jovanovich, New York, 1973

In Search of Our Mothers' Gardens: Womanist Prose, Harcourt Brace Jovanovich, San Diego, 1983

Living by the Word: Selected Writings 1973–1987, Women's Press, London, 1988

Meridian, Harcourt Brace Jovanovich, New York, 1976

Once: Poems, Harcourt, Brace & World, New York, 1968

Possessing the Secret of Joy, Harcourt Brace Jovanovich, New York, 1992

Revolutionary Petunias and Other Poems, Women's Press, London, 1988

Same River Twice: Honoring the Difficult: A Meditation on Life, Art, and the Making of the Film 'The Color Purple', Ten Years Later, Washington Square Press, New York, 1997

The Temple of My Familiar, Harcourt Brace Jovanovich, San Diego, 1989

The Third Life of Grange Copeland, Pocket Books, New York, 1988

Warrior Marks: Female Genital Mutilation and the Sexual Blinding of Women (written with Prathiba Parmar), Harcourt Brace Jovanovich, San Diego, 1996

You Can't Keep a Good Woman Down: Stories, Harcourt Brace Jovanovich, New York, 1981

Naomi Wolf

The Beauty Myth: How Images of Beauty are Used Against Women, Anchor Books, New York, 1991

Fire with Fire: The New Female Power and How it will Change the 21st Century, Random House, New York, 1993

ACKNOWLEDEGMENTS

Special thanks must go to the following people: the management of Qantas, in particular Stephen Thompson and Barbara Stewart; Tim Curnow, my literary agent, for his belief in the project; Jane Burridge and Alison Urquhart, 'The Other Women' involved in my work; Judith John-Story from Beyond International; Susan Morris-Yates and Andy Palmer for their initial encouragement; Angelo Loukakis and Belinda Budge for their backing and good judgement; Jude McGee and Belinda Yuille for their calm and classy editing; Gillian Harvie for her professional transcribing and word processing; Bob Pugh, Jane Galvin-Lewis, Deirdre and Von Bair, Nancy Grossman and Arlene Raven, who were my special New York back-up and cheer squad. And finally all the women in the book who submitted themselves and their lives to my scrutiny.

If I have left anyone out please blame the vagaries of the menopause.